A Sure Thing

A Sure Thing

WHAT WE

BELIEVE

AND WHY

CORNELIUS PLANTINGA, JR.

Bible Way   CRC Publications
Grand Rapids, Michigan

ACKNOWLEDGMENTS

The Education Department is grateful to Dr. Cornelius Plantinga, Jr., associate professor of systematic theology at Calvin Seminary, for writing this book. Dr. Plantinga is also the author of two doctrinal studies for adults: *A Place to Stand* and *Beyond Doubt.*

We are also grateful to Laurie Sienkowski and Paul Stoub, free-lance artists of Grand Rapids, Michigan, for illustrating this book.

5 4 3
Library of Congress
Plantinga, Cornelius, 1946–
  A sure thing.

  (Bible way)
  1. Youth—Prayer-books and devotions—English.
  2. Reformed Church—Doctrines—Juvenile literature.
  I. Title. II. Series.
  BV4850.P55   1986   242'.83   86-8280

  ISBN 0-930265-27-0

"NOW FAITH IS

BEING SURE OF

WHAT WE HOPE FOR . . ."

—HEBREWS 11:1

PREFACE

A Sure Thing . . . What We Believe and Why is written especially for Christian teenagers who want to know more about what their church believes and confesses. It is written to help your own faith and hope in God become "a sure thing."

When you study this book, you will be learning "the language of faith." By this I mean the special words the church uses when it talks about what it believes and what the Bible teaches. These words are the basic ideas of the Christian faith, as taught in Reformed/Presbyterian churches. Knowing these words certainly won't save you—only the Holy Spirit, working in your heart, can do that. But knowing these words will give you a better understanding of what you believe with your heart, and will help you grow as a Christian.

This book is not hard to use. Notice from the table of contents that it teaches you the words of our faith systematically, beginning with teachings about God and ending with teachings about the last things. Each week features four short selections for you to read at home, either with your family or by yourself, followed by activities that will help you think about what you've read. Finally, you may join with other young people from your church to talk about what you've learned.

Learning the language of our faith takes some work, but it doesn't have to be dull; in fact, you'll find this book interesting and very much related to your daily lives as young Christians. The author is Dr. Cornelius Plantinga, Jr., Associate Professor of Systematic Theology at Calvin Seminary. Besides being a teacher, he's also a father of two teenagers on whom he's tried out this book, just to be sure that what he wrote would be clear and interesting.

God bless you in your learning. May it help you be "sure of what we hope for" as God's people.

Harvey A. Smit
Director of Education

CONTENTS

GOD

THE
ATTRIBUTES
OF
GOD

DAY 1

GOD IS

MYSTERIOUS

Scripture

(Jacob) had a dream in which he saw a stairway resting on the earth, with its top reaching to heaven, and the angels of God were ascending and descending on it. There above it stood the Lord, and he said: "I am the Lord, the God of your father Abraham and the God of Isaac. . . . I am with you and will watch over you wherever you go. . . .

When Jacob awoke from his sleep, he thought, "Surely the Lord is in this place, and I was not aware of it." He was afraid and said, "How awesome is this place! This is none other than the house of God; this is the gate of heaven."

—Selections from Genesis 28:12–17

Teachings

We all believe in our hearts
and confess with our mouths
that there is a single
and simple
spiritual being,
whom we call God—
  eternal,
  incomprehensible,
  invisible,
  unchangeable,
  infinite,
  almighty;
  completely wise,
  just,
  and good,
  and the overflowing source
    of all good.

—Belgic Confession, Article 1

A great Christian writer once asked us to imagine something. Imagine, he said, that some night when you are home alone you begin to believe that there is a fierce, person-eating tiger in your bedroom. You would be afraid. In fact, if you are normal, you would be terrified because you would be in great danger.

But now imagine something slightly different. You are in a dark house and in a spooky mood. And you begin to believe that there is a corpse in your bedroom. Once more you would be afraid, but in a weird and special way. It is not that you are in much danger. After all, dead bodies do not hurt you; they haunt you and fill you with dread.

The same thing happens to people when they believe that a ghost or a mighty spirit is nearby.

Probably people have felt this way about God from near the beginning of time. Early in the Bible we find evidence of such feelings. At a place he calls *Bethel* Jacob senses that someone from beyond has mysteriously visited him. He feels haunted and afraid. The one who has visited Jacob is so strange, so alien, that Jacob probably feels like fleeing. He feels awe. And the place where he feels it, therefore, seems awesome or awe-ful.

It is hard for us to get this feeling about God. We say God's name so often and worship God so regularly and hear so much about God that he does not seem very awesome. He seems almost like an unseen great-uncle in another country. We get the feeling of awesomeness about God only at certain times and in certain places. If we are alone at night and hear the wind come mysteriously through the trees, we may think of God. If we attend the funeral of someone we love, we may feel the strangeness of death and the mystery of God. Or suppose we step into a large Roman Catholic church. We see statues and smell candles. We sense an atmosphere that is strange and awesome to us. We may feel surrounded by the secret things of God.

A mystery is something puzzling, secret, or unknown to us. We read mystery books, watch mystery movies, and observe mysterious persons.

Multiply this a thousand times in thinking of the mystery of God. Even when we love God and trust that God loves us, we still cannot see him or know everything about him. Even when we cannot imagine the world without God, we are often puzzled by his ways with the world.

Still, God has made himself partly known to us. By his speaking and acting God has let us know something of who he is and what he wants. Thus we know that God is good and great and triune. We know that God wants our obedience and trust.

When we say that God is good or great or triune, we are listing some of God's *attributes*. Attributes are things true of someone. When we know some of God's attributes, we can praise and even imitate him. We can partly understand and try to describe God.

I say "try to describe" because God is in some ways indescribable. To say that God is good, for instance, is a little like saying that the Atlantic Ocean is a long swim.

To tell the truth, we will never understand some things about God. That is because God is great beyond all our imagining and holy beyond all our power to think of him. God is terribly and awesomely real. He is indescribably good and great. He is triune.

In all these ways and more God is a mystery.

Prayer

O God, help us overcome our fear. Show us who you are and what you want. Show us not only your mystery but also your great love. Amen.

DAY 2

GOD

IS GOOD

Scripture

The Lord is good to all;
   he has compassion on all he has made.
The Lord is righteous in all his ways
   and loving toward all he has made.
My mouth will speak in praise of the Lord.
   Let every creature praise his holy name
   for ever and ever.

—Psalm 145:9,17,21

Teachings

I trust him so much that I do not doubt
   he will provide
     whatever I need
     for body and soul,
and he will turn to my good
     whatever adversity he sends me
     in this sad world.

—Heidelberg Catechism Q & A 26

"**G**ood" is a word so common we use it without thinking. "How do you feel this morning?" your parent asks. "Pretty good," you reply. Then at school an English composition comes back with your teacher's comments on it. One of them, in a margin, is "good." After school you do some work around your house. "Thanks," says your parent. "Good job."

A common word—*good*. But there are times when you really mean it. You've been out all day hiking, or working, or cross-country skiing. Every muscle aches with pleasant tiredness. Every bone has gone off duty. At night you climb slowly into your bed, squirm deliciously till it nests and cradles you perfectly. You whisper your prayer to God and then let everything in the world fall away into drowsy nothingness. A bed on a tired night can feel so good.

Or suppose you've been playing tennis or basketball. It's an outdoor court, and the drinking fountain hasn't worked for years. So you wait for a drink till you get home. Water is a common gift for most of us. But when you are really thirsty, when not just your tongue and lips and throat but your whole body craves liquid, then even water can be incredibly good. It's an overflowing fountain of good.

One more example: you settle into a beanbag with a book. Sometimes you don't feel like reading, but this time you've found a book you can't close. You begin to care deeply about the characters. The places and adventures in the book make you feel new things. The whole story moves you outside of yourself in some wonderful way. A good book can be incredibly satisfying.

Goodness is what satisfies us, feeds us, fills us to the brim. That is the way we have been created by God. We have a built-in desire for beds, thirst-quenching liquids, good books, good food, even good people. What's good is whatever God created us to want.

Did you ever notice that the psalms speak of God himself as what we want? Psalm 42 compares God to water. A deer "longs for flowing streams." The deer wants water as a drink, as a bath, possibly as an escape from hunters. God, says the psalmist, is like a stream. God is like water that quenches, cools, and removes us from danger. We *thirst* for God.

Another psalm (63) compares God to food. God is like a feast for some starving, hunger-crazed person. The person wants as much of God as he can get because God is good. We *hunger* for God. We long for God because we belong to him.

Do these sound like strange ideas? Perhaps they are. Perhaps that's because we do not hunger and thirst for God enough. But something we do in church shows our desire for God—and also shows God's way of meeting it. At the Lord's supper mature believers take a piece of bread in hand and lift a cup to their lips. They say, "This is the body of Christ. This is the blood of Christ." Then they eat and drink. There is no doubt they are eating bread and drinking wine or juice. Still, in some mysterious way believers are also consuming as much of God as they can get. They are satisfying their hunger and thirst for God—because God is so good.

Psalm 145 speaks of God's goodness. The Lord is kind to the poor, just in opposing the wicked. He has open ears for our prayers and open hands to hold out to us good things. The Lord "satisfies the desire of every living thing." The Lord, in other words, is good.

But, once more, the point of saying this is not just to admire or appreciate. The point is to worship and give thanks. For whatever goods we have— beds, drink, food, good people, even God himself—are a sheer gift. A never-ending gift. God is an overflowing fountain of good.

That is why we want him.

Prayer
O Lord God, even when we are not thinking of you we need your goodness. For every good gift, for life itself, thank you, God. Amen.

DAY 3

GOD

IS GREAT

Scripture
Praise the Lord!
For it is good to sing praises to our God. . . .
He determines the number of the stars,
   he gives to all of them their names.
Great is our Lord, and abundant in power;
   his understanding is beyond measure.
The Lord lifts up the downtrodden,
   he casts the wicked to the ground.

—Psalm 147:1,4–6 (RSV)

Teachings
I trust him so much that I do not doubt
   he will provide
      whatever I need
      for body and soul,
   and he will turn to my good
      whatever adversity he sends me
      in this sad world.

He is able to do this because he is almighty God;
he desires to do this because he is a faithful Father.

—Heidelberg Catechism Q & A 26

My newspaper today featured a front-page picture of a very large fireman bending over a very small girl. The girl had been in a house fire and had breathed in a lot of smoke. By the time she was carried out she wasn't breathing at all. So the fireman knelt at her side, pinched her nostrils shut with his thumb and first finger, placed his mouth over hers, and breathed into her lungs the breath of life.

Sometimes we think of kneeling, stooping, and crawling as signs of weakness. A slave kneels before a master. A person who has gotten old and tired walks stooped over. Someone who is being humiliated in a book or movie crawls in front of his tormentor.

But kneeling or stooping can also show strength, the strength of goodness. The small girl I mentioned above received mouth-to-mouth-resuscitation from a strong man. In the same way a person who cares for a tiny pet or who rescues someone younger and smaller or who cares for someone old or sick is showing strength.

Worldly people often get this mixed up. They think of kindness as a weakness. Sometimes they sneer at goodness. But anybody who has ever been picked up by powerful arms or who has *felt* a parent's struggle to nurse a sick or dying person—anybody like that knows that kindness, goodness, and compassion are great strengths.

20

One of the odd and striking things about God is that his goodness so often shows itself in kneeling, stooping, and bending. Of course, God is great without doing these things. The Bible keeps telling us, for example, of God's powerful deeds in nature. God cracks open great mountains; he shakes the whole earth till it rumbles and splits. He stretches out the heavens and tramples on the waves of the sea (Job 9:8). God possesses unimaginable strength, intelligence, resourcefulness, and power. God is incredibly vast, majestically strong, galactically great. That is part of the reason people fear God.

But our psalm for today (and, by the way, also the one for yesterday) tells us that God's greatness includes his stooping, his bending toward us. "Great is our Lord, and abundant in power" (v. 5). Then, in the very next verse, the psalmist writes, "The Lord lifts up the downtrodden."

Some of God's children are downtrodden. People tread on them. Careless people walk all over them. The downtrodden eagerly look for friends, but others tell them to get lost. They need food, but others grab even the little they have. Lacking proper homes and education and parents, these people always seem to have someone's foot in their face. They are like human cigarette butts or crab apples. Other people like to crush or squash them.

God lifts up the downtrodden. It is part of God's *greatness* to do this. He lifts squashed people to their feet, throwing off the wicked who have been walking all over them. God's greatness is the muscle behind his goodness.

God's greatness is awesome. People fear it. But it is also kind. God bends over to feed young ravens, young children, young people. Because God is high, he can lift up and straighten out crushed people.

For all God's downtrodden people, one day in the city of David a Savior is born. A baby is born in a cow shed. God stoops over to place a tiny child in the world.

All of heaven's greatness lies there wailing in the straw. What must we think of that?

Prayer

O God, you are great beyond all of our thinking. You are the almighty one. But you are also our loving Father. Reach down to us and all your children. Through Jesus Christ, our Lord, Amen.

DAY 4

GOD

IS TRIUNE

Scripture

My prayer is not for them alone. I pray also for those who will believe in me through their message, that all of them may be one, Father, just as you are in me and I am in you. May they also be in us so that the world may believe that you have sent me.

—John 17:20–21

Teachings

Q. Since there is but one God,
why do you speak of three:
Father, Son, and Holy Spirit?

A. Because that is how
God has revealed himself in his Word:
these three distinct persons
are one, true, eternal God.

—Heidelberg Catechism Q & A 25

People often compare things. Some jokes and riddles, for example, depend on comparisons. Suppose someone asks, "When is a frog like a baseball player?" (when it catches flies). For the joke to work, a frog and a baseball player have to be alike in some way. They have to be comparable.

In the fine work of great writers comparisons help make stories interesting to read. In John Steinbeck's story *The Red Pony* a boy named Jody receives a colt as a gift. Steinbeck tells us that the new pony's coat was "rough and thick as an airedale's fur." Later, Jody brushes and curries his pony so that "his coat lay as smooth and gleaming as orange-red lacquer." Finally, Jody wants to train the red pony never to fall on top of him. Why? "He had seen that happen to men before, had seen how they writhed on the ground like squashed bugs, and he was afraid of it." In the author's mind, dog's fur, paint, and bugs are interesting comparisons for horsehair and people.

The Bible is full of comparisons. God is compared to a rock. Jesus is compared to a shepherd. You and I, who are members of the church, are compared to the limbs of a human body.

One of the most mysterious things about God is that God is both one and three. There are three persons in God—the Father, the Son, and the Holy Spirit. But there is still only one God. When Christians say this, they are stating the doctrine of the Trinity. They are saying that God is *triune*.

But what would that be like? What is a good comparison for the triune God?

People have thought about this for centuries. Some have suggested that God is like water. After all, water has three forms—solid, liquid, and vapor—but is still only one substance. Maybe God is like that.

Others have said that God is like a man who has three roles to play. God is like an actor. The President of the U.S., for instance, has to play the role of president. But he may also have to play the role of husband (to his wife) and father (to his children). He is therefore one man with at least three roles. Is God like that?

No. In fact, neither of these comparisons is a very good one. In the first comparison, the three forms of water are actually not very much like persons. None of them can think or love, for example. And in the second comparison, the president, even with three roles to play, is still only one person. God, on the other hand, is three persons.

Suppose we think of a better comparison. Think of three persons in a family. They are very much alike. Birth, blood, and marriage tie them together. The family members may look like each other. Further, they know each other deeply and love each other. They share memories, experiences, hopes, and plans. If anyone or anything (such as a mugger or a tornado) threatens them, they turn to face this threat together. They are three persons, but one family unit.

In a way, God is like that. God is like an extraordinarily close family. The three persons in God are only one divine family or Trinity.

But the Bible gives us the best comparison. In today's passage the Father and Son together are compared to the church. (In other places the Spirit is included.) Does it seem like an odd comparison? The church, after all, contains so many sorts of persons. And some do not seem very much like God.

Still, this is the Bible's comparison. God is three persons, but there is only one God. The church is many persons, but there is only one church. That is, across the world and across the centuries there is only one group of persons who call Jesus their Lord.

God is like the church. Or, better, the church is like God. Do you think the church ought to be even more like God than it is?

Prayer

Triune God, you are greater than anything we can imagine and good to us in more ways than we know. Turn toward us, and let your love come to us, we pray. Amen.

HOMEWORK

Vocabulary
Please study the following words and definitions until you know them well enough to explain them on your own.

1. doctrine: the church's teachings, based on the Bible, about God and our salvation

2. confessions: organized, carefully written statements of doctrine approved by the church

3. Belgic Confession: the oldest confession of the Reformed church (1561); consists of 37 articles or statements of Reformed doctrine

4. Heidelberg Catechism: a popular confession of the church, used primarily to teach doctrine. This sixteenth-century confession includes 129 questions and answers about the Apostles' Creed, the Ten Commandments, and the Lord's Prayer.

5. attributes of God: God's characteristics or qualities, such as goodness and greatness. God's attributes help us understand, praise, and imitate God.

6. goodness of God: an attribute of God; means that he satisfies the needs of all his creatures

7. greatness of God: an attribute of God; means that God is awesome. God's greatness is the muscles behind his goodness.

8. triune: being at once a triple and a unit. To say that God is triune is to say that God is three persons (Father, Son, and Holy Spirit) but only one God. That is, God is a *Trinity.*

Questions
Please answer the following questions on a separate sheet of paper. Use the readings from each day to help you. *Be sure to bring the completed assignment, along with this textbook, to class.*

Day 1: Write three things that you don't know about God, things that make him "mysterious."

Day 2: Read Psalm 145. Then write down at least half a dozen specific examples the Psalm gives of God's goodness.

Day 3: Give an example from Psalm 147 of two quite different ways in which God shows his greatness.

Day 4: How is the Trinity like a family? Like a church?

Summary

Talk with your mom or dad about a time when they—or your entire family—felt God's goodness or greatness in a special way. Write a *brief* version of his or her answer.

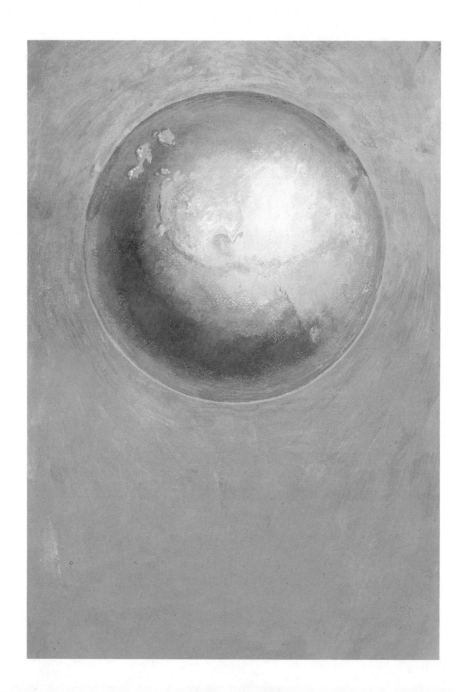

2

GOD

ACTS

IN

CREATION

DAY 1

GOD'S SOVEREIGNTY

IN CREATION

Scripture

In the beginning God created the heavens and the earth. Now the earth was formless and empty, darkness was over the surface of the deep, and the Spirit of God was hovering over the waters. And God said, "Let there be light," and there was light.

—Genesis 1:1–3

Teachings

In the beginning, God—
Father, Word, and Spirit—
called this world into being
out of nothing,
and he gave it
shape and order.

—*Our World Belongs to God,* 8

We all do hundreds of things we hardly ever think about. We vibrate our eardrums, beat our hearts, pump our blood. We multiply cells, expand lungs, mix stomach juices with swallowed Big Macs. We sneeze in dusty rooms, blink in bright sunlight, yawn in a boring class, hiccup for no known reason.

But even though we are the ones who do these things, we seldom think about them. Why? Because they are all involuntary. That is, we do not do them on purpose. They are things we do because, like all animals, we have bodies. You could almost say that heart beating and blood pumping and cell multiplying are things we don't really *do* at all. Instead, they happen to us or in us.

But there also are a great number of things we do on purpose. We deliberately choose *this* tape and not that one. We intentionally cut a piece of cloth or wood to size. We purposely think up our first computer program. We do such things because, unlike snails and slugs, we are persons. To be a person is to *act* in intentional and orderly ways.

When we act in these ways, we are like God! The triune God, the God of three persons, is supremely the God who acts. God the Trinity is bursting with purposeful activity. God is alive with plans, programs, and designs. Even if some of God's acts are hidden from us, even if some occur in mysterious ways, still we know from reading the Bible that God is the great actor in the drama of the universe.

The first act of God we know about is *creation.* As we know, the Bible begins with a simple, but magnificent, statement: "In the beginning God created the heavens and the earth." It is hard for us to grasp this. What was it like without a universe? Why did God see fit to create one? How can we imagine the great bursts of godly power that lit up the stars, swung moons into orbit, and delicately balanced the earth on its axis? How can we imagine the thoughts of the first man and woman as they gazed around at a brand-new world, watching birds and animals at play and feeling inside themselves the stirrings of life?

We cannot really imagine these things very well. But we do live in the world that has come from these beginnings. What a world it is! God designed and then built the universe out of his sheer intelligence and stunning power. Christians believe, moreover, that God built the universe out of nothing. There was no universal lumberyard where God had a charge account, no stone quarry, no pet store. The striking truth is that God made not only the universe but also the materials out of which he made it. This is part of what we mean when we say that God is *sovereign*. Sovereignty means that God is supreme and in control. The universe *reveals* God's attribute of sovereignty.

Think of the result! We have been created with five senses so that we may know and take delight in God's creation. In five ways we *sense* that God has acted in creation. We see a beautifully dressed autumn tree, smell a fresh loaf of warm homemade bread, touch a puppy's velvet coat, hear the lonesome call of a bird, taste the juices of a perfectly roasted slab of meat.

All these things—and millions more—come from God. Christians see, smell, touch, hear, and taste God's creation as if there were signs and signatures all over it that said "Made by God."

Can you understand now why the psalmists keep telling us to praise him?

Prayer
We praise you, O Lord. We praise your goodness and greatness in creation. We praise your holy name. Through Jesus Christ, Amen.

DAY 2

GOD'S GOODNESS

IN CREATION

Scripture
God saw that the light was good . . . God saw that (the land and seas were) good . . . God saw that (the plants and trees were) good . . . God saw that (the sun, moon, and stars were) good . . . God saw that (the creatures of sea and sky were) good . . . God saw that (the land animals were) good . . . God saw all that he had made, and it was very good.

—Genesis 1:4,10,12,18,21,25,31

Teachings
In the beginning
everything was very good.   —*Our World Belongs to God,* 9

G od acted sovereignly in creation. In an incredible explosion of activity God spread out the heavens, dug and filled the oceans, planted the great gardens and forests. God launched birds, stocked lakes with fish, and set animals free to cruise the earth. And, last, God made human beings to work and play, worship and serve, love and laugh. He made them like himself to do these things and then rest.

Why did God create? Was he lonesome? No, within the holy Trinity God already enjoyed life, zest, and an overflowing of love. Was God absentmindedly doodling in creation—the way we do, sketching out houses and stick people to amuse ourselves when we are bored? No, the universe shows every sign of having been created on purpose. Did God tell himself he *had* to create or else he couldn't be God? No, God was free either to create or not to create. He is sovereign. It was up to him whether to make a universe.

Why, then? Why did God create? We do not know all the reasons. But one reason is this: God created because he is *good*. To be good means in part that you want to share what you have with others. Parents do this when they make room for children. They want to share their life, their love, their laughter, their faith, their home with smaller persons. They want to share *themselves.*

So it is with God. In creation God made room for others. God had already existed without beginning or limit. But at creation God began a great experiment. God began to share his life and existence with whales and frogs, birch trees and bluegrass. And God made persons like himself. The God who was overflowing with goodness opened his home to guests.

Many of us have been guests in somebody else's home. It is often a wonderful experience. A good host or hostess welcomes you with a restful place to sleep, nutritious and attractive food, interesting things to see and do. A host or hostess *makes room* for you in a generous way. This practice is called *hospitality.* It flows out of human goodness. It is, after all, not so easy to be hospitable. You have to do extra work to make your guests feel at home. You might have to sleep on the couch. You have to take responsibility for your guests and try to protect them.

But in any case human hosts do not create their guests. They simply welcome guests that already exist. God went a step further. He made a whole universe in order to have things and persons he could love—and that would love and praise him in return. God's goodness shows itself in his creative hospitality. God has made room in his life for you and me.

Now notice one more thing. In a strange and wonderful way God passed along his own goodness to his creation. The whole first chapter of Genesis rings with the word *good*. Not only is God good; God also saw that what he had made was good. Then he saw again that it was good. And again and again. All of it good. At last God stepped back, looked over all that he had made room for, and called it *very* good.

Can you see why it is good for us in turn to make room for others?

Prayer

O God, everything you have made is good. Thank you especially for creating human beings to share life and love with so great a God as you. Help us to open our lives and make room for others. In Jesus' name, Amen.

DAY 3

GOD'S GREATNESS

IN CREATION

Scripture
"Where were you when I laid the earth's foundation? . . . Who marked off its dimensions? . . . Who shut up the sea behind doors? . . . Who cuts a channel for the torrents of rain, and a path for the thunderstorm . . . ?

—Job 38:4,5,8,25

Teachings
God formed the land, the sky, and the seas,
making the earth a fitting home
for the plants, animals,
and humans he created.
The world was filled with color, beauty, and variety;
it provided room for
work and play,
worship and service,
love and laughter.

—*Our World Belongs To God,* 9

The other day my family and I visited the Detroit Zoo. It was the sort of cool, clear summer day that seemed to make even caged animals glad to be alive. We watched a hippo repeatedly open its great pink mouth, as if he expected to have his four teeth cleaned and checked by a hippo dentist. A sixth-month-old polar bear cub did endless belly whoppers into a small diving pool. Seals and sea lions swam fifteen-yard freestyle races. Monkeys studied and groomed each other's fur. Prairie dogs commuted underground back and forth from the suburbs to the center of prairie-dog city. In a family of lynx the children romped and fought, their mother occasionally separating them with a large paw. The father lynx simply watched in cool aloofness.

Why are animals fun to watch? Partly because they are so much like us. Or we are like them. Also, partly because animals are so different from each other in size, color, shape, speed, and habits. Some are massive and slow, like living trucks. Others are so small and quick you wonder how the zoo people ever caught them. Some are striped, some spotted, some flecked, some dappled. The Asian giraffes we saw were marked with rust-colored rectangles on beige fur. Animals come in almost indescribable variety.

Did you know that zoologists have colorful names even for groups of animals? A group of lions is called a *pride* of lions. (Perhaps we can guess why.) Then there is a gaggle of geese, a peep of chickens, a knot of toads, a parliament of owls, and a clash of rhinos. All this clashing, gaggling, peeping, knotting, and priding tell us how marvelously different animals are from each other—and what fine imaginations zoologists have.

But their imaginations are nothing like God's. It is a sign of God's greatness that he has created such incredible *kinds* of things. And such vast numbers of things—billions of stars, galaxies, solar systems, fiery comets, deadly rays, planets circled by moons. Countless plants and kinds of plants. Numberless birds and kinds of birds.

In a place like Canada's Banff National Park visitors can listen to a chorus of wolves or to the roaring of the Athabasca River. They can peer at awesome, soaring peaks or at the depth of sky-blue waters—or at the one reflected in the other. They can hike across places so wondrously beautiful that the Creator of the heavens and the earth seems to have settled there in all his mystery and glory. God made Banff.

And God made us. How remarkable the way he does it! Each of us starts as a single cell that comes from the union of a sperm and an egg. Then that cell divides into two, then four, then eight, then sixteen, on and on to millions and billions of cells. A great scientist once pointed out that at a certain stage in this process one particular cell appears. This one cell, as it divides, will become a human brain. Everything needed to learn to talk, to write, to play music or softball is in that one cell. All we need to learn to argue or give up an argument; every ability to be surprised, thoughtful, or bored; every raw material for thinking, imagining, or planning—all of it is in this single cell that keeps dividing and dividing until one day it becomes that trillion-cell wonder, the brain.

It is a work of God's greatness in creation.

Prayer
God, our Father, you are greater than anything we can think or imagine. All praise to you! In Jesus' name, Amen.

DAY 4

GOD'S IMAGE

IN CREATION

Scripture

Then God said, "Let us make man in our image, in our likeness; and let them rule over the fish of the sea and the birds of the air, over the livestock, over all the earth, and over all the creatures that move along the ground."

So God created man in his own image, in the image of God he created him; male and female he created them.

—Genesis 1:26–27

Teachings

As God's creatures we are made in his image
to represent him on earth,
and to live in loving communion with him.
By sovereign appointment we are
earthkeepers and caretakers:
loving our neighbor,
tending the creation,
and meeting our needs.
God uses our skills
in the unfolding and well-being of his world.

—Our World Belongs to God, 10

I mages. They are all around you. You get up in the morning and peer into a mirror. What peers back at you is not you but your image. You look into a camera viewfinder or watch a favorite person on TV. You gaze at a reflected mountain upside down in a lake. You have a dental X ray taken or make a photocopy of a school report. In all these cases you are dealing with images.

An image is a likeness of something. Often, as in mirrors, it is a reflected likeness. Some images, as in great portraits, are beautiful. Some are funny, as in cartoons. A few (in good computer games, for example) are exciting.

In addition, images are often very powerful. They can deeply influence your thinking and feeling. Why do you suppose TV advertisers often show you a wealthy or a happy person using a certain product? Why do rulers of some countries plaster their picture up on every wall, fence, and billboard? Why does the second commandment in the Bible tell us we must not make a "graven image" of God?

After God had made day and night, after God had created land and seas, plants and trees, moons and stars, birds and fish and land animals—after all that, God did one final thing. God made an image. God made a likeness, a reproduction, a reflection of himself. God made human beings.

It's a scary and difficult thought—that we humans are like God. What could it mean? After all, we have bodies and faces, but God has no body at all. So how could we look like him? Also, we are persons who often do or say what is wrong. God never does. So how could we resemble God in our acts or speech?

Yet we do. Look at the Genesis verses at the top of this reading. One way we resemble or image God is in our *ruling*. God has made us responsible for taking good care of the earth, making sure that water and air are clean, for instance, and that forests and other natural gifts are protected. God wants us to use soil intelligently and to handle animals well. God is, of course, the ultimate ruler over all these things, but he has seen fit to share his ruling by giving us a part to play in it. We are earth-rulers or earth-keepers.

Now look at verse 27. Being created male and female is also part of what it means to be in the image of God. Of course, God is not male or female. God is a family of three wonderfully fellowshipping persons: Father, Son, and Holy Spirit. But we human beings can have a similar fellowship—not only with God but also with each other! Because we are male and female we can have families. We can know and love other human beings intimately. And our *loving fellowship* images God.

As a matter of fact, according to the New Testament, whenever we *act rightly*—showing kindness, for example, or helping someone who isn't attractive, or telling the truth—we are imaging God. To act like God is to show God's likeness to the world.

Have you ever noticed that it is sometimes hard to visualize a person you deeply love? Sometimes we can get a better picture in our minds of somebody we don't know very well than of a person we are very close to. God is the one we must love above all. And we cannot picture God at all. Yet at times we can see what God is like. We see his image in the ruling, fellowshipping, and right action of human beings. We see him especially in Jesus Christ, who is not only human but also divine and is therefore the perfect image of God.

And when we imitate Christ, we can tell what God is like not only by looking at Christ himself. We can also tell by looking in a mirror.

Prayer
Thank you, O God, for making us like yourself. Help us to be good images of you so that others can see you in us. In Jesus' name, Amen.

HOMEWORK

Vocabulary
Please study the following words and definitions until you know them well enough to explain them on your own.

9. Our World Belongs to God: a "contemporary testimony" that the Christian Reformed Church has approved for use in its congregations. This testimony is intended to help us serve the Lord in the world around us. It addresses such concerns as abortion, nuclear war, ecology, etc.

10. sovereignty of God: the attribute of God which means that he is supreme and in control.

11. creation: the sovereign act of God by which he brought into being the whole universe from nothing. Creation shows God's sovereignty, goodness, and greatness, as well as his image in us.

12. image of God: the likeness of God in human beings. We see the image of God in us by our ruling over creation, by our fellowship with each other, and by any right actions we do. The image of God means being like Christ.

Questions
Please answer the following questions on a separate sheet of paper. Use the readings from each day to help you. *Be sure to bring the completed assignment, along with this textbook, to class.*

Day 1: How is God's sovereignty shown in creation?

Day 2: How many times is the word *good* mentioned in Genesis 1? What does this tell us about God?

Day 3: Suppose you had to convince someone who doubted God's greatness that God was truly awesome and wonderful. Where might you take that person? What could you show him or her? Explain.

Day 4: Describe three ways in which you "image" or resemble God.

Summary
Find a few verses from a psalm that describe God's greatness in creation. Ask someone in your family for help, if you wish. Write down the location of verses you found and be ready to tell the class how these verses show God's greatness in creation.

3

GOD

ACTS

IN

PROVIDENCE

DAY 1

GOD

PROVIDES

Scripture

"The God who made the world and everything in it is the Lord of heaven and earth and does not live in temples built by hands. And he is not served by human hands, as if he needed anything, because he himself gives all men life and breath and everything else."

—Acts 17:24–25

Teachings

Our world has fallen into sin;
but rebellion and sin can never dethrone God.
He does not abandon the work of his hand;
the heavens still declare his glory.
He preserves his world, sending seasons, sun and rain,
upholding his creatures,
renewing the earth,
directing all things to their purpose. —*Our World Belongs to God*, 4

An animal shelter is a noisy and busy place. It is also a sad place. Row after row of abandoned or abused animals bark, whine, yip, howl, and meow. Nobody wants them.

Each of these animals has a history. Perhaps one of them was once given to a child as a pet. For the first few weeks everybody in the house played with the newcomer. But then school started, or people got busy some other way, and the pet was gradually neglected. Nobody gave the animal a bath or a grooming. Nobody bothered to train or discipline it. No one provided the right diet or proper veterinary care. Because of such carelessness a pet that was once the center of attention in a home became an unwelcome nuisance.

Some such animals stray away. Others are driven out into the country and pushed out of a car. Some are allowed to run the neighborhood in packs. When these abandoned creatures end up in animal shelters, a few are adopted. Most have to be killed.

One of the greatest tragedies of the world is that some children are treated in similar ways. Careless parents conceive these children but do not really want them. Some kill them before they are born. Others abandon live babies in trash cans or on the steps of churches. Still other parents allow their children to grow up in their houses but never give them strong, loving care. For example, they don't ever read to them or play with them when they are small. They don't keep them clean. They don't hug them or hold them or tell them they are important and loved. Some of these parents even smash their children in the face or lock them in dark closets for days.

These are parents who have created children but have not provided for them. Day by day their children suffer. Their minds and spirits and bodies and feelings gradually crumble because nobody takes care to nourish and support them.

To provide for somone is to show *providence*. You can show it by supporting a person's life with food, education, love, a house, even discipline.

All good providers, including our parents, learn their providence from God. God acts in creation, but then he also acts in providence to take care of his creation. He makes provision for summer and winter, springtime and harvest. He gives both rain and sunshine so that grains and fruits and green plants—and all the creatures who feed on them—may continually grow and be nourished.

By providing these things God *preserves* his creation. He never abandons it. He never turns his back on it. Like a father who holds a child's head above water, God faithfully upholds what belongs to him. He provides for life to reproduce, flesh to heal, humans to know and love him. God provides antibodies to fight infection, spiders to fight flies.

He even provides firemen to fight fires. Did you ever consider why most of us live safe and healthy lives? Why do people fight fires, set broken bones, help abused children, dam floods, imprison criminals, grow beans, teach children, fix teeth, sell clothing? What if nobody were willing to do any of these things? What if nobody cared? Suppose everybody went on strike at the same time. Civilization would collapse!

But this doesn't happen because God is at work in his world. He preserves it. And he often does this by empowering *us* to do his work. Every garbage collector, every judge, every forest ranger, every traffic cop is acting for God in preserving his world.

God takes care of what he has made. That is why we trust him.

Prayer
Dear God, thank you for the way you take care of your world. Thank you for food, clothes, caring parents. Thank you for other providers and for civilization. Thank you for life itself. In Jesus' name, Amen.

DAY 2

GOD HAS

PROVIDED RESCUE

Scripture
The Lord said, "I have indeed seen the misery of my people in Egypt. I have heard them crying out because of their slave drivers, and I am concerned about their suffering. So I have come down to rescue them from the hand of the Egyptians. . . ."

—Exodus 3:7–8a

Teachings
While justly angry,
God did not turn his back
on a world bent on destruction;
he turned his face to it in love.
With patience and tender care he set out
on the long road of redemption
to reclaim the lost as his people
and the world as his kingdom.

—*Our World Belongs to God*, 19

Because of his sovereign greatness and goodness God preserves the world. But why is this necessary? Why can't the world preserve itself? To answer this we have to remember two things. One is that we are not our own. We and our world belong to God. God is the creator. We are only creatures. Even our casual language tells us we forget this at times. Our friends wave goodbye and say, "Take care!" Clerks in stores tell us, "Have a nice day!" (Try saying back, "Sorry, I have other plans.") Actually, we cannot do these things. We can't really take care of ourselves. And whether we have a nice day depends on many things and people outside our control. The truth is that we depend entirely on God.

The other thing to remember is that our world is sinful. Way back at the beginning Adam and Eve pushed their way out of God's arms in order to be on their own. They wanted to belong to themselves, rule themselves, run their own garden. Everyone knows the tragic result. Sin entered the world and began to spread like an oil slick. Since that time the human story has always included war, kidnapping, rape, murder, child abandonment, cruelty, racism, drunkenness, divorce, disease, and other miseries. God's world has been constantly threatened and at times almost wrecked by sin.

But God has kept on preserving his world. Sun and rain and fruitful seasons have continued in their rhythm. And one more thing: God has provided rescue for sinners.

We all know how a person can get himself in trouble. A teenager wanders off in a wilderness area; rangers have to search for her. A drunk and disorderly man nearly drowns in a lake; lifeguards have to swim out and haul him in. A rock climber breaks all the rules of safe climbing and needs a rescue team to get him down the mountain.

Now think back over what you know of the Bible. Again and again we read similar stories. God's people get themselves in terrible trouble. Then God rescues them. Almost at once, by sin and foolishness the people again get themselves enslaved, captured, hurt, and miserable. And again God comes to the rescue. Trouble and rescue. Sin and salvation. Over and over that is the pattern. If the human story includes more sadness and wreckage than we can imagine, it also reveals—in a way that is equally hard to imagine—that God keeps on coming back to rescue his children.

God saved Noah from the flood. God promised Abraham blessing for the whole world. When Joseph's brothers sold him like an animal, God used this sin to save the whole family from starvation. When that family and its children got enslaved in Egypt, God "heard them crying out" and "came down to rescue them." The Israelites in the desert kept telling their children the story of this mighty exodus. But they also complained about the food. So God sent them manna. Along the years God gave them laws, a temple, priests, prophets, kings. In great battles he delivered them from enemies left and right.

When at last the Israelites went miserably off into exile, God rescued a faithful few. And to them and to the whole world God one day sent a Savior, who is Christ the Lord.

When human beings killed him, God raised him. Since then God has poured out his Spirit, raised up his church, and equipped millions of men and women to spread the gospel and to fight sin. History is, in fact, the death struggle of the raging forces of evil on the one hand and the rescuing God on the other. And history tells us that the God who has rescued before will do it again.

Does any of this come home to us? It does. Is it an accident that you and I have been given families who love us? Is it an accident that we have been baptized into the church where we can hear the rescue stories and believe them? Or does God purposely have rescue in mind for *us*?

Prayer
Almighty God, thank you for working in so many ways in our lives to rescue us from sin and evil. Come for rescue again, O Lord, every time we struggle with evil. In Jesus' name, Amen.

DAY 3

GOD IS PROVIDING

WHAT IS GOOD

Scripture

We know that in all things God works for the good of those who love him.

—Romans 8:28

Teachings

Q. What do you believe when you say, "I believe in God, the Father almighty, creator of heaven and earth"?

A. . . . I trust him so much that I do not doubt

he will provide
whatever I need
for body and soul,
and he will turn to my good
whatever adversity he sends me
in this sad world.
He is able to do this because he is almighty God;
He desires to do this because he is a faithful Father.

—Heidelberg Catechism Q & A 26

Every day you read about it in the newspaper. Or see it on TV news. You read about and see evil.

Some evils are caused by human beings. We have experienced many of them ourselves. Someone cheats by shoving into line ahead of you. Some adult steals from you by refusing to pay for the newspapers you delivered. Another student spreads a vile story about you. Or somebody mocks you because she thinks you are stupid or fat or no good at anything. Mockery hurts and gnaws at you for a long time after it happens. Most kids would rather be slugged than mocked.

In the larger world that we read about or see on TV, human evils are as great or even greater. Every Christmas, it seems, we read about a family that scraped together enough money to buy their children a few gifts—only to find some night that a thief has stolen every one of them. I once read a news account of some robbers who burst into a Utah tape and record store. One of the thugs forced customers to drink a caustic drain cleaner that burned their esophaguses and stomachs. Another stomped a ballpoint pen down through a man's eardrum into his skull.

Such things are so wicked and painful that we can hardly stand even to hear about them. But terrible events happen every day in our sinful world, and sooner or later we come to know it. Without doubt the most famous example of human evil in the twentieth century is the Nazi holocaust, the slaughter of six million Jews in Europe in World War II. Some were starved or beaten or kicked to death. Others were machine-gunned so that they would topple over into the burial ditches they had been forced to dig themselves. Some had to submit to medical experiments designed to see how much pain a human being could suffer before dying. Many, including children, were gassed and then incinerated.

Large numbers of these Jews believed in God. Over and over they prayed. *Why?* they asked. Why is this happening? O God, why do you allow this? Some who suffered, or who saw the suffering, just quit believing in God.

While humans cause much of the evil in the world, fearful evils also happen in nature. Floods, earthquakes, tornados, drought, and hurricanes threaten millions. Some evils of nature happen in our own bodies. A person is born with brain damage. A child develops leukemia. A loved father or mother dies terribly of some other dreaded disease.

Once more, believers ask *why.* Sometimes they do not ask it. They shout it or howl it or scream it into the night. If God is so great and good, if God acts in providence to preserve his children and rule his world, then *why?*

We do not always know. And it is foolish to pretend to know when we don't. We sometimes think we can tell what good reason God might have for allowing evil, but often we only guess. Maybe God allows people great freedom to do both evil and good because else they wouldn't be humans at all, but only robots. Maybe God doesn't turn all guns into salami and all bullets into bubbles because then the world wouldn't be real and couldn't be counted on. Maybe God allows diseases and tornados to make us depend on him or to make us more courageous. Maybe God sometimes sends punishments on a whole nation. Or maybe there are times when a person's suffering—and the way he handles it—draws *others* closer to God.

It is hard to say in a particular case. Often we do not know exactly why God permits a certain evil. But we do know this: just as a doctor must sometimes hurt you in order to help you, so God is always working with us for good. Even when we can't see it or tell it. That is sometimes hard to accept. But no God, and no good, would be even harder to accept.

We know one more thing. Our Lord Jesus Christ himself, as he died inch by inch from his fatal wounds, shouted "My God, my God, why have you forsaken me?"

Two days later he was alive again and speaking peace to his disciples. God *does* act against evil and for good. It is part of his providence.

Prayer

O Lord, our world is dangerous. Please protect and keep us from evil. If we must suffer, be close to us. Through Jesus Christ, our suffering Lord. Amen.

DAY 4

GOD WILL

PROVIDE CONTROL

Scripture
Then Jesus came and said to them, "All authority in heaven and on earth has been given to me. Therefore go and make disciples of all nations, baptizing them in the name of the Father and of the Son and of the Holy Spirit, and teaching them to obey everything I have commanded you. And surely I will be with you always, to the very end of the age."

—Matthew 28:18–20

Teachings
The faithfulness
of our great Provider
gives sense to our days
and hope to our years.
The future is secure,
for our world belongs to God.

—*Our World Belongs to God*, 13

If you are normal, you are sometimes afraid. Our fears differ, but we all have them. You head off to a new school. You don't know what's there, or even who's there. You feel the flutterings of fear in your stomach. The same is true of getting used to a new home in a new neighborhood or getting used to a new stepparent.

Some people are afraid of high places, or closed-in places, or even wide-open places. They have phobias. Some kids are clutched with fear at the sight of asparagus or brussels sprouts. Some are afraid to fly.

Many people are afraid of losing their health, or their job, or their spouse. And most of us are afraid of walking around in certain neighborhoods after dark. We are also afraid of some animals. And of some people. And of getting lost. When we are lost, a fear rises up in us that becomes a panic if we do not fight it. In fact, it might be the panic, not the lostness, that ends up hurting us.

But perhaps the greatest of all twentieth-century fears is that of nuclear war. At first only the USA had nuclear capability. Then the Soviet Union gained it. Soon other nations, one by one, were added to the list of those with the ability to blow creation away. The world's fear is that not only smart college students but also crazy terrorist groups will develop nuclear capability and use it to bend great nations to their will.

Meanwhile, the two superpowers, the USA and the USSR, race to see who can surpass the other in nuclear destructive potential. They bargain and bicker. They accuse and defend. The two nations have been compared to two men, both drenched with gasoline and locked in a small room, who argue with each other about who has more matches.

One of the special treasures of the Christian faith is God's assurance that world events—even the nuclear arms race—are under control. God is the sovereign Lord of history. Nobody gets elected president or premier unless God permits and controls it. Nobody stockpiles weapons or reduces those stockpiles unless God sees fit to allow it. No nation rises or falls except by God's purpose. We live in God's world.

What does this mean? We have already seen how God provides. He has acted in the past to rescue his people and in the present to work for good. In fact, he does both these things all the time. All along he works steadily through the rhythms of nature to preserve and support life. What he does is all part of God's great world plan that centers in the work of Jesus Christ. And it stretches out into the future. God has a plan for "the fullness of time" to make sure the magnificent death and resurrection of Christ have the results God wants—peace and love and the final safety of God's people and his world.

What does this mean for *us*? It means we may be confident in spite of our fears. God is at work in our world by the Holy Spirit. God is speaking to the world by his Word. God is saving the world through his church. Over all, God is in control. God *will* act in providence to bring our world to the end he has in mind.

Will that include nuclear war? Many Christians believe God will never permit such a war; he will not give human beings the terrible power to bring the world to its last chapter. Others believe God might permit it, but only if it is the way *he* has chosen to end the world's story.

We do not know. But we *do* know the world is in God's hands. We are therefore free to grow and love, marry and work, worship and serve. That is because we know that whatever happens, whatever and whomever we fear, nothing in the world can ever separate us from the love of God.

He is in control.

Prayer
O God, you have the whole world in your hands. And you have us. Help us to trust you so completely that we may live our lives without fear of any enemy. Through Jesus Christ, Amen.

HOMEWORK

Vocabulary
Please study the following words and definitions until you know them well enough to explain them on your own.

13. providence: the care God shows for his creation. God preserves our world, rescues his people, works for good, and controls history. Providence lets us trust and thank God.

Questions
Please answer the following questions on a separate sheet of paper. Use the readings from each day to help you. *Be sure to bring the completed assignment, along with this textbook, to class.*

Day 1: Mention six things that we tend to take for granted in our day-to-day lives which actually come from God and are signs of his providence. Why does God provide these things for us?

Day 2: Why can't the world preserve itself? (2 reasons)

Day 3: What reasons can we give for all the terrible suffering and evil in our world—why does it happen?
What promise can you find in today's Scripture and confession?

Day 4: What would you say to someone who is constantly worried about the possibility of a nuclear war? Write a short paragraph on this.

Summary
Almost every family has a "rescue story" in its history—a time when God saved them from trouble or provided for them in a special way. Talk to your family about this. Briefly describe (in writing) the main thing that happened to you or to someone in your family. Be ready to share your "story" with the class.

4

GOD

   SPEAKS

      IN CREATION

         AND

            PROVIDENCE

DAY 1

GOD

SPEAKS

Scripture

"Every valley shall be raised up,
 every mountain and hill made low;
the rough ground shall become level,
 the rugged places a plain.
And the glory of the Lord will be
 revealed,
 and all mankind together will see it.
 For the mouth of the Lord
 has spoken."

—Isaiah 40:4–5

Teachings

We know him by two means:
First, by the creation, preservation, and government
of the universe. . . .
Second, he makes himself known to us more openly by his holy and divine
Word. . . .

—Belgic Confession, Article 2

S uppose your friend calls you on the phone. Suppose the President or Prime Minister addresses the nation. Suppose a preacher delivers a sermon or a sports fan yells an insult or a teacher presents a lesson or a comedian tells a joke or a parent praises a child or a group discusses an idea or a sergeant barks a command or a TV announcer brings an "important message" about a new product—a combination dessert topping and floor wax.

What do all these people do? They *speak*.

Speaking is so common we don't even think about it. We begin speech so early in our lives we cannot remember learning it. We hear so much speaking we unconsciously tune much of it out.

Yet there are times when the power and importance of speech impress us. If you travel in a foreign country, for instance, you may become frustrated because you cannot speak the language. Or if you have a speech defect, you may have to struggle to overcome it. If you think you must criticize something a person has said or done, you notice how important it is to choose your words carefully.

Speech is a gift of God to human beings. Animals cannot speak—at least not as well as we can. Speech lets us inform others. It lets us persuade, question, command, even entertain. By speech people have declared war, preserved history, confessed sin, preached the gospel, made promises, and greeted friends. Sometimes people speak just for the fun of it. And sometimes they misuse the powerful gift of speech by mocking a kind act or by taking God's name in vain or by telling a sneaky lie.

Speech is so important to how we think, feel, and act that ordinary human life would be unimaginable without it.

The Bible tells us that God speaks. The same God who gives speech also speaks himself. We recall that God's speaking brings the world into existence. Over and over in Genesis 1 we read the words "And God said. . . ." When God speaks, things happen.

But God speaks in providence as well as in creation. Why? God wants to *get through* to his human creatures. Even after they rebel against him and fall into sin, he wants to be in touch with them, in fellowship with them. God is a personal, active, caring, saving, communicating God. And his creatures cannot know his will or hear his plans or be frightened by his warnings or comforted by his forgiveness unless he speaks and they listen.

So the Bible is full of God's providential speaking. God gives commands and asks questions. God makes covenants and in wonderful ways promises a Savior. God calls prophets and appoints priests, judges, and kings. In the New Testament God the Father announces Jesus' birth and declares his love for him at Jesus' baptism (Luke 3:22). Jesus himself speaks for the Father and as his Son. He forgives sins, drives out demons, converses with his friends, comforts the poor, rebukes some of the Pharisees. After Jesus' resurrection the Holy Spirit teaches the disciples what to say and do.

God speaks. In creation and providence the Father, Son, and Spirit command, declare, question, comfort, teach, forgive.

But how? After all, even though our text for today says "the mouth of the Lord has spoken," we know that God the Father does not really have a mouth. So how can he speak?

God has his ways. He arranges for people to have mysterious dreams and visions. He speaks through the beauty and design of his created world. He speaks by way of meaningful events. It seems in the Bible as if God sometimes speaks by creating thoughts in the minds of certain believers. In biblical times God spoke most often by sending someone to speak for him—a prophet, an apostle, a messenger, even his own Son. All of what these people say for God is the word of God; the part of their message that is written down in the Old and New Testaments is the Bible.

Does it still happen, do you think? Does God still speak?

Prayer

O God, thank you for not leaving us alone in this world. Thank you for speaking to us. In Jesus' name, Amen.

DAY 2

GOD SPEAKS

IN HIS WORLD

Scripture

The heavens declare the glory of God;
  the skies proclaim the work of his hands.
Day after day they pour forth speech;
  night after night they display knowledge.
There is no speech or language
  where their voice is not heard.
Their voice goes out into all the earth,
  their words to the ends of the world.

—Psalm 19:1–4

Teachings

We know him by two means:
First, by the creation, preservation, and government
of the universe,
since that universe is before our eyes
like a beautiful book
  in which all creatures,
  great and small,
  are as letters
  to make us ponder
  the invisible things of God:
   his eternal power
   and his divinity.

—Belgic Confession, Article 2

A young shepherd watches his flock by night. In the stillness of the long watch he leans on his staff and gazes into the evening sky. He sees hundreds of stars, maybe as many as two thousand. As always, some seem bright, some faint, a few hazy or milky. A number of stars appear to be doubled up with others. Parts of the sky look like great fields of stars, the individual lights combining into a huge cluster.

Here and there the shepherd thinks he spies star patterns that look like dippers, dragons, camels, or hunters. He observes that certain familiar stars appear in a different place than they did only a few months before. But from long experience he knows that when the seasons come around again, these stars will be back in the same section of sky where they used to be.

This particular night, while the shepherd watches, an eerie thing happens. Near the top of the quarter moon a brilliant star disappears behind the darkened part of the moon, only to reappear on the light side of it a few minutes later. The shepherd is awed, humbled, impressed. And into the Judean night he whispers the name of God.

As the hours pass, the shepherd waits for the sun to rise and his watch to end. Gradually the sky in the east lightens and blushes pink. Then the great flaming ball of light begins its climb. It seems full of fire and excitement for a new day. It is like an eager runner, straining at his starting blocks. Or it is like a joyful young husband who comes out of his dark tent and stretches his arms toward the sky and the new day in his life. Glancing at the climbing sun that will soon bathe everything in its inescapable heat, the shepherd once more turns in his thoughts to God.

Day and night. Light and darkness. Sun and stars. The shepherd thinks about them. Are not these the things God made by speaking at creation? And now here they still are for us to see and feel—great, silent things full of God's mystery and beauty. They are so regular you can plan your life by them. Surely something of God comes through in the watches of the night or in the heat of the noontime. At last the shepherd sits down to turn his thoughts into a song:

> The heavens declare the glory of God;
> the skies proclaim the work of his hands.
> Day after day they pour forth speech;
> night after night they display knowledge.

So it is for us. God speaks in his world. In the design of the evening sky, in the color and variety of 685,000 kinds of insects, in the growth of 250,000 species of plants, in the birth of a human child whose tiny ears are shaped to catch the sound of a mother's voice—in all these things, and in countless others, God speaks.

God speaks his power in the endless crashing of surf against coastal cliffs. God speaks his reliability in the regular rhythm of day and night, light and darkness. God speaks his providential care in the design of grasshoppers that look like leaves to their enemies and in the hitchhiking of young beetles who get to their homes on the backs of bees. A number of Christians have suggested that God speaks his sense of humor in the design of the duckbilled platypus, one of the earth's oddest-looking mammals.

God speaks in his world. And his world includes us. From the incredible complexity of our brains to the simplicity of our little toes our bodies reveal the thought and work of God. But God also speaks in our thoughts and feelings. That is why we long for him even when we do not know it. That is why we do not find it hard to believe in God even though we cannot see him. That is why we know the difference between right and wrong.

God speaks in us.

Prayer
O God, the heavens declare your glory and the skies proclaim the work of your hands. Thank you for speaking to us in your world. Amen.

DAY 3

GOD SPEAKS

IN HIS WORD

Scripture

"As the rain and the snow
  come down from heaven
and do not return to it
  without watering the earth
and making it bud and flourish,
  so that it yields seed for the sower
    and bread for the eater,
so is my word that goes out from my mouth:
  It will not return to me empty,
but will accomplish what I desire
  and achieve the purpose for which I sent it."

—Isaiah 55:10–11

Teachings

Second, he makes himself known to us more openly
by his holy and divine Word,
as much as we need in this life,
  for his glory
  and for the salvation of his own.

—Belgic Confession, Article 2

As we have seen and heard, God speaks in his world. In the beauty, order, and caretaking of nature God declares his goodness, greatness, and sovereignty. In our own human longing for God and in our knowledge of right and wrong, God says that we belong to him and that he wants us to act like his children. In other words, God's speaking and acting *reveal* who God is and what he wants.

God speaks in his world. But he also speaks in his word. Are the two kinds of speaking connected?

They are. We can see how they are connected by looking at the Bible text for today.

In the Isaiah text at the head of this page God first talks about rain and snow, about the water that descends from the clouds. What does it do? It moistens the dry earth so that corn, wheat, rye, soybeans, and other nourishing things can sprout and grow. The grains we eat in cereals and bread come up from the earth because water comes down from heaven. One *purpose* of rain is the watering of crops. If the earth is saturated, the water that collects in ponds and field puddles does not ordinarily evaporate back into the atmosphere until it has done its life-giving work. The falling and rising of water tell us that God is good and that he wants to preserve life on the earth.

In the same way, says God in verse 11, my word comes to earth from heaven, accomplishes its purpose, and then returns to me. In world and word there is the same pattern. Things come from God, do their work, and return to him. Their mission is accomplished.

But what is the purpose or mission of God's speaking in his word? Why doesn't God just speak in his world? After all, we can tell a great deal about God from what he says in his world. Isn't it enough?

No. The reason it isn't enough can be said simply and sadly: human beings have sinned and fallen away from God. They have lost their ability to see and hear God clearly in his world.

One of the terrible things about sin is that it blinds us to God's glory in creation and providence. It also deafens us so that we can no longer hear God speak. That is why people look at the starry sky without thinking of God. People listen to the wind moving mysteriously through the trees and do not hear the voice of God.

Sin has blinded and deafened us to God. But the fall into sin way back at the beginning has also interfered somehow with creation itself. Things in nature are no longer perfectly good. The rain and snow that come down from heaven sometimes cause terrible floods. Or sometimes they quit coming altogether. Then fields dry up, topsoil blows away, and people suffer from drought and famine. We and all the rest of creation have been badly damaged by sin.

That is why God speaks not only in his world but also in his word. He wants to get through to us. So he sends prophets and preachers to warn us, challenge us, comfort us. More clearly than nature can these people tell us who God is and what he wants. They spell it out. They especially tell us something nature never could—how we can be saved from sin. They bring the saving Word of God. Isaiah is a prophet who does this. Your own minister is a preacher who does it. Isaiah preaches in the Bible. Your minister preaches from the Bible.

God speaks in his word. By influencing certain human beings to say what he wants them to say, God *addresses* us. He questions and commands. He announces his rescue plan. Then we *respond* to God by answering, obeying, and praising him.

In this way the word of God accomplishes its purpose. It does not return to God empty, but accomplishes what he desires and achieves the purpose for which he sent it.

Prayer

O God, you never give up. When people can no longer read what you say in nature, you find another way. In this, and in everything, you are incredibly great and good. In Jesus' name, Amen.

DAY 4

GOD SPEAKS

BY HIS SON

Scripture
In the beginning was the Word, and the Word was with God, and the Word was God. He was with God in the beginning. . . . The Word became flesh and lived for a while among us. We have seen his glory, the glory of the one and only Son, who came from the Father, full of grace and truth. —John 1:1,2,14

Teachings
God remembered his promise
to reconcile the world to himself;
he has come among us
in Jesus Christ.

—Our World Belongs to God, 29

When poets want to compare two things, they often use a *metaphor.* They say things like this: "The road was a ribbon that wound around the mountain." Or, "Morning is a new sheet of paper for you to write on." Or even, "The Lord is my shepherd."

Perhaps you know about metaphors from your literature classes in school. A metaphor compares two things that are otherwise not very much alike. Poets aren't the only ones who use metaphors. Everyone does. In fact, some metaphors have become so common we hardly notice that they are comparisons: "He's a star." "He's a pig." "This car's a lemon." "You're off-base" (or off-track, or off your rocker). "It's in the bag." "This reading is a piece of cake."

One wonders what foreigners think of our metaphors. They must find some of them puzzling!

But, puzzling or not, metaphors are useful things. While they are still new to us, they help us see an object or a person in a fresh way. They delight us with a pleasing or surprising comparison.

The Bible is full of metaphors. Our bodies, for example, are called "temples of the Holy Spirit" (1 Cor. 6:19). The word of God is compared to a "double-edged sword" that cuts us to the heart (Heb. 4:12). Faith is said to be a "shield" against everything Satan can throw at us (Eph. 6:16).

Some of the best and most interesting metaphors in the Bible have to do with God and God's Spirit. For example, as stated above, "The Lord is my shepherd" is a famous metaphor. But in the Bible God is also compared to a rock (Ps. 18:2), to flowing streams of water (Ps. 42:1), to fire (Heb. 12:29), to a bird (Ps. 17:8), to a nursing mother (Isa. 49:15), to a husband (Hos. 2:16), and to human fathers, kings, judges, and lords. The Spirit of God is compared to a wind (John 3:8).

So it is with Jesus Christ. The Bible uses a number of metaphors for him, especially in the gospel of John. Jesus is "the light of the world" (1:9). He is "the bread of life" (6:35). He is a grape vine (15:1). And, as our text says, Jesus is the Word of God.

What could that metaphor mean? How could a person be like a word?

Let's see. Suppose someone said, "Do you want to know leadership? Think of George Washington!" "Do you want to know what wickedness is? Think of Hitler!" "Do you want to know what honesty is? Think of Abe Lincoln!" Do you see what is going on here? We connect a person with a certain word if the person is a striking example of what the word means. A word can be *lived out* or *embodied* in a person. Honesty, for instance, was embodied in Abe Lincoln.

Now let's try some of our questions again. Do you want to know what truthfulness is? Think of Jesus Christ. All the words and qualities—all the attributes—that apply to God may be seen in action in the life of Jesus. Love, goodness, and greatness are embodied in him. These qualities, as the Bible puts it, "became flesh and lived for a while among us." In fact, whatever God wants to say to us is said by the life and teaching of Jesus. God's *Word* to us is this person. God speaks by the Son of God.

What does God say by way of Jesus? One day Jesus calmed a storm. It was God's way of saying he is sovereign over nature. One day Jesus multiplied bread and fish to feed a great crowd. It was God's way of saying that he would nourish his people and care for them. One day Jesus was nailed to a tree by wicked people. By this event God tells us how great our sin is. But he also tells us that his love and power to overcome it are even greater.

God speaks in his world. God speaks in his word. God speaks especially by his Son. And what God says by his Son is the greatest story ever told.

Prayer

God our Father, no words in the world could ever say how great and good you are. But you have said it in Jesus Christ, your Son. Thank you, O God, for your Word that became flesh to live among us. In Jesus' name, Amen.

HOMEWORK

Vocabulary
Please study the following words and definitions until you know them well enough to explain them on your own.

14. God's speaking: God's communication to us. God speaks in his world, in his word (including the Bible), and by his Son. God's speaking tells us that God is a personal, caring, and saving God. When God speaks, we ought to respond.

15. God's word: what God says in his speaking. Some of what God says is written down in the Bible. That is why the Bible is sometimes called God's Word. Everything important about God is "lived out" by his Son, Jesus Christ. That is why he is sometimes called the Word of God.

Questions
Please answer the following questions on a separate sheet of paper. Use the readings from each day to help you. *Be sure to bring the completed assignment, along with this textbook, to class.*

Day 1: Where does God speak (2 places)? Why does he speak? What does God's speaking tell us about him?

Day 2: Supply your *own* examples of how God speaks his power, his reliability, his providential care, his creative variety, his attention to the smallest detail, his sense of humor.

Day 3: In what forms do we hear God's word? Why does God need to speak to us with words? What can words tell us that creation (the world) can't?

Day 4: How can Jesus, a person, be the Word?

Summary
How should we respond to God's speaking in his world? How should we respond to God's speaking in his word?

5

GOD

SPEAKS

IN THE

SCRIPTURES

DAY 1

THE INSPIRATION

OF SCRIPTURE

Scripture

But as for you, continue in what you have learned and have become convinced of, because you know those from whom you learned it, and how from infancy you have known the holy Scriptures, which are able to make you wise for salvation through faith in Christ Jesus. All Scripture is God-breathed.

—2 Timothy 3:14–16a

Teachings

We confess that this Word of God
was not sent nor delivered by the will of men,
but that holy men of God spoke,
being moved by the Holy Spirit,
    as Peter says.

Afterwards our God—
    because of the special care he has
    for us and our salvation—
commanded his servants,
the prophets and apostles,
to commit this revealed Word to writing.

—Belgic Confession, Article 3

During the Vietnam War many American soldiers were captured and imprisoned by the enemy. One group of soldiers told part of their story when they were finally released. They told how they had been painfully beaten up. They described stinking food and hopeless sleeping conditions. They recalled how many times they had prepared themselves to die, certain that their enemies would either torture them to death or else casually shoot them through the brain.

One additional agony these prisoners suffered was loneliness. Their captors purposely kept them apart so they could not encourage each other or plan escapes. Each prisoner had to sit in his own miserable cell. There was nothing to do, nothing to read, nobody to talk to.

But a number of these prisoners were Christians. And as they sat on the floor of their cells, fearful and lonely, they tried as hard as they could to recall passages of Scripture they had memorized when they were young. One man could recall Psalm 23. Another knew several other psalms and the Beatitudes. A number of prisoners remembered John 3:16. And a few knew a lot more.

Gradually they worked out a system of communication. They would tap in code on the walls that separated their cells. At first they tapped names, addresses, and simple greetings. Then they tapped encouragement. They tapped warnings. And they tapped out as many Bible verses and passages as they knew, each man adding as much as he could recall to the general treasury of Scripture.

By the time these Christians were released, they had put together hundreds of verses of Scripture. They had assembled their own Bible. One of them later said that this activity saved their sanity and probably their lives.

The apostle Paul knew what it was like to be in prison. He also knew what it took to encourage another Christian. So Paul writes to Timothy, "Continue in what you have learned . . . how from infancy you have known the holy Scriptures." Then he adds a strange claim. "All Scripture," he says, "is God-breathed."

The first few words present no problem. "Scripture" means writing. "Bible" means book. The Bible is therefore a book of Scriptures or writings. It is the part of God's word that is written down and treasured by the church.

But what does that second part of Paul's sentence mean? "All Scripture is God-breathed." Does Paul picture God as taking a big breath and then exhaling the words of Scripture? Or does he picture the Scriptures as already written and God blowing into them the breath of life to make them lively and helpful? Whatever picture Paul has in mind, he is talking about the *inspiration* of Scripture.

What he means is this: for over a thousand years God breathed his thoughts and words into human writers. From the earliest book of the Bible to the latest, God inspired the Bible's writers. Some were history writers. Some were poets. Some wrote laws and lists, or put down collections of wise sayings. Some wrote about the life of Jesus. Others were letter writers. None of these writers was perfect. All used their own language and style. Each colored what he wrote with some of his own personality. But deep in the hearts and minds of these writers God was at work, influencing them, moving them, inspiring them.

The result is God's breathed-out Word, the Bible. Just as a lifeguard resuscitates a nearly drowned swimmer, so God breathes life into dying human beings by his written Word. The Bible tells people of God's presence, God's purpose, God's Son, and our salvation.

That is why prisoners of war struggle to recall it. That is also why it speaks to you and me. The Scriptures are the very breath of God.

Prayer
O God, thank you for the word from you that comes to us in the Scriptures. Inspire us to hear you speaking in the Bible. Amen.

DAY 2

THE AUTHORITY

OF SCRIPTURE

Scripture
Above all, you must understand that no prophecy of Scripture came about by the prophet's own intepretation. For prophecy never had its origin in the will of man, but men spoke from God as they were carried along by the Holy Spirit
—2 Peter 1:20–21

Teachings
We receive all these books
and these only
as holy and canonical,
for the regulating, founding, and establishing
of our faith.
—Belgic Confession, Article 5

N ew Englanders tell a story about an old man who lived outside a certain town. This man was an expert electrician. In fact, when he was young, he designed the electrical system for the town. He figured out how lines and circuits could best be arranged to bring cheap and plentiful electrical energy to the town's citizens.

But the townspeople did not treat the man well. When he got to a certain age, they fired him and replaced him with younger electricians. In effect, the town told the old man to get lost. So he moved out to a nearby woods. Nobody saw him or heard from him.

Then, one day, the town's power failed. Lights flickered and went out. Refrigerators warmed up. Heaters cooled down. TV sets went dark and silent. The town was in a panic. And none of its young electricians seemed to know how to solve the problem.

Then one of the town commissioners remembered the old man in the woods. Possibly *he* could find a way to restore power. He was an authority on the town's electrical system. After all, he had thought it up in the first place.

So the old man was brought to the central power plant. He walked around slowly for a few moments, shining his flashlight here and there. Finally he pulled a little hammer out of his pocket, walked over to one main circuit, and tapped on it. Instantly the lights went on and power surged through the whole system. The old man went back to his home in the woods.

Three weeks later the mayor received a bill. On it the old man charged the town $1,000.05 for his work. This is how he listed the charges:

　　5¢ tapping
$1,000 knowing where to tap

The old man was an authority on the town's power system. Why? Because he was its author. The system *came* from him.

The Christian church says the Bible is the authority for our faith and our lives. Why? Because God is its author. The Bible gets its authority from its author. What the Bible says, God says. That is why the Bible is an expert on how we must think and act. That is why the Bible has power to influence and help us. That is why the Bible has the right to give us orders that we must obey. *God* speaks through the Bible. And of course God is the supreme authority in the universe. After all, he thought it up in the first place.

The Scriptures are like one of the round, metal speakers in a radio or TV set. If the President or Prime Minister addresses us, we hear him through one or two of those speakers. But the speaker by itself is not authoritative for us. The real authority is instead the person who speaks to us *through* the speaker.

So it is with the Scriptures. As our text says, the Scriptures do not come just from people. Human writers do not themselves have the power to help or command us. Instead, "men spoke from God" as they were carried along, or inspired, by the Holy Spirit.

That is why Christians study the Bible and take it so seriously. It is God's speaker. It speaks with God's authority. Christians are people who stand in the world with this *book* in their hands. We obey its commands. We open ourselves up to its comfort. We thrill to its great passages of hope. And through the Bible we come to know Jesus Christ, our Savior.

Even Jesus himself read and obeyed the Bible. So must we. It is our authority because of its author.

Prayer
Dear God, our heavenly Father, you are the one who speaks to us through the Scriptures. *You* are our authority. But you are also our loving Savior, through Jesus Christ your Son. Amen.

DAY 3

THE INFALLIBILITY

OF SCRIPTURE

Scripture
Jesus answered them, "Is it not written in your Law, 'I have said you are gods'? If he called them 'gods,' to whom the word of God came—and the Scripture cannot be broken—what about the one whom the Father set apart as his very own and sent into the world?

—John 10:34–36

Teachings
Therefore we must not consider human writings—
   no matter how holy their authors may have been—
equal to the divine writings. . . .

For all human beings are liars by nature
and more vain than vanity itself.

Therefore we reject with all our hearts
everything that does not agree
with this infallible rule.

—Belgic Confession, Article 7

The marathon is a twenty-six-mile race for endurance runners. It tests a person's speed, stamina, courage, and even intelligence. To win a marathon a person obviously needs speed: that's the name of the game in every race, short or long. But a marathon runner needs stamina as well—that is, the strength to keep up speed over a great distance. He or she also needs courage to endure pain as the body burns up not only every ounce of its fat but also small amounts of muscle tissue. And a marathon runner needs intelligence in order to make up and follow a "race plan"—that is, a strategy for using speed, stamina, and courage in some way that will actually win the race.

But runners are only human. Some make mistakes in their race plan. Others follow their race plan perfectly—except for the part at the end that calls for them to cross the finish line first. These runners simply lack winning speed, stamina, and courage. So a few of them try to cheat. In the 1972 Olympics at Munich, a runner sneaked into the race at mile twenty-five. He had not bothered to run the first twenty-four miles. This, of course, gave him a small advantage. He used it to cross the finish line first, but he did not win the race. He was disqualified as a cheater.

The fact is that most runners do not win. By cheating, or by making a strategy mistake, or simply by failing to keep up, a runner can easily fall short of his or her goal. Runners are not *infallible*.

The Bible is. When the church says in its confessions that the Scriptures are infallible, it means three things. It means, first, that the Bible does not cheat or deceive us. It means, second, that the Bible makes no mistakes in bringing God's Word to us. In the third place it means that the Bible does not fail to reach its goal. The Bible, if we may say so reverently, is a winner.

Let's take these meanings of infallibility one at a time. First, the Bible does not cheat or deceive us. It is honest and truthful. In this respect the Bible differs from a lot of other books. Many books, after all, tell you lies. Some say the Christian church is for weaklings and fools. Some say it is OK to hurt someone if it will help you get what you want. A number of books suggest that making a great deal of money is the best thing to do with your life. Some books give twisted accounts of love and sex. Human beings often lie. Some of the clever ones publish their lies in books.

But the Bible is truthful. It comes from human beings, but ultimately it comes from God. And God doesn't lie. We can therefore depend on the Scriptures.

Second, the Bible makes no mistakes in bringing God's Word to us. It makes no error in doing this. We therefore say that it is "inerrant." Like a runner who makes and follows a perfect race plan, the Scriptures faithfully present Jesus Christ and God's rescue plan for fallen people.

This does not mean, of course, that there are only plain, boring facts in the Bible and no personal interpretations of these facts or interesting stories about them. As we know, the Bible uses parables, stories, metaphors. Matthew, Mark, Luke, and John offer four accounts of Jesus, each a little different from the others. And we know that the Bible writers lived in the ancient world. They believed that the sun revolves around the earth and that the earth is flat. No matter. So far as the *message* of the Bible is concerned, its Scriptures make no mistake.

Third, the Bible does not fail or fall down in reaching its goal. It achieves God's purpose of helping to save believing women, men, children, and teens of every race and of all times and places. That is, besides being honest and accurate, the Bible is effective. It works. People get rescued by taking the Bible's message to heart. They also learn how to please and thank their rescuer.

The Scriptures, as our text says, cannot be "broken." They cannot fail, or fall, or falter, or be false. They are the infallible Word of God.

And they are meant for you and me.

Prayer
Lord God, let the same Holy Spirit who inspired the writers of the Bible help your word find its way into our hearts. Through Jesus Christ, your Son, Amen.

DAY 4

THE PROPER

USES OF SCRIPTURE

Scripture
All Scripture is God-breathed and is useful for teaching, rebuking, correcting and training in righteousness, so that the man of God may be thoroughly equipped for every good work.   —2 Timothy 3:16–17

Teachings
The Bible is the Word of God,
record and tool of His redeeming work.
It is the Word of Truth,
fully reliable in leading us
to know God and have life
in Jesus Christ.   —*Our World Belongs to God,* 35

One of my friends recently told me about a man who was packing for a long trip. The man's wife asked him if he was ready to go. "Almost," he said. "But there is still a corner in one suitcase to fill with what's left: a guidebook, a lamp, a mirror, a hammer, a book of good poetry, a bundle of old letters, a hymn book, a sharp sword, and a small library of sixty-six volumes."

"But how will you get all *that* in your suitcase?" his wife asked. "Like this," said the man, as he placed his Bible in the few inches of remaining space and then closed the suitcase.

What this story tells us, of course, is that the Bible is many things at once. And it has many *uses*: it guides us, lights up the world through which we walk, reflects the face of God like a mirror, teaches us the early history of Israel, and so on.

Some people use the Bible in ways never intended by its writers. For example, some people carry a pocket Bible for good luck. Some treat the Bible as if it were a magic crystal ball or a deck of fortune-telling cards: they close their eyes, flip Bible pages at random, and let their finger drop blindly to a place on some page. Underneath their finger is the text they will use to guide their decisions for the day. (What do you do if the text only says something like "And Uz was the brother of Buz"?)

A few people spend their time fooling around with the Bible, thinking, for example, about who was the shortest man in the Bible (either Bildad the Shuhite, or else the Roman soldier who slept on his watch). Some people even make up sports quizzes about where the Bible refers to such things as tennis ("Joseph served in Pharaoh's court") or baseball ("In the big inning"), and so on.

But all this is foolishness. We must not use the Bible for things outside its purpose. The Bible is not a handy guide to boat building, animal habits, astronomy, or the exact age of the earth. Surely the Bible is not our magic book or fortune-teller.

So what *is* the Bible for? What are its proper uses?

First, the Bible tells us the truth about God, the world, and how they are related to each other. The Bible is a kind of tourist's guide to the universe. We read the Bible to become informed, to get good information about who God is and who we are in God's world. Our task is to receive and believe this information.

Second, the Bible tells us not only what to believe but also how to behave. The two are connected. For instance, it is *because* we believe that God is great and good that we worship him and seek to imitate him by being good to others—especially those who are unpopular and weak. As our text for today says, the Bible teaches and trains us in righteousness. It is like an athlete's training manual or a runner's race plan. Our task is to follow the manual.

Third, the Bible lifts us and helps us with our problems. The same Holy Spirit who inspired the Scriptures now inspires us when we read them so that we are filled with hope. The Bible *encourages* believers. Our task is to take such encouragement to heart.

Fourth, as we mature, the Scriptures guide us to become intelligent citizens, to spend our money properly, to choose a job and mate in a Christian way, and so forth. Of course, the Bible cannot answer all our questions. For example, it cannot tell us which person to marry or to vote for in an election. But it can tell us what *sort* of person to marry or vote for. In this way the Bible is a guide to all of life. Our task is to let it lead us.

Finally, the Bible is the book that helps us become personally close to God our Father and Jesus Christ our Savior. We must therefore trust them and give ourselves over to them.

For all these reasons we must read and know the Scriptures. The Scriptures are the main place that the God of the universe speaks. And when God speaks, we must listen and believe.

Prayer

O God, when you speak, help us listen. Teach us through the Bible how to love and serve you better. Through Jesus Christ, Amen.

HOMEWORK

Vocabulary
This week's words are very important in helping us understand the Bible. Please study them extra carefully. If your teacher is giving a unit test after unit 1, also begin reviewing the vocabulary and questions of each week.

16. Bible: the book that contains the writings, or Scriptures, that Christians recognize as the written Word of God.

17. inspiration of Scripture: the process by which God "breathed" into the biblical writers what he wanted them to write. God moved, influenced, inspired them by the Holy Spirit. The same Holy Spirit now inspires us to receive and believe the Bible.

18. authority of Scripture: The power of the Bible to influence our believing and acting. Because the Bible is our authority, it can even give commands that we must obey. The Bible is authoritative because God is its author and because only in the Bible do we find Jesus Christ, our rescuer.

19. infallibility of Scripture: the quality of the Bible that means it will not *fail*. By the Bible's unfailingness or infallibility we mean it does not deceive us, make mistakes in presenting God's word, or fail to reach its goal of helping people get saved and then lead thankful lives.

Questions
This is the last time we'll be telling you to write your answers out on a separate sheet of paper and to bring your assignment and textbook to class. You will still have to do these things, of course, but you shouldn't need any more reminders from us. This week's questions follow:

Day 1: Review the definition of *inspiration* above. What word in 2 Timothy 3:16–17 means "inspired"? What words in Article 3 of the Belgic Confession describe what we mean when we say the Bible is "inspired"?

Day 2: Review the definition of the authority of Scripture. Why do Christians study the Bible and take it so seriously? How should we respond to the authority of the Bible?

Day 3: Review the definition of the infallibility of Scripture. In what three ways is the Bible infallible? What good does it do you to know this?

Day 4: Mention three improper uses of the Bible and five proper uses of the Bible.

Summary
Write a paragraph in which you describe the place of the Bible in your life. (How important is it to you? How often do you read it or hear it read? How is it helpful to you?)

HUMANITY

6

THE

HUMAN

TRAGEDY

DAY 1

WHAT IS WRONG

WITH US?

Scripture

When the woman saw that the fruit of the tree was good for food and pleasing to the eye, and also desirable for gaining wisdom, she took some and ate it.

—Genesis 3:6

Teachings

Early in human history
our first parents listened to an intruder's voice.
Rather than living by the Creator's
word of life,
they fell for Satan's lie
and sinned!

—*Our World Belongs to God*, 14

Something is wrong with us human beings, and we know it. We know that when we watch TV or read the front page of a newspaper, we often see or read bad news. A gang in Los Angeles sprays a birthday party with gunfire, killing four teenagers. An arsonist in Toronto sets fire to a house while people are sleeping in it. Some macho bully robs an elderly man and snaps his brittle old bones with terrible kicks and punches. Two powerful nations talk frighteningly of nuclear war. Yet another government official is accused of wasting or stealing the citizens' money. A drunk driver careens over a curb and smashes into a child on a tricycle.

On it goes, day after day, year after year, all across the country, all across the world. We are talking, of course, about sin and misery. Together they make up what we call *evil*. Nobody can miss evil. Everybody knows about it. As a matter of fact, all of us who read this know about evil from our own experience. Sometimes we suffer from it; sometimes we make others suffer from it.

Why? After all, everybody knows that evil things are hurtful. So why don't people just stop doing them?

Experts guess at the reasons. Some say the reason we hurt each other is that we have not yet outgrown our animal past: we are part beast and part human. Education, they insist, is what we need to make us more fully human.

But that is not right. Animals are not as cruel or sly as humans. They don't torture each other, for instance. So in some ways we ought to be not less but more like animals. And education is not the solution to our problem either. Wrongly used, it just turns dull criminals into smart ones.

Others say what's wrong with us is that we cannot get what we want—money, for example, or a feeling of power over others, or personal freedom to do as we please. We are therefore frustrated and angry and show it by the hurtful ways we act. These people believe that more money or power or freedom will solve our problems.

But that is not right either. In the first place, if people want money or power or freedom, they will have to take them from others. Then *those* people will be frustrated and angry. In the second place, most people who get what they want are still not satisfied. They keep wanting more money or power or freedom, thus raising the same old problem all over again.

Christians believe what the Bible teaches—that there is a better and deeper explanation of human trouble with sin and misery. The first human beings, as we learned in lesson 2, were created good. In fact, they were made to image God by being powerful rulers, loving companions, joyfully obedient children of God.

But they sinned. They stumbled and fell. And like a chain of dominoes, all of us who come after them have been toppled by their fall. We stand or fall together.

Or think of it like this: parents pass on certain traits to their children. Your eye, skin, and hair color, for instance, come from your parents or, through them, from your grandparents. Even some diseases can be inherited.

The tendency to do wrong instead of right is something like that. Like a hereditary disease it is passed down the generations. We are born with it. And every day we see, read about, or suffer the symptoms of our human disease: lying, stealing, murder, war, divorce, ridicule of others.

Here is yet another way to think of it: the human race is like a great palace in ruins. We were built by a master builder. You can still see some of the soaring greatness and noble goodness he built in. In fact, that is why everybody in our world wishes things were different from the way they are. People remember what our house used to be like.

But we have wrecked our house. We now see crumbling, sagging, rusting, and ruin. And we seem powerless to fix these things. Every repair we make needs repairs itself.

If only the master builder would come back! Without him, the human story can only be called a tragedy.

Prayer

O God, we cannot be healed of our human disease unless you heal us. We cannot live in our house unless you rebuild it. Through Jesus Christ, our Lord, Amen.

DAY 2

LISTENING

TO THE GREAT DECEIVER

Scripture
"You will not surely die," the serpent said to the woman. "For God knows that when you eat of it your eyes will be opened, and you will be like God, knowing good and evil."

—Genesis 3:4–5

Teachings
Early in human history
our first parents listened to the intruder's voice.
Rather than living by the creator's
word of life,
they fell for Satan's lie
and sinned!

—Our World Belongs to God, 14

Did you ever notice that evil is always advertised as good? When people want you to do something wrong, they hardly ever say, "Try it! You'll hate it! It's a rotten thing to do!" They never suggest that you lie or cheat or steal or mock somebody just because it's wrong and hurtful. They never advertise some foolish or useless thing on TV as being foolish and useless.

No, people dress up evil as good. They put a good face on it. They say, "Try it! You'll like it!" They say, "Let's do it just for the fun of it." They say that if you lie, you'll protect yourself. If you steal, you'll enrich yourself. If you cheat, you'll get ahead. If you mock somebody, you'll feel better yourself. And, of course, fun, protection, riches, getting ahead, and feeling better can all be good things.

Evil imitates good. It cannot show its true face. Evil always wears a mask. We see this already near the beginning of the human story. Part of the tragedy of the fall is that Adam and Eve listen to the Great Deceiver. (Genesis calls him a serpent, but according to Revelation 12:9 he is really Satan or the devil.) The Great Deceiver's best trick is to make evil sound good. He could sell kryptonite to Superman.

As we know, the first human beings were free and full of bliss in loving and serving God. The only thing God did not permit them to do was eat fruit from a mysterious tree called "the tree of the knowledge of good and evil."

It is on this tree that the Great Deceiver centers his sales pitch. Look, he says to Eve, God wants to keep all the power for himself. *He* wants to decide what's good and what's evil. That is why he put this tree off limits. If he says eating its fruit will be the death of you, he lies. God just wants to protect himself. God is a liar, says Satan. "For God knows that when you eat of it your eyes will be opened, and you will be like God, knowing good and evil" (Gen. 3:5).

Can we step back from these familiar words and see what is going on here? It's the oldest trick in the world. It's dressing up evil as good. Satan, the Great Deceiver, points out all the *good* things you get if you disobey God. "Your eyes will be opened" and you will "know good and evil." Satan means you will be able to *decide for yourself* what is good and what is evil. You can make your own rules, run your own garden, do what you want.

In this, says Satan, "you will be like God." And who doesn't sometimes want to play God, or be God, or be like God? It's the top position in the universe! Satan conveniently forgets to mention, of course, that Adam and Eve are already like God. They have been made in God's image and likeness.

So the Great Deceiver sets his trap. The bait is something that, like all bait, looks good. Everything for the human race now depends on whom Eve believes. Will she trust the God who made her and who awakened her to all the light, peace, and joy of life in God's world? Or will she trust the devil who is all dressed up in his borrowed Halloween costume?

We know what happened. We also know it still happens all the time. Evil imitates good. Kidnappers disguise themselves as trusted adults, perhaps as police or family friends. Child molesters tell their victims they love them and that the two of them share a special secret. Liars insist they are telling the truth. Thieves and cheats pretend they are winners. TV programs present silly or violent people as heroes.

Satan himself, says Paul, still "masquerades as an angel of light" (2 Cor. 11:14). When you trust and obey the Great Deceiver, sooner or later you become his slave. It is part of the human tragedy.

Prayer
Unmask evil for us, O God, so we see it as it really is. Then let us turn to you for the only true good there is in the world. Through Jesus Christ, our Lord, Amen.

DAY 3

GREAT

PRETENDERS

Scripture
Pride goes before destruction,
    a haughty spirit before a fall.

—Proverbs 16:18

Teachings
Apart from grace
we prove each day
that we are guilty sinners. . . .
Looking for life without God, we find only death,
grasping for freedom outside his law,
we trap ourselves in Satan's snares;
pursuing pleasure, we lose the gift of joy.

—*Our World Belongs to God,* 15

Satan is a great deceiver. But humans are great pretenders. Everyone pretends now and then to be someone she isn't. Most of the time it is nothing but fun. You imitate someone's voice or wear a crazy hat. You strut across a floor or slink around a corner. You talk confidently about a subject you know nothing about. Do any of these things and you are a pretender. Actors are pretenders. Some politicians are pretenders. Some people who say they are late for school because their alarm didn't go off are pretenders.

Pretending is often full of good humor. But sometimes it isn't. When most countries had kings instead of presidents or prime ministers, *pretenders* were a problem. It was very important to protect the king (especially if he was a good one) from pretenders. Who were these dangerous people? They were persons who tried to unseat the king and enthrone themselves. Sometimes pretenders would gather an army and try to fight the king. Sometimes they would make foolish campaign promises to the people. A pretender would lay claim to the king's throne. That is, he would pretend to be king himself. A good example of a pretender in the Bible is King David's handsome son Absalom.

The story of the fall in Genesis is the story of human pretenders to God's throne. This is one of the times when pretending is not funny. The Great Deceiver tells our first parents that they can "be like God, knowing good and evil." As we have learned, this is a promise that they can decide for themselves what is good and what is evil. That is, it is a promise that Adam and Eve can take God's place.

Trembling with ambition, our first parents pretend to be God. The sad result of this foolishness is the fall heard around the world. For Adam and Eve cannot handle the position of God. They are not up to it. They are, after all, only human.

Can you understand what is tragic about this? Adam and Eve pretend to be someone they are not. Like a teenager who boasts to his class that he will get a TV star to visit school—and then has to admit that he was only dreaming—so the first human beings try pathetically to go beyond their limit. They are tripped up by pride. They fall for pride. That is, they try to go beyond who they are (*images* of God) and be someone they are not (God).

> Pride goes before destruction,
> a haughty spirit before a fall (Prov. 16:18).

We have seen this kind of falling all around us. A teenager tells all his friends he is a great high diver. When the test comes, he actually does a humiliating belly-whopper. Or worse, he has to climb back *down* the ladder. Or picture an over-confident water skier who attempts a casual beach landing. He ends up tumbling head over heels along the beach, his skis stopped dead where their rudders have dug into the sand. Or imagine a child who thinks she can copilot a jumbo jet.

We human beings want so much to be great that we fool ourselves into thinking we are like God. It is a sad and sorry part of the human tragedy. For the truth is that we *are* great if only we do not try to be great pretenders.

Our greatness shines out instead when we reach for God and say "Father."

Prayer

O God, our Father, save us from foolish pride. Save us from being great pretenders. O God, let us instead be your sons and daughters. Through Jesus Christ we pray, Amen.

DAY 4

NAKEDNESS

AND CLOTHING

Scripture
The man and his wife were both naked, and they felt no shame. . . . Then the eyes of both of them were opened, and they realized they were naked; so they sewed fig leaves together and made coverings for themselves. . . . The Lord God made garments of skin for Adam and his wife and clothed them.
—Genesis 2:25; 3:7,21

Teachings
They forget their place;
they tried to be like God.
But as sinners they feared
the nearness of God
and hid from him.
—Our World Belongs to God, 14

The fall brought shame. The texts above tell us how it happened and what God did about it. These texts show us the history of the human race. They tell us of creation, fall, and redemption. They tell us about perfection, then tragedy, then rescue. The texts tell us about nakedness, and shame, and graceful clothing.

Adam and Eve are at first perfectly innocent and unembarrassed in their nakedness. They have nothing to fear, nothing to hide, nothing to cover up. In their nakedness and in their innocence the man and the woman can look at each other and see that they belong together. They are a perfect match. There is nothing to laugh at, no one to hurt. Their nakedness is a sign that nothing is wrong. When Adam and Eve look at each other, all they see is a person to love. That is the way God made them—to be together in his image. The man and the woman are as free in their nakedness before each other as they are in their nakedness before God.

But then the fall. The first blush of shame spreads across the face of the human race. We all know what shame feels like. Shame is a red face, a downcast eye, an awful feeling of being all wrong. Here is its very beginning. Adam and Eve disobey God "and then the eyes of both of them were opened, and they realized they were naked; so they sewed fig leaves together and made coverings for themselves."

As a wise Christian once said, nakedness looked good on perfect human beings. But now things change. With great sorrow and mystery the Bible writer tells us that "they realized they were naked."

What does this part of the fall mean? It means much more than just physical nakedness, much more than embarrassment. Adam and Eve discover *shame*—shame before God, shame before each other, shame as each looks at the self he or she had never really seen before. Now they feel like hiding from God. Now they scramble to pin the blame on someone else. Now they frantically cover up so that they can no longer see their own shame. "They sewed fig leaves together and made coverings for themselves."

Clothing is born. It is still with us. We wear clothing not only for warmth and comfort, not only for color and shape to delight us. We wear clothing to cover up. We need a covering. We need physical secrets. Why?

Because we are no longer good enough to be naked. Public nakedness is too dangerous. It tempts us to hurt other people or to use them for selfish pleasure. Public nakedness would tempt us to ridicule each other. In a perfect world it would not matter if your body was fat or thin or unusually shaped. We would rejoice in such differences the same way we enjoy the difference between a banana and a pear. But in a world that mocks and hurts we need clothing.

Ashamed of themselves, Adam and Eve do the best they can to cover up. They weave pathetic little garments out of fig leaves.

And then a strange and wonderful thing happens. The God they have disobeyed comes back to them. The God they have tried to get rid of brings a gift. The God whose grace is deeper than our sin "made garments of skin for Adam and his wife and clothed them."

Can we see what a wonderful thing this is? Can we see what a surprising and graceful God we have? The man and the woman find themselves naked and ashamed in a suddenly cold and frightening world. Pathetically they shiver in their homemade clothes. *They should never have needed any clothing at all.* But here comes God with better and more durable clothing for their shame. Life in sin will be hard and painful. God knows the man and the woman will need good clothing for it. So the Lord God makes graceful clothing for guilty people.

This is the God to whom we are not enemies but loved children. This is the God of amazing grace in the middle of human tragedy.

Prayer

O God, we often feel alone and ashamed. But you are the God who covers us with your amazing love. We praise your name. Amen.

HOMEWORK

Vocabulary

20. evil: the combination of sin and misery that we see in the world around us. Evil originated in the angel world but comes to us through the fall of Adam and Eve.

21. the fall: the event in which our first parents disobeyed God and thus brought evil into the world.

22. tragedy of the fall: the fact that the fall happens not to unimportant creatures (whose fall wouldn't matter so much) but to people made in God's image. The fall is also tragic because it includes trickery, foolishness, pride, and disastrous results.

23. shame: a sense of humiliation after sin. People who are ashamed feel as if they'd like to crawl under something or have some covering hide them from view. The fall brings shame into the human race.

Questions

Day 1: Mention two false explanations of "what is wrong with us." What chapter in the Bible gives us the right explanation?

Day 2: Explain how Satan deceived Adam and Eve by dressing up evil as good. Give two examples of how TV programs sometimes present evil as good.

Day 3: What did our first parents pretend to be? Why? Name one way we pretend to be more than what we actually are.

Day 4: Which of the Bible verses for this reading show innocence? Shame? God's grace?

Summary

What evidences of sin and misery do you see in your own world: your school, community, home? Mention a couple of specific things you've observed in others or in yourself.

7

ORIGINAL

SIN

DAY 1

ORIGINAL

SIN

Scripture
Sin entered the world through one man, and death through sin, and in this way death came to all men, because all sinned. —Romans 5:12

Teachings
We believe
that by the disobedience of Adam
original sin has been spread
through the whole human race.

It is a corruption of all nature—
an inherited depravity which even infects small infants
   in their mother's womb,
and the root which produces in man
   every sort of sin. —Belgic Confession, Article 15

Suppose you like to draw or paint. Your art teacher has you learn art technique by making pencil copies of interesting photographs. You look at something already done and do it all over again. You do a photocopy.

Now suppose you become skillful enough to enter an art contest. But the rules forbid copies. The rules say you have to hand in "an original pencil drawing or watercolor." An *original*. It means, of course, something you invent. It means something that begins with you. This watercolor or drawing must arise from your own brain, your own imagination. Then it must pass through your nerves and hands and fingers onto a surface. You must come up with something original.

The Christian church speaks of original sin. We mean the sin that had its origin or beginning in Adam and Eve. Sin started with them, but, sad to say, it did not end with them. Adam and Eve's sin is reproduced in all of us. Their sin is the original photograph. Our sins are the reprints, the reproductions, the photocopies.

Of course, an art student can choose whether or not she wishes to copy a photograph. There seems to be much less choice with sin. We do not choose to imitate Adam and Eve when we sin; we just *do*. It is as if we cannot help it. It is as if we are infected with sin while we are still in our mother's womb. We are born with the tendency to sin.

Have you ever noticed, for instance, that little children are naturally selfish? A two-year-old will sometimes try to grab all the toys in the room, even if he cannot possibly hold them all at once. Children have to be shown and told and taught how to share generously with others. Selfishness comes naturally; generosity must be learned. That is why Shel Silverstein's "Child's Prayer" is only half-funny:

Now I lay me down to sleep.
I pray the Lord my soul to keep.
If I should die before I wake,
I pray the Lord my toys to break.
So no other kid can play with 'em.

Let us go further. Just as an original drawing comes from inside a person, so sin comes out of our own hearts and minds and imaginations. Sin is imitation of others, all the way back to Adam and Eve. But it is also more than that. For when sin comes from the inner self, from that deep inner place where we are proud or angry or envious of others, then sin is original all over again.

Let me try to say this another way. When we sin, we do copy others at times. We see how they cheat or sass somebody, and we imitate them. But when we *want* to do that, when we decide to sass or cheat, the sin becomes ours. Something old and bad and deep inside us awakens. And the sin that appears is our original sin.

It is as if a hundred students made drawings of one photograph. Each did it in his own way. Each added her own touches. The result would be a hundred *original copies*.

That is the terrible thing about sin. Sin reproduces itself in countless new ways. Sin makes copies. Sin has children and grandchildren. Sin is a root with a thousand branches. Sin is a river with a million side streams. Sin is a contagious disease with a billion new victims. Sin, in other words, corrupts the whole world with wickedness, sadness, and guilt. And it finds a home in us.

The doctrine of original sin tells us that sin is universal, that it reproduces itself in original copies, and that it is miserably hard to get rid of. When we understand that, and when we begin to understand our own guilt for sin, then we can start to see why the Christian church speaks with longing for a savior.

Prayer

O God, we have gotten into a terrible mess by sinning. We know we all do our part and that sin just gets worse and worse. But we also know the gospel—that Jesus Christ came into the world to save sinners. Let him come for us. Amen.

CORRUPTION

Scripture
To the pure, all things are pure, but to those who are corrupted and do not believe, nothing is pure. In fact, both their minds and consciences are corrupted.

—Titus 1:15

Teachings
Q. Then where does this corrupt human nature come from?
A. From the fall and disobedience of our first parents,
    Adam and Eve, in Paradise.
This fall has so poisoned our nature
    that we are born sinners—
    corrupt from conception on.

—Heidelberg Catechism, Q & A 7

T he Bible has a big vocabulary for sin. It uses metaphors and colorful language to describe the many ways in which sin reproduces.

For example, sometimes the Bible writers think of sin as *unfairness* or *injustice*. Perhaps you recall the word *iniquity*, which means the same thing. Here sin means not treating others as equals. Sin is grabbing and killing a poor man's single lamb. You do it because he is poor and weak and you are rich and powerful. It is unfair.

Sometimes sin is *trespassing* or *transgressing*. God's holiness or God's law is pictured as a piece of land. When we step across the border of it, we trespass. We tread on holy ground. We go beyond our limits. We sin as Adam and Eve did in trying to be as God.

Or sometimes sin is pictured as missing a target, or stumbling and falling, or getting all dirty, or wandering off the right path and getting lost.

What the Bible writers are telling us with this rich language is that sin is everywhere. Sin seeps into every part of the human house, like an over-flowing sewer that cannot be plugged. It is not just that we commit wrong acts (we trespass). It is also that we fail to do right acts (we miss the target by a mile). We commit wrong and omit right.

Further, it is not just that our acts are wrong (like beating up a smaller and weaker person). It is also that our words are often wrong: we lie, for example, or brag, or mock someone who is clumsy. And it is not just that our words and deeds are often wrong. Even our thoughts show that sin has seeped in. We secretly think we are better than others, for instance, even if we don't dare say it. Or we envy someone who is smarter or richer. Or we wickedly look down on a person of another race.

To sum up, sins are of thought, word, and deed. They are sins of omission and commission. A sin is in fact anything at all that displeases God and does not match up with his will for us.

But the Bible writers do not talk just about sins in the plural. Often they talk instead about sin, in the singular. They see sin as a huge force or power that floods into human life like an army—destroying kindness, smashing justice, deceiving children, hurting old people, wrecking families, drowning the poor, pulling down good rulers and propping up bad ones, bribing the police, and ruining everything good.

When this power shows itself in our own homes, when it conquers us as persons, we think, talk, and act like sinners. In fact, it is not only that we are sinners because we sin. It is also that we sin because we are sinners. When sin is inside us, when it floods our hearts, then sins flow forth from sin. Sin is the sewer; sins are all the gunk and junk that flow from it.

The word for this seeping, flowing power of sin is *corruption*. Original sin corrupts us.

Of course, hardly anybody ever shows the worst of such corruption. If all human sewers gushed full force all the time, life would end in a miserable flood of evil. That is why God checks the floods. He holds them back. He partly plugs our sewers. As an army corps of engineers controls the pollution of an oil spill in the ocean, so God controls human pollution by laws and civilization, by customs and teachings and the good influence of believers. When God does this, we say he gives *common grace*. Common grace controls corruption.

Still, corruption makes us guilty and miserable. And common grace will not save us. That is why Jesus Christ must be the Savior not only for our sins but also for our sin. He must rescue us from the corruption of original sin.

Prayer
Father, thank you for holding back sin in our world. Jesus, thank you for dying to take away *my* sin. Amen.

DAY 3

GUILT

Scripture

O LORD, do not rebuke me in your anger
  or discipline me in your wrath. . . .
My guilt has overwhelmed me
  like a burden too heavy to bear.

—Psalm 38:1,4

Teachings

God requires that his justice be satisfied.
Therefore the claims of his justice
must be paid in full,
either by ourselves or another.

—Heidelberg Catechism, Answer 12

Q. Can we pay this debt ourselves?

A. Certainly not.
  Actually, we increase our guilt every day. —Heidelberg Catechism Q & A 13

E very so often you read in a newspaper about a person who has done some terrible thing but feels no remorse. Perhaps this person murdered a whole family in the middle of the night. But he is not sorry, not remorseful, not even very interested in what he did.

Decent people are shocked by such accounts. They find it hard to believe that a person would do something so wicked as mass murder; and they are very upset when such a murderer shows no remorse. It's frightening. It's not normal. In fact, doctors have a special name for people like that. If a person can feel no love and no guilt, a doctor may call him a *psychopath*. Psychopaths are deformed human beings—just as deformed as if they had been born without arms and legs.

Ordinary human beings feel guilty when they do wrong. Some sensitive people feel guilty even when they *haven't* done anything wrong. Did you ever wake up from a dream feeling guilty but unable to remember why?

Occasionally people feel guilty when they just come *close* to wrongdoing. Children, for example, sometimes feel terribly guilty when their parents divorce—even though these children had nothing to do with the tragedy. Police who are called upon to use a gun in their work may afterwards feel so guilty that they get sick. Some are even tempted to commit suicide. Even though their use of a gun was entirely justified, they still feel *unclean*.

These examples help us see that *being* guilty and *feeling* guilty are different things. Usually they go together: if a person is guilty of a crime or sin, she will feel guilty. But not always. A murderous psychopath is actually guilty but feels no guilt at all. On the other hand, the child of divorcing parents may feel awfully guilty but actually be innocent.

I think we all know what guilt feelings are. We have felt them. But what is guilt itself?

To be guilty is to have broken a law, human or divine. It is to be responsible or blameworthy for a crime or sin. In a court of law nobody asks at first whether you *feel* guilty. People want to know instead whether you plead guilty and whether you are guilty. That is, they simply want to know whether you did the crime you are accused of having done.

Original sin includes guilt. In fact, original sin includes two parts. One is corruption, the poisoning or polluting of humanity by sin. The other is guilt. We are originally *guilty*. That is, our original sin deserves a judge's guilty verdict and a court's penalty.

The Heidelberg Catechism uses an interesting word for our guilt. The catechism calls it *debt*. Think of it like this: because we belong to God, we owe him our time, our energy, our service, our total obedience. Think of all this as worth, say, a million dollars a day. The first day we hardly think about God. By the next day we therefore owe God not only a new million but also the old million dollars *plus interest*! In only a few weeks our debt would overload our pocket calculators. In several months it would make the national debt look like pocket change. Our debt, growing heavier and heavier every day, would soon be staggering. Its burden would break our backs and buckle our knees.

Who on earth could pay this debt? Who in heaven's name could step in to lift our burden?

Prayer
Heavenly Father, we know that we are guilty in your sight. We owe you so much we can never repay you. Thank you for your Son, who pays our debt and sets us free. In his name, Amen.

DAY 4

MOMENTUM

Scripture

The Lord saw how great man's wickedness on the earth had become, and that every inclination of the thoughts of his heart was only evil all the time.

—Genesis 6:5

Teachings

Q. But are we so corrupt
   that we are totally unable to do any good
   and inclined toward all evil?
A. Yes, unless we are born again,
   by the Spirit of God.

—Heidelberg Catechism Q & A 8

When you watch a basketball game on TV, you may hear the commentator say something about *momentum*. Suppose the Celtics are playing the Lakers. The Celtics have been winning. Their defense has been tight and stingy. Their shot selection has been wise. And they have been intercepting passes by magic. But then, in a seven-minute stretch in the third quarter, the Lakers begin to get their act together. They start swishing baskets from impossible angles. They launch lightning-fast breaks. Their defense becomes even stickier and stingier than that of their opponents.

And the commentator says, "The momentum has changed."

He means, of course, that the game is now going the Lakers' way. It's as if someone has tipped the court so that everything naturally flows toward the Lakers' basket. The Celtics, meanwhile, find themselves facing an uphill battle.

Momentum is an amount or quantity of motion. You know that if a car—or especially a train or ship—is just barely moving, it may still be extremely hard to stop. It's so large. It's so heavy. Even when moving slowly it has a great deal of momentum.

Human life has a kind of momentum as well. For instance, if you are asked to wash a family car, you might, like Tom Sawyer's friends, start to have some fun at it. You can see your progress. You can make your parents smile and shine. You can accidentally spray your brother.

In fact, you get into the spirit of car washing and offer to take on the other car on the driveway. Then the car next door. Soon you are dreaming of starting a neighborhood car wash. You have gotten good momentum going. In fact, sports, schoolwork, home chores, good deeds—all these things succeed when you get into the swing of them, when you get moving, when you gain momentum.

Unfortunately, human life includes not only good but also bad momentum. Once a person is going in the wrong direction, it is hard to stop. It's hard for a smoker to smoke just one cigarette. It's hard for a dieter to eat just one potato chip. It's hard for a liar to stop lying. These people have bad momentum going.

Original sin in its corruption and guilt has bad momentum. Our debt to God snowballs. Our corruption increases. A whole society can gain bad momentum.

I think we can see why this is so. It is because the things in us that can go right or wrong are all hooked together. These things are our thoughts, words, deeds, and feelings. It's as if all these things are hooked together by cables, gears, and pulleys. For example, if we hate someone, we might also dream about some deliciously bad thing happening to him. We might also want to curse this person or gossip about him. If things get even worse, we might try to trip him or take a swing at him. Feelings are tied to thoughts. And thoughts are tied to words and deeds.

Strangely, we not only hurt people we hate. We also hate people we hurt. If we hurt someone, we have to tell ourselves that she had it coming. Why? Because she's so hateful. So we begin to hate this person even more. And so on, round and round.

The Bible says we do this because our *hearts* are "inclined to evil." We have evil at our core. We have evil in the inner place where our feelings, thoughts, words, and deeds come from and where they are tied together. Bad momentum is the result of a heart that is inclined or tipped away from God.

That is why the Bible says we need surgery. We need a heart transplant. To have a new heart is like being born again.

Prayer

O God, you are the one who makes our hearts clean and new. Break our bad momentum. Turn us around. And give us the joy of salvation through Jesus Christ our Lord. Amen.

HOMEWORK

Vocabulary

24. original sin: the corruption and guilt that the human race has inherited from Adam and Eve. The doctrine of original sin tells us that sin is universal, that it keeps reproducing, and that it is extremely hard to get rid of.

25. corruption: the seeping or flooding power of sin. Sin seeps into every part of human life, staining and spoiling thoughts, words, deeds, feelings, and inclinations.

26. common grace: God's way of partly stopping corruption so that human life can continue. Common grace explains why unbelievers often show good behavior—better than that of some Christians.

27. guilt: what we have when we break God's law and deserve the law's penalty. Guilt includes not only what we have when we do wrong; it also includes what we have when we fail to do right. When we fail to do right, guilt is called *debt*.

Note: Please review the vocabulary section of lesson 6.

Questions

Day 1: How are our sins like "original copies"? What does the doctrine of original sin tell us about sin?

Day 2: In what two ways do we human beings sin? What is corruption, and what keeps it under control?

Day 3: What are the two parts of original sin? What's the difference between being guilty and feeling guilty?

Day 4: Give an example of how one sin can lead to another and another and another, and so on.

Summary

Talk with your family about Bible passages that assure us that our sins are forgiven and that God loves us. List the location of at least one such passage below.

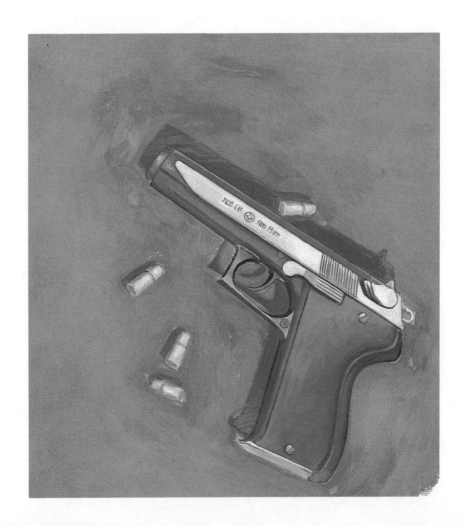

8

MISERY

MISERY

Scripture

Lamech said to his wives,
"Adah and Zillah, listen to me;
    wives of Lamech, hear my words.
I have killed a man for wounding me,
    a young man for injuring me.
If Cain is avenged seven times,
    then Lamech seventy-seven times."

—Genesis 4:23–24

Teachings

Q. How do you come to know your misery?
A. The law of God tells me.

—Heidelberg Catechism Q & A 3

As I write this, all the newspapers in the United States are filled with the story of a man who shot four teenagers in New York. Here is what happened: the man was on his way home from work on a subway train. Four teenagers surrounded him. First they asked him for the time. Next they asked him for a match. Finally they asked him for five dollars. "Sure," said the man, "I've got five dollars for each of you." Then he pulled out a gun and shot the four youths, one after another. All had to be hospitalized. One is still paralyzed from damage to his spinal cord.

When the man who did the shooting gave himself up, he discovered that he had become a hero. People sent him money and promised legal help. Newspaper writers said the man had done something terribly necessary. Strangers wrote to say they would have done the same thing. People are, after all, sick and tired of being hassled and threatened in public places. They feel trapped and frustrated when streets and subways are unsafe. They hate it when young toughs mug them. Finally an ordinary man had done what a lot of citizens would have liked to do. An ordinary, soft-spoken citizen blew four muggers away.

All this happened several weeks ago. By now more of the story has come out. The subway "hero" had been mugged once before, and his muggers had gotten off with small jail sentences. This angered and frustrated the man so much that he bought a gun, carried it illegally, and waited for a chance to use it. If the law would not take revenge on bullies and thieves, then he would have to do it himself.

Meanwhile, as it turns out, all four of the teenagers had been wanted by the police. Three of them were carrying sharpened screwdrivers. All had mugged before. They were dangerous people.

More has come out: the youth who is paralyzed comes from a Christian home. His own father was killed by muggers years ago. So the boy's mother tried to raise him herself—but soon ran into trouble. The young man began to hang around with a street gang. He became a thief. And one day he got himself shot on a subway train. Now his mother prays for him and for the man who shot her son.

This situation is full of *misery*. Misery is the pain, the suffering, the wretchedness that comes from sin. Misery is the fallout from the fall.

Anyone can see the misery in the case we are describing. The paralyzed teenager lies miserably in a hospital bed. He'll never walk again. His mother is wretched. The citizens who live in fear of muggers are miserable. Even the "hero" who shot the teenager may end up in jail for taking the law into his own hands. Misery all around. In sin nobody wins.

From the time of the fall the world has been full of misery. Much of it is caused by violence. One man injures another. So the second man injures him—only more so. Then the first man gets back at *him*—on and on in endless rounds of violence, revenge, and misery. Sometimes people even boast of the revenge they have taken and the misery they have caused:

> I have killed a man for wounding me,
>   a young man for injuring me.
> If Cain is avenged seven times,
>   then Lamech seventy-seven times.

Does it sound as if it might have happened in a subway?

The reason we hate sin and misery is that we know their opposites. We know what's right and joyful. We know God says "Do not steal," "Do not kill." We know Jesus Christ says "Love your neighbor as yourself."

How do we come to know our misery? The law of God tells us.

Prayer

O God, for all the miserable people of the world we pray. Stop sin by your powerful grace. And ease misery by the spread of your gospel and the knowledge of your law. Through Jesus Christ, our Lord, Amen.

DAY 2

THE MISERY

OF DISORDER

Scripture
In my inner being I delight in God's law; but I see another law at work in the members of my body, waging war against the law of my mind and making me a prisoner of the law of sin at work within my members. What a wretched man I am!

—Romans 7:22–24

Teachings
All spheres of life—
marriage and family,
work and worship,
school and state,
our play and art—
bear the wounds of our rebellion.

—*Our World Belongs to God*, 17

Misery comes in many kinds. The pain that comes from violence and revenge is miserable. So is loneliness, especially in the feeling of being cut out or shut out. Poverty, divorce, unemployment—all these are miseries. In fact, as our confession says, every sphere or area of human life shows the wounds of our rebellion.

The misery I want to talk about today is, like the others, a very old one. I want to talk about disorder.

As we recall from the story of creation, God did his great work one step at a time. He did things in order. Each time God called his creation "good," he meant that it had turned out as he intended. It was a custom creation, made to order.

Thus, as God arranged things, each part of creation meshed smoothly with the others. Sun, moon, and stars traced the pattern God had drawn for them. Animals grazed and romped together. The human beings loved God and clung to each other. Everything was in harmony. All was at peace. The whole creation was orderly and at rest.

Sin brought disorder. It disturbed the peace. Sin brought noise into the music of creation. It caused disorder between God and Adam and Eve. The human beings who had been made to walk with God and lean on God began instead to fear God and to hide from him (Gen. 3:10).

Sin also caused disorder between the man and the woman. They had trusted each other. They had been companions. But after the fall they began instead to blame and accuse. And the man began the long, sinful history of bossing his wife around (Gen. 3:12,16).

Sin caused disorder, too, between human beings and the rest of creation. God's original order was for Adam and Eve to keep the earth—sowing, tilling, and reaping good food from it. But after the fall thorns and thistles began to crowd out the crop. Soil got rocky and dry and hard to cultivate.

Sin even caused disorder inside each human being. The man and the woman began to feel the terrible difference between what they should do and what they did do. In our text for today Paul talks about the same thing. It is something we have all felt. Paul talks about how we know what's right; we even want what's right. But somehow we still end up doing what is wrong. It is as if there are two persons inside us, each battling the other for control. Paul is finally so frustrated with being a battleground for these two persons that he roars out his misery: "What a wretched man I am!" The misery of disorder.

What God ordered in creation humans have disordered by sin. Why, still today, do school rooms and court rooms have to "come to order"? Because our natural inclination, after the fall, is toward unruliness. Why do police and military commanders have to give orders? Because if everybody did what he wanted, there would be chaos—a lot of people would get drunk and disorderly, for instance. Why does a basketball referee have to keep control of a game? Because we cannot even *play* well unless rules are obeyed. Why do citizens sometimes demand a return to "law and order"? Because otherwise a whole society can turn into a riot.

God likes things done decently and in good order, as the Bible says. God's law is in fact a way of restoring order to a fallen creation. When God says "Love me above all and your neighbor as yourself," he is calling us to order. He is calling us to trust and obey. For there's no other way to be happy than with God's law and order.

Prayer
O God, help us to see and feel the joy of living within your boundaries and within the security of your law. In Jesus' name we pray, Amen.

DAY 3

THE MISERY

OF ESTRANGEMENT

Scripture
So the Lord God banished him from the Garden of Eden to work the ground from which he had been taken.

—Genesis 3:23

Teachings
Although Adam and Eve were expelled from the garden
and their work was burdened by sin's effects,
God held on to them in love.
He promised to crush
the evil forces they unleashed.

—Our World Belongs to God, 20

On TV news you sometimes hear an item like this: "An east-side man barricaded himself in his home today and held off police for three hours after slaying his estranged wife and her lover."

His "estranged" wife. Who is that?

An estranged wife is a woman who has become separated from her husband. There has been some terrible break in the marriage, and the couple has split up. Each person becomes in some way a stranger to the other. The husband and wife are therefore *estranged*.

Estrangement is a human misery that comes from the fall. It is an example of disorder. We were meant to be at home with God, with others, and in God's world. But now, without Christ, people are strangers to each other, and to God, and even to nature.

Let's see if we can understand this a bit better. When Adam and Eve sinned, the Bible tells us they were "banished" from the garden. To be banished is to be put out, thrown out, sent away. To be banished is to be estranged. The person who is banished is treated as an enemy instead of a friend, as a foreigner instead of a citizen, as a stranger instead of a son or daughter. When the Bible tells us that Adam and Eve were banished from the Garden of Eden, it is not just saying they were removed from a piece of real estate. No, the Bible writer is trying to tell us much more. He is telling us that the human beings were separated from all that is bright and joyful and welcome and secure. Adam and Eve were banished from *home*. And they were estranged from *God*.

Many of us have only a tiny hint of what this might be like. Thank God, many of us have loving homes. And we know that God loves us. We don't feel so terribly estranged. We have hardly ever been banished from any place but the refrigerator.

Still, if we think back to times of loneliness, we can start to get the feeling. Suppose there is a group you want to be with. But they don't want you to be with them. Whether politely or not, they tell you to get lost. You pretend you don't care. But you do. It hurts. It hurts a lot. You feel cut out, unwanted, banished, estranged.

Or think what it's like to have done something really wrong. Your mother is angry with you. Your conscience bothers you. You say things you don't mean. Until you get matters cleared up, you feel estranged from your own family and somehow even from yourself.

Now multiply this feeling a hundred times. It is the human misery of estrangement. People are estranged from God: they flee from God, or fight God, or find talk of God embarrassing.

People are estranged from each other—parents from children, husbands from wives, friends from friends, nations from nations. The misery is not just separation but what separation brings with it: estranged people often fear and try to hurt each other. And that causes more misery.

We are even estranged from nature. We fear wild animals. They fear us. We pollute air and water. They take their revenge in damaging our health. We are not at home in God's world.

We are even estranged from ourselves. Sometimes we can't believe we actually do and say the things we do. We take ourselves by surprise. We disappoint ourselves. We are sometimes strangers to ourselves.

The Bible tells us about these estrangements. But it also tells and shows us how they are overcome. Jesus our Savior shows us. For example, he purposely loves strangers and enemies—a scuzzy little sinner named Zacchaeus, a prostitute, a demon-possessed lunatic. Jesus loves people whom others hate. And one day Jesus tells the story of a young man who ran away from home and became a stranger to everybody who loved him. The prodigal son, as he's called, is a picture of the misery of estrangement. But in the prodigal's father Jesus also shows us a picture of the amazing grace of God, who opens his arms and his home to welcome us back and welcome us in.

Estrangement. Homecoming. This is the good news of the gospel.

Prayer
Overcome our misery by your amazing love, O God. And spread your reconciling love to others and to the whole world. Through Jesus Christ our Savior, Amen.

DAY 4

THE MISERY

OF DEATH

Scripture
The Lord God commanded the man, "You are free to eat from any tree in the garden; but you must not eat from the tree of the knowledge of good and evil, for when you eat of it you will surely die." —*Genesis 2:16–17*

Teachings
Looking for life without God, we find only death. —*Our World Belongs to God, 15*

People hate death. Except when people are very old or very depressed or in terrible pain, they do not want to die. They cling to life. They shrink from death. People pray and struggle and spend money and see doctors. They try everything they can think of to fight off death.

Even Jesus hated death. When Jesus' friend Lazarus died, Jesus did not explain that this was necessary. He did not try to accept Lazarus's death. Jesus wept. And when Jesus turned to face his own death, he wept again. He struggled with God the Father. Jesus showed that he himself feared and hated death.

Why? The reason is that death is an enemy. Death is an enemy because it is a kind of estrangement. And estrangement is a kind of disorder. And disorder is a kind of misery.

It is true, of course, that people also find death interesting. They read about it. They make and watch plays and movies about death. They wonder about what lies beyond death. For example, in Stephen Crane's *Red Badge of Courage* the hero, Henry, pauses in battle to peer into the open, staring eyes of a dead man. Crane writes that Henry is "trying to find the answer to *the* question." That is, Henry is trying to read in the dead man's eyes the answer to the question of whether there is life after death.

People think about death more than they admit. Even some children's prayers have a central place for death:

If I should die before I wake,
I pray the Lord my soul to take.

And some children's songs are really about death, even though you wouldn't notice it at first:

Ring around the rosies, pocket full of posies.
Ashes! Ashes! We all fall down!

Dust to dust. Ashes to ashes. We all die.

But even though death fascinates people, it also frightens them. Why? Death brings pain. People often suffer before they die. People always suffer when their loved ones die. Some of us have had to suffer the death of a mother or father. It hurts more than anyone could ever explain. You never know how much you love a person until the person has died. Then you know.

Even those of us who have not lost a loved one can imagine a tiny bit what it must feel like. For when we imagine one of our parents dying, we feel like weeping. It is too painful even to think about.

Death brings pain. That is because death is an estrangement. Death is a separation, a ripping, a tearing of life. *Death should never have happened.* If Adam and Eve had not sinned, and if we would not sin, we human beings would not die.

Death is a misery that comes from sin. The penalty for disobeying God in the Garden of Eden was death. We are talking here not only about physical death. We are talking especially about *spiritual* death—the estrangement from God that people experience when they try to live without him. Spiritual death includes loneliness, fear, guilt, violence, suspicion, and a feeling that life has no meaning. The name for final spiritual death is hell.

But once more God has a way past this misery. God's solution to death is another death! Jesus dies and rises so that we will never spiritually die. We will never be estranged from God. Nothing in the whole universe, says Paul, can separate us from the love of God.

Think once more of the parable of the prodigal son. At the end, why does the father want singing and dancing and feasting? Why is there a great, noisy, joyful party?

It is because a son who was dead has come alive again. For the misery of death this is the good news of the gospel.

Prayer
O God, we fear and hate death. We try not to think about it. Save us through Jesus Christ so that even though we die, we shall still live forever. And, O God, hold and keep our loved ones who have already died. Through Jesus Christ, our Lord, Amen.

HOMEWORK

Vocabulary

28. misery: the pain and suffering that come from sin; the fallout that comes from the fall. Among the fallen world's miseries are disorder, estrangement, and death.

29. disorder: the loss of harmony and right relation in the universe. Disorder shows up in relations between God and humanity, between some humans and others, between humanity and nature, and even within individual human beings.

30. estrangement: a disorder in which persons or things that ought to be friends become strangers instead. For example, when people are estranged from God, they see God not as a loving father but as an embarrassment or even an enemy.

31. spiritual death: the estrangement from God that people experience when they try to live without him. Hell is the ultimate spiritual death.

Questions

Day 1: Pick out one sentence which you think best says what the reading for day 1 is trying to prove. Write the sentence out.

Day 2: Name four kinds of disorder that sin brings into our world. How can order be restored in our lives?

Day 3: From whom and from what does sin estrange us? How can estrangement be overcome?

Day 4: How do physical death and spiritual death differ? How do death, estrangement, and disorder all fit together? How has God provided a way to escape death?

Summary

"God whispers to us in our pleasure, but shouts to us in our pain." Talk with your family about what this means; then write a brief explanation below. Give an example if you can.

9

COVENANT
OF
GRACE

DAY 1

THE SHINING

FACE OF GOD

Scripture
"The Lord bless you
   and keep you;
the Lord make his face shine upon you
   and be gracious to you;
the Lord turn his face toward you
   and give you peace."

—Numbers 6:24–26

Teachings
While justly angry
God did not turn his back
on a world bent on destruction;
he turned his face to it in love.
With patience and tender care he set out
on the long road of redemption
to reclaim the lost as his people
and the world as his kingdom.

—Our World Belongs to God, 19

Several years ago in Tennessee a girl was born without a face. There was a story about it in the *Reader's Digest*. The newborn girl had a healthy heart and lungs, strong arms and legs, and a well-formed digestive system. But where her face was supposed to be there was only "a shapeless mass of wet mucous membranes, with only a ragged opening for breathing and feeding."

People who saw this child were stunned into silence. Some shielded their own faces with their hands and turned away. Others gasped or cried.

Then, one day, a hospital supervisor called a meeting of all those who took care of the faceless child. "I don't want to hear any more talk about this baby's appearance," said the supervisor. "Her name is Alice, she has a purpose in this world, and we're going to treat her like any other newborn patient."

These were brave words. The truth was that Alice's road toward happiness would run uphill. Alice's mother was a frightened, unmarried teenager. Alice's father wanted little to do with his deformed daughter. Other relatives thought of Alice as "an evil omen."

But one strong and kindly woman took an interest in Alice. This woman, Thelma Perkins, was a nurse in the hospital where Alice spent much of her early life. Mrs. Perkins often held and cuddled the child that others feared. She talked to Alice and patiently fed her through the opening in her head. "I've held enough babies to know when they wanted love," she said, "and Alice needed a lot of it."

Mrs. Perkins was right. Alice's own mother was not mature enough to care for her daughter. After all, Alice would need years of patient, skillful attention. She would need at least a dozen operations. For example, surgeons would have to build a whole new mouth for Alice and try to form a nose—both of those from "extra" bones and tissues in Alice's body. For years Alice would look strange. She would need strong, loving parents to help her cope with pain, frustration, blindness, and the cruel comments of stupid persons. She would need protection. She would need caring people to teach her, help her, and tell her again and again that she was loved. Alice's mother couldn't handle all this.

Therefore, Thelma Perkins and her husband, Ray, agreed to become Alice's foster parents. Foster parents are people who give parental care (feeding, clothing, sheltering, loving) to children who would otherwise be without it. Ray Perkins patiently taught Alice how to walk. After many months Alice could explore the house by "hooking her thumb in Ray's pocket and walking beside him." Thelma Perkins helped the blind child learn to get around in the house and yard without getting hurt. Both helped her deal with the thoughtlessness of people who care too much about what a person looks like on the outside. As a matter of fact, other children have sometimes been kinder to Alice than adult strangers have been:

> At Sunday School one morning, a woman seeing Alice for the first time blurted, 'Who's that monster?' 'That's just Alice, ma'am,' said a little girl standing nearby. Then she took Alice by the hand and led her off to class.

The main people in Alice's life are Ray and Thelma Perkins. They have shown *grace*: that is, they have shown lovingkindness to a person in misery. They have acted like God. Alice has no eyes. She cannot see their faces. But if she could, she would see the shining of graceful light and love.

On February 7, 1983, Mr. and Mrs. Perkins legally adopted Alice as their own child. "She's always been my little girl," said Thelma. "The paperwork just made it official."

That paperwork is what we call a covenant of grace.

Prayer
O God, we are all your adopted children. Now bless us, we pray. Bless us and keep us and make your face shine on us and be gracious to us. Through Jesus Christ, our Lord, Amen.

DAY 2

COVENANTS:

OFFICIAL LOVE

Scripture
"I will establish my covenant as an everlasting covenant between me and you and your descendants after you for the generations to come, to be your God and the God of your descendants after you. The whole land of Canaan, where you are now an alien, I will give as an everlasting possession to you and your descendants after you; and I will be their God. . . . Every male among you shall be circumcised."
—Genesis 17:7–8,10c

Teachings
The Creator pledged to be God
to Abraham and his children,
blessing all nations through them
as they lived obediently before him.
—Our World Belongs to God, 22

Suppose a man and a woman get married. You may have seen it happen. On their wedding day the two people stand solemnly before God and their families and friends, and they make promises to each other. If they are Christians, each promises to love the other till death. Each promises to help and encourage the other, even if one of them gets hurt or ugly or sick. Then they exchange rings. The ring is a sign of their love and a seal on their promises. And they kiss. The public kiss is also a sign of their love and a seal on their promises. After the kiss the minister declares them husband and wife. "What God has put together," says the minister, "let nobody else pull apart."

Can you see what has happened? The man and woman have made a *covenant*. That is, they have made a solemn agreement with each other. You could also call it a *pact*. The main idea is that they bind themselves to each other with vows, or promises. To make the binding strong they do it in public. They do it in front of witnesses—including God. They give each other signs and seals of their pact. They receive a marriage certificate that makes their pact legal. Neither could say later that they were just kidding.

As anyone can tell, marriage is a very serious thing. It is joyful, of course. But it is also weighty and deep. Two people who know each other and love each other do this serious thing. They make their love official. They make it legal. They have it signed, sealed, and witnessed in public. They make a covenant.

Why? Why not just live together? Why risk public promises? Why bother with rings and kisses?

People marry because this covenant helps to make their love *secure*. People are weak and sinful. If they did not bind themselves together with weddings, the man might leave as soon as he saw someone he liked better. Or the woman might leave if her husband got crippled or lost his job. People need security. They need to know the other person will not abandon them. They need to be able to trust and depend on their spouse. If they are going to share all their secrets; if they are going to trust another person not to dump them when they fail; if they are going to give themselves in love and sexual intercourse to another person; if they are going to make plans, and children, and a home, and a life together—then they will need as much security as possible.

That is why God made marriage. And adoption. And many other covenants. In fact, in the Bible God is making and renewing covenants all the time. He *himself* makes covenants with people he loves. With God the situation is like that with Mrs. Perkins and Alice. You remember that Mrs. Perkins said Alice was always her little girl. The paperwork just made it official.

Think of covenants in the Bible in this same way. Genesis 15 and 17 tell us that God made a covenant with Abraham. That covenant is renewed with Moses at Mount Sinai (Ex. 19–24) and fulfilled in the New Testament by the work of our Lord Jesus Christ. The Bible tells us of other smaller covenants too. Some are like adoptions. Like a parent, God rescues his children and then makes a solemn promise to take care of them. He adopts them. The rainbow covenant with Noah is like this (Gen. 9:8–17).

But sometimes a covenant looks more like a marriage. In the book of Hosea, for instance, it is as if God marries his people. Sometimes a covenant looks like a pact between a king and his subjects. He will be their protector and helper. He will help them grow and prosper. Meanwhile, they must obey him. The covenant has two parts: one part is the promise made by God the King. The other part is the duty of people to obey. Then the whole arrangement is strangely signed and sealed by circumcision.

This arrangement, like a wedding or an adoption, makes love official. It allows for security. It also allows for blessing. Now stop and think: Can you imagine any way in which blessings and security might be connected with each other?

Prayer

O God, you are the one who seeks your children in order to protect and bless. You are great and good. For Jesus' sake, Amen.

PROMISES

Scripture

"I will make you into a great nation
 and I will bless you;
I will make your name great
 and you will be a blessing.
I will bless those who bless you,
 and whoever curses you I will curse;
and all peoples on earth
 will be blessed through you."

—Genesis 12:2–3

"The promise is for you and your children and for all who are far off—for all
whom the Lord our God will call."

—Acts 2:39

Teachings
God holds this world
in sovereign love.
He kept his promises,
sending Jesus into the world.

—*Our World Belongs to God,* 5

You recall that the fall brought miseries. Life fell apart. Humans became strangers to God and to each other. People even became estranged from themselves. And death entered the world. Cain killed Abel, Lamech sang his revenge song, and the flood drowned wicked people. Then, by the end of Genesis 11, all the proud people who tried to crowd God out of the world by building the Tower of Babel—all these people were scattered in confusion across the earth. The early part of the Bible shows us sin, disorder, estrangement, death, and scattering.

What is astonishing is that God does not give up or get out. He does not say, "To hell with this world." No, the world is not sent to hell. Like an adoptive parent, or a spouse, or a just and kindly king, God comes not with hell but with grace.

Grace is lovingkindness for miserable people. It comes even to people who are miserable because of their own sin. Grace is undeserved favor for sinners. And God specializes in grace.

Let's think of some examples of grace in our own lives. Suppose you owe a library fine but don't have to pay it. There's a grace period. Suppose you "say grace" before a meal. It's a way of saying thanks for food you do not really deserve. Suppose someone trips or insults you on the playground. You later do something strange: you bring that person a gift. That's grace (and maybe self-protection!).

Take a more serious example. Suppose you shoplift something from a department store. Shoplifting is wrong, and you know it. Still, in some crazy, dangerous mood you do it anyway. And a store detective catches you!

You feel miserable. The detective describes the juvenile detention center—a jail for teenagers. Then your parents come down to pick you up. You feel even more miserable and ashamed. Finally the store detective stands up and says, "I'm going to let you off with a warning. Don't try to steal anything again." Grace. You should have been punished, but you weren't.

Then your father says, "I'm deeply unhappy about what you did. But I know you're sorry. And I still love you. I'm going to spend more time with you." Grace. A graceful promise.

All such graces are learned from God. When God makes a covenant of grace with Abraham, he makes his love official. His is a saving love that people do not deserve. It is offered in *promises*. These promises are packages of grace that are to be opened in the future. (One of them is opened on Christmas Day.) The first promise package appears in Genesis 3:15. God promises Adam and Eve that he will "crush the serpent's head." This means God will finally crush the misery they and we deserve.

In Genesis 9:11–17 God promises Noah that he will never again destroy the whole earth with a flood. In Genesis 12 God promises Abraham that the great nation of Israel will come from him and that God will provide a wonderful land in which this nation can grow. God also promises that by means of this nation in this land he will bless *other* nations. That, in fact, turns out to be the most important promise of all. God wants to save and bless the whole world! He wants to bless all who are scattered, all who are "far off."

God is a promise maker. Unlike some human beings, God is also a promise keeper. What God says he will do, he actually does.

We depend on this. As a matter of fact, as a thoughtful Christian by the name of Lewis Smedes once said, only one thing in the world tells us we will never be abandoned or left alone. Only one thing tells us our world will not end in a smoking ruin. Only one thing tells us God wants to forgive our sins and make us clean. That one thing is the promise of God. It is the main part of the covenant of grace.

If we can't count on God's promises, then we can't count on anybody's.

Prayer
O God, you are full of grace and light and love. Thank you for your packages of grace, for your promises of grace, for your covenant of grace. Through Jesus Christ our Savior, Amen.

DAY 4

OBLIGATIONS

Scripture

Then God said to Abraham, "As for you, you must keep my covenant, you and your descendants after you for the generations to come. This is my covenant with you and your descendants after you, the covenant you are to keep: Every male among you shall be circumcised."

—Genesis 17:9–10

Teachings

As covenant partners
called to faithful obedience,
and set free for joyful praise,
we offer our hearts and lives
to do God's work in his world.

—*Our World Belongs to God*, 6

The covenant of grace has two parts. One part includes all the graceful promises of God. God will never leave us or forsake us. God will supply graceful clothing when we are naked, guilty, and ashamed (Gen. 3:21). God will bless all the nations through Israel and, now, through Jesus Christ and the church. God will bring the world to a just and loving end.

God promises all this in his covenant of grace. It is his way of making love official. This is the "paperwork" that Mrs. Perkins talked about. God always loves his people. But because God wants us to feel secure—like an adopted child, or a marriage partner, or a person devoted to a just ruler— God makes his love official. God makes promises. God covenants with his people. A covenant is God's way of planning and controlling our future. He does this by promising his love and then signing and sealing his promise with the strange ceremony of circumcision in the Old Testament and baptism in the New Testament.

So what do *we* have to do? Do we simply say thanks? Do we just take God's gifts and ask for more? Do we simply notice how gracious God is and let it go at that?

No. Covenants, as I said earlier, have two parts. The first part is God's. But the second part is ours. True, in some covenants (like the one with Noah) God makes the promises and that's it. But in the main covenant in Scripture (the one with Abraham) we have a role to play as well. This is' true not only in the Old Testament, where Moses acts for God's people (Ex. 19–24). It is also true in the New Testament, where Jesus Christ takes the place of Moses in acting for God's people (Heb. 3:5–6). In both cases there is something that we, God's people, have to do.

In Genesis 17 God tells Abraham what this is. God lists again all the gifts he offers: children, land, blessing to the nations. Then God turns to Abraham. "As for you . . . ," he says. "As for you." What must Abraham do?

"As for you, you must *keep* my covenant—you and your descendants." Covenant making is God's part. Covenant keeping is ours.

What does that mean? It means we have *obligations*. But what are those obligations?

Suppose someone does a kind deed for another person. The person who has been helped might say "Much obliged!" I'm *obliged* to you. I have an obligation to you.

An obligation is something you owe. If you hurt someone, you owe that person an apology. You are obliged to say "I'm sorry." If you are late with a library book, you owe a fine. It's your obligation. If you are a son or daughter (and who isn't?), you owe your parents obedience. And when someone does a kind deed or shows grace to you, you owe them thanks and gratitude.

So it is with Abraham and us. God gives grace. We have obligations. God makes a covenant. We must keep his covenant. We do our part through obedience, trust, and thanks. Because God is Parent and King, we owe him obedience. It is our obligation. Because God is our Savior, we must trust him. Because God is graceful, we owe him thanks. Obedience, trust, and thanks are our covenant obligations. As we will see later in our study, we can fulfill these obligations especially by prayer and by keeping God's law.

For now, simply notice how the two parts of the covenant are signed and sealed. To Abraham, God says, "Every male among you shall be circumcised." In the New Testament Peter says, "Repent and be baptized!" (Acts 2:38). Like a wedding ring or a wedding kiss these two acts are signs and seals of promises and obligations.

Prayer
Help us, O God, to keep covenant with you. Let us obey, trust, and thank you as our Ruler, Father, and Savior. Through Jesus Christ, Amen.

HOMEWORK

Vocabulary

32. covenant: a solemn agreement or pact. In a covenant there are always promises on one side and often obligations on the other. Covenants are usually signed and sealed, sometimes by strange acts.

33. grace: lovingkindness to a person in misery, especially when a person is miserable because of his or her own sin. Grace is then undeserved favor or kindness.

34. covenant promises: God's promises in the covenant of grace that he will love his people, protect them, and help them. God also promises to bless the whole world through his people.

35. covenant obligations: the duties God's people owe to God. These are especially obedience (because God is Parent and King), trust (because God is Savior), and thanks (because God shows grace).

36. circumcision: the Old Testament sign and seal of the covenant of grace.

Questions

Day 1: How is the adoption of Alice a covenant of grace? Where's the grace in this? Where's the covenant?

Day 2: Why does God make covenants with the people he loves?

Day 3: List four things God promises in the covenant of grace. Also mention one promise of God that is especially meaningful to you.

Day 4: What are the two parts of the covenant of grace? What are our obligations to God?

Summary

Read Genesis 17:1–11. Identify the covenant partners, the covenant promises, the covenant obligations, and the covenant sign. Then tell when this covenant of grace was renewed and when it was fulfilled (see the reading for day 2). Finally, tell to whom the covenant promises of God are now given (see Gal. 3:6–9) and what the sign of the covenant is today.

III

CHRIST,

SPIRIT, AND

SALVATION

10

INCARNATION

DAY 1

WHO IS

THIS?

Scripture
He said to his disciples, "Why are you so afraid? Do you still have no faith?" They were terrified and asked each other, "Who is this? Even the wind and the waves obey him!"

—Mark 4:40–41

Teachings
God remembered his promise
to reconcile the world to himself;
he has come among us
in Jesus Christ,
the eternal Word made flesh.

—Our World Belongs to God, 24

Twice in a recent film the hero, who is being tortured by the enemy, stretches out his arms as if being crucified. The hero is a violent, revengeful man. He is not at all like Jesus Christ. Yet the film wants us to connect him to Christ—to think of this hero as suffering for his people. The filmmakers can make more money that way.

That's because Jesus Christ is the most famous person in the world. Thousands of books, plays, essays, and poems have been written about him. Hundreds of great artworks depict him. Millions of people know his name, even if only as a pair of curse words. People sing about him; children pray to him; politicians claim him for their cause. All history snaps like a twig at his birth, so that events are measured according to whether they come before Christ or after him. And more than a billion people across the world, including you and me, are named after him.

Yet there is a lot of confusion about Jesus Christ. Some people think of him as a kind of communist rebel. Others believe he was more like an American businessman. Some have thought of him as a good man but not a great one. They think he was a pretty good teacher, for instance, who was clearly right about many things but wrong about others. A number of unbelievers have seen Jesus Christ as a magician, or even as a madman. Years ago a few people even thought Jesus never existed. They believed he was a mythical figure like Hercules or Robin Hood or Superman. And then, in every age since Jesus' birth there have also been many who have believed in him, who have turned to him and whispered "Lord."

Why all the confusion? One reason is that people are not always perfectly honest. They do not want to believe what is true if it will not help them make money or act important or feel right about what they are doing. So they turn Jesus into a movie actor or a communist rebel or a hard-driving businessman. Such people want a Silly-Putty Jesus who can be twisted and shaped to become whatever god they like.

But another reason for uncertainty about Jesus Christ is that he is frankly a mysterious person. The gospel of Mark shows us that people were confused about him from the beginning. Some people who saw or heard Jesus thought that Elijah had returned. Others got Jesus mixed up with John the Baptist (8:28). His townspeople assumed he was only the local carpenter (6:1–6). Enemies dismissed him as a demon-possessed lunatic (3:22). And everywhere Jesus went, he seemed to astonish and bewilder people, even his own disciples. They kept saying things like "What is this?" and "Who is this?" (1:27, 4:41).

The Bible gives a hundred answers to these questions. Who is this? He is both the lamb of God and a shepherd. He is a suffering servant but also a lord. He is a convicted criminal but also a judge. He is the savior who did not save himself, the defender of the weak who did not defend himself. He is the living water who almost died of thirst. He is the king of creation whom thugs pinned to some two-by-fours. He is the light of the world who was snuffed out—only to flame up gloriously again. He is our Lord and our God.

Who is this? Out of all these biblical answers let us think of three that are especially important to the church. In the next three readings let us recall that Jesus is the *Christ*, that he is *Immanuel*, and that he is *one of us*.

Prayer
Lord Jesus, may we always know you and love you and serve you. Amen.

DAY 2

JESUS IS

THE CHRIST

Scripture

Jesus and his disciples went on to the villages around Caesarea Philippi. On the way he asked them, "Who do people say I am?"

They replied, "Some say John the Baptist; others say Elijah; and still others, one of the prophets."

"But what about you?" he asked. "Who do you say I am?"

Peter answered, "You are the Christ."

—Mark 8:27–29

Teachings

God holds this world
in sovereign love.
He kept his promise,
sending Jesus into the world.

—*Our World Belongs to God*, 5

For centuries they dreamed about it. In the deserts and villages, along the seas and hills, Israelites told of a coming time when God would make things right. With his mighty arm God would shake his people free again, just as he had in the exodus. God would burst the chains that bound his people to the Babylonians or Romans. God would arrest all the terrorists who had hijacked his loved ones.

In Israel itself the rich would no longer squeeze blood money out of the poor. The strong would no longer make tracks across the faces and chests of the weak. Lame people would begin to dance. Blind people would gaze hungrily at a world they had never seen before. The deaf would listen with wonder to the songs of larks and lyres. Deserts would be turned into fragrant gardens, bayonets into gardening tools, enemies into friends. Jerusalem would be at the center of the world, and all the kings of the earth would come there to bow and pay their respects. Covenant promises and obligations—broken and forgotten—would at last be fulfilled. A *messianic age* was coming.

The Israelites got this idea from prophets. The prophets got it from God. But the prophets did not speak only of a coming messianic age. They spoke also of a particular person, an individual, who was to come. It was from this person that the age to come took its name. For over the years people began calling this expected person "Messiah."

Who was this person and why was he called "Messiah"?

The prophets described Messiah in many ways. Sometimes they talked of the one to come as if he would be a great warrior king. As David had slain the Philistines, so the Messiah, the new David, would slay God's enemies (Isa. 63:1–6). On the other hand, the one to come would be a man of sorrows who would be slaughtered like an animal for the sins of others (Isa. 53). He would be a king or a servant, but in any case he would be "anointed." That is, like kings and priests in the Old Testament, he would

126

have oil poured over him as a sign that God had picked him out for special work. Or, like a prophet (Isa. 61), Messiah might be anointed with the very Spirit of God poured out on him.

The important thing to know is this: the Hebrew word that was used for the person to come, *Messiah,* meant "the anointed one." Greek-speaking Jews used the word *Christ* instead. No Jewish child of God could hear one of those words without a lump forming in his throat. The Messiah was coming! The Christ! The anointed one! He would be the greatest of men, a kind of twig growing out of the trunk of David that would finally dwarf David himself.

Or else, as the prophets sometimes put it, the one to come would be a branch growing out of *the Lord* (Isa. 4:2). Messiah would be the "Mighty God" (Isa. 9:7) or God-with-us (Isa. 7:14) or the Lord himself suddenly coming to his temple (Mal. 3:1).

Messiah, in other words, might be human or he might be divine. In either case he would be brilliantly great.

Centuries later a traveling teacher talks with his followers. People have been asking about him and his miracles. "What is this?" they ask. And "Who is this?" At last the teacher turns to look at his own disciples. There is perhaps a pause and a silence. Then the question comes—a question like a shot to the heart: "Who do *you* say I am?"

The answer that comes back carries the weight of centuries. Isaiah and the prophets are in the answer. The longing of the generations is attached to it. Peter's own life depends on it. Peter's answer has become famous and has become ours. *"Su ei ho Christos,"* he says. "You are the Christ."

Who is this? He is the one who was to come. He is the Christ. Messiah has arrived at last.

Prayer

Christ, our Lord: You are the one for whom people have waited. You are the one in whom all the hopes and fears of all the years come together. We praise your name. Amen.

DAY 3

JESUS

IS IMMANUEL

Scripture

The Lord himself will give you a sign: The virgin will be with child and will give birth to a son, and will call him Immanuel.

—Isaiah 7:14

Teachings

He is the long-awaited Savior,
fully human and fully divine,
conceived by the Spirit of God
and born of the virgin Mary.

—*Our World Belongs to God*, 24

A man named Walpole once wrote a fairy tale called "The Three Princes of Serendip." In this tale the princes make a number of wonderful discoveries by sheer accident.

Today similar wonderful accidents are named after the princes. Finding a delightful thing you were not looking for is now called "serendipity." You get a wrong number—and make a lasting friend. You hunt for a lost softball—and find a twenty-dollar bill instead. You sit down to some math problems—and discover to your amazement that you are having fun. Serendipity.

Something like that happens when Jesus Christ appears. God's people had been longing and looking for Messiah. Hundreds of years earlier, the prophets had pointed to a warrior king or a suffering servant or even God himself as the one to come. But gradually the last two of these possibilities began to fade from people's minds. By the time of Jesus' birth most people thought Messiah would be a politician. They believed the Christ would be a mighty, royal man who would lead a revolt against the Romans. He would be a revolutionary war hero who could make things hot for Herod and Caesar.

We can imagine, then, why people did not at once recognize Jesus as Messiah. He certainly didn't look or sound much like a royal rebel. He seemed to speak more of peace than of war. He advised trigger-happy young rebels to love their enemies. He stated that the meek, not the mighty, would inherit the earth. And when he entered Jerusalem on Palm Sunday, he sat on the back of a borrowed donkey.

It was like a President or Premier arriving for a summit conference and waving to the crowds from one of those rusted junkers you get from Ugly Duckling or Rent-A-Heap.

What is this? Who *is* this?

Gradually it began to dawn on people—first the disciples and then the others—that this carpenter from Nazareth was no ordinary man. He did not teach the way the scribes did—repeating old answers year after year. He taught as one who had real and personal authority. In addition, he forgave not only sins committed against him but also those committed against other people. (To understand how unusual that is, suppose some-body stole your bike and a stranger came up to the thief and said, "I freely forgive you.")

Jesus healed people who were hopelessly crippled or blind. One time he performed an exorcism—the casting out of a demon—and the demon-possessed man seemed weirdly to *know* him from somewhere: "What do you want with me, Jesus, Son of the Most High God?" (Mark 5:7). He had calm control over the powers of nature: "Who is this? Even the winds and waves obey him." Yet his life seemed to end in ruins. He was simply erased by the Romans. His very dead body was laid to rest by heartbroken followers.

A couple of days later two women made their way through the dawn to his tomb. They were carrying things that would keep death from smell-ing like death.

> Suddenly Jesus met them. "Greetings," he said. They came to him, clasped his feet and worshiped him.   (Matt. 28:9)

Later, the man who has become famous as "Doubting Thomas" (as if "Doubting" were his first name) met the risen Jesus. With a startled glance Thomas choked out his confession: "My Lord and my God!" (John 20:28).

Women worshiped him. Thomas called him "God." A prophet had said the Christ would be Immanuel—that is, "God with us." But people had forgotten about this possibility.

Now for the disciples and us it is the world's greatest serendipity. People had looked for a man. They got God-in-disguise, the second person of the Holy Trinity in flesh and blood. People had looked for a man who could become king. What they got was a King who had become a man. Before he left, the King told his disciples he was Immanuel: "I will be with you always," he said, "to the very end of the age" (Matt. 28:20).

Who is this? Jesus is Immanuel to the end of the world.

Prayer

Lord Immanuel, be with *us* till the end of the age. Surround us, support us, lead us, and comfort us, we pray. Amen.

DAY 4

JESUS IS

ONE OF US

Scripture

For we do not have a high priest who is unable to sympathize with our weaknesses, but we have one who has been tempted in every way, just as we are—yet was without sin.

—Hebrews 4:15

Teachings

As the second Adam he chose
the path we had rejected.
As our representative,
serving God perfectly,
and loving even those who scorned him,
Christ showed us how
a righteous child of God lives.

—*Our World Belongs to God,* 26

Some things cannot be understood till we experience them. Take hunger, for instance. We read of it or see hungry people on TV. But few of us understand hunger from the inside. Few of us know what it feels like to crave potato peelings, or to gnaw on shoe leather, or to fill our stomachs with leaves, grass, and dirt.

Or take fear. Most of us have been startled. We have had uneasy nights during tornado watches or violent thunderstorms. But what about people who have been hijacked by terrorists? What about a teenager who is abducted by a kidnapper or rapist? What about small children who are beaten almost to death by their own parents? They know the sick feeling, the paralysis, the silent scream of real fear. We do not.

Years ago a reporter by the name of John Howard Griffin wrote a book about his experiences in the southern U.S. Griffin was a white man who knew the wickedness of racism only by reading about it or by seeing the signs that said things like "Whites Only" or "Colored Waiting Room." Griffin knew that gas stations often had three restrooms: "Men," "Women," and "Colored." He knew all this but did not fully understand it because he did not know how a victim of racism feels.

So Griffin arranged to get his hair and skin dyed black. The job was done well enough that he could pass for a black man. He also learned to talk and act the way a black man was expected to talk and act in those days. He then set out across the South.

The results were predictable—and yet Griffin *felt* them for the first time. Stupid young toughs called him "nigger." The word hit him like a hammer. People pushed him around. Police and others looked at him suspiciously, as if being black made it somehow likely that he was a wanted man. One white man with whom Griffin hitchhiked told him dirty stories; he seemed to think blacks were especially fond of them.

As a black man Griffin began to understand what it is to be humiliated, or else to have people look right through you—as if you were a windowpane instead of a person. Some things cannot be understood till we experience them.

Earlier we learned that God speaks by his Son. Jesus Christ is the Word *incarnate,* that is, the Word made flesh. We have just been reminded that he is the Christ and Immanuel. What we must now bring to mind is that Jesus is a human being of flesh and bone and blood. He knows from the inside what it is to be human.

The eternal Son of God, who already had a glorious divine life, took on our flesh. He was born from a human mother in a cow shed in Bethlehem. A person who was already divine became a person who was human as well. Christmas is the celebration of the incarnation of the eternal Son of God.

Why did he do it? Why did the Son of God become man? The Bible does not tell us in so many words. One reason may be that if humans fell into sin, then it would be fitting for a human to pay the price to get us out of sin again. A second Adam ought to pay the debt run up by the first Adam.

But there is more to it than that. As a human being, Jesus could show us how to live, how to serve God perfectly. As a bird can show other birds where food is without scaring them away, so the human Son of God can safely lead us to our heavenly Father.

Finally, the Son of God became man to share our condition with us. He learned what it means to be tempted by pride and power. He *learned* obedience to God! He learned, like John Howard Griffin, what it's like to be taunted, shoved aside, and beaten up. He was crucified, dead, and buried.

Perhaps God could not understand us from the inside if he were not a man. Certainly we could not understand very much of God unless one of our race were also divine. Some things cannot be understood unless they are experienced.

Who is Jesus? Who is this? He is the divine Son of God incarnate. He is one of us.

Prayer

Jesus, our Lord, we thank you for becoming one of us not only to save us but also to know our struggles. Amen.

HOMEWORK

Vocabulary

37. messiah: the Hebrew word for "the anointed one." In the Old Testament this person was an expected warrior king, suffering servant, or even God himself. He would bring reconciliation, peace, and prosperity. The Greek word for Messiah means "the Christ."

38. messianic age: in the Old Testament, the age to come, when God would make things right by means of his anointed one, or even by his own appearance.

39. Immanuel: Hebrew word that means "God with us."

40. incarnation: the Christmas event in which the eternal Son of God took on human flesh.

Questions

Day 1: Mention half a dozen different ways that people have answered the question "Who is Jesus?" Why don't people all believe the same things about Jesus?

Day 2: Name several Old Testament passages that (a) show that the coming Messiah would be human; (b) show that the coming Messiah would be divine (God).

Day 3: What kind of Messiah were the Jews of Jesus' day expecting? What did Jesus do that revealed that he was Immanuel ("God with us")?

Day 4: What three reasons does the author give for Jesus' becoming a human being?

Summary

Ask one other adult in your family to answer this question: Who is Jesus? Write down his or her answer.

11

ATONEMENT

SACRIFICE

Scripture
He is the atoning sacrifice for our sins, and not only for ours but also for the sins of the whole world.

—1 John 2:2

Teachings
Q. What do you understand by the word "suffered"?
A. That during his whole life on earth,
   but especially at the end,
   Christ sustained
     in body and soul
     the anger of God against the sin of the whole human race.

This he did in order that,
   by his suffering as the only atoning sacrifice,
   he might set us free.

—Heidelberg Catechism Q & A 37

We have seen and heard of it so often it no longer surprises us. But it is strange. Planted like a scarecrow in the center of our religion is an ugly, humiliating thing. People wear it on a chain like a charm. Churches mount triple-size replicas of it twenty feet off the ground. Two-year-old Catholics learn how to touch out the pattern of it on their own heads and chests. We have gotten used to it. But it is still a strange and ugly thing.

A torture rack is the main symbol of the Christian faith: a cross. Christians see Jesus Christ not just as Messiah, but as crossed-up Messiah. He is not just Immanuel, but God with black eyes and a split lip and a beard matted with other men's spit. He is not just one of us, but a scapegoat for all of us—like the kid in a class that everybody blames and mocks and kicks around.

It is all very strange. The apostles went up and down the Mediterranean basin preaching "Christ crucified." People thought they were crazy. Who else would dream of *celebrating* the death and humiliation of their God? Who else would think there was universal power in a rubbed-out preacher, dead weight hanging from spikes on a dreary afternoon?

It is strange, but true. God deals with sin by the sin of Romans and Jews. God conquers death by death within the holy Trinity. God overcomes misery by the misery of his Son. Because of the capital punishment of Jesus Christ, last-minute pardons are issued for us. By his scarred hands and spiked feet we are healed.

The whole process is called *atonement*. It means putting right what sin puts wrong. It means repairing a broken relationship. It means making amends for sin, paying the price to cover the damages. The Bible and the church, in fact, use a number of words for what happens in atonement— words such as *reconciliation, redemption, satisfaction, sacrifice.*

Today let's take the last one: *sacrifice*. Jesus Christ's death on the cross is an atoning *sacrifice*.

We know the idea of sacrifice from various areas of human life. Somebody wants to sell a two-year-old auto below book price. Her newspaper ad says, "Owner anxious to sell: will sacrifice." A dying patriot declares, "My only regret is that I have but one life to sacrifice for my country." A young Olympic swimmer sacrifices her social life in order to swim endless laps of backstroke, dreaming of medals and glory. A baseball player comes to the plate in a tied game, the bottom of the ninth, with a runner on first and nobody out. He lays down a sacrifice bunt.

When you sacrifice, you give up something of value in order to get something of even greater value.

Throughout the Old Testament we read of God's people bringing their sacrifices to God as an atonement for sin. They would give up something of value—an animal that might otherwise have been a meal—in order to get something of greater value: forgiveness and peace with God.

And so, on Good Friday, Jesus the Christ groans and suffers through the, hours of official torture. He is pinned, probably naked, to a Roman crosspiece. Pontius Pilate's joke in three languages is tacked up over his head. He suffers heat and flies and searing pain. He suffers the sneers of bystanders—the kind of people who like to crack jokes and munch popcorn at an execution. He suffers a terrifying sense of abandonment by God his Father. At one point he recites the words of Psalm 22:

> My God, my God, why have you forsaken me?
>   Why are you so far from saving me,
>   so far from the words of my groaning?

The Son of God sacrifices his life for something he wants more: the lives of you and me. It is the strangest event in the history of the universe.

But for us it is also the mightiest and most gracious.

Prayer

O God, your love for us is greater than anything we can think or feel. We can say thank you, but it is not enough. Still, we say it. Thank you for your love. Amen.

SATISFACTION

Scripture
God presented him as a sacrifice of atonement, through faith in his blood.
He did this to demonstrate his justice. — Romans 3:25

Teachings
We believe
that Jesus Christ is a high priest forever
according to the order of Melchizedek—
    made such by an oath—
and that he presented himself
in our name
before his Father,
to appease his wrath
with full satisfaction
    by offering himself
    on the tree of the cross
    and pouring out his precious blood
    for the cleansing of our sins,
    as the prophets had predicted. — Belgic Confession, Article 21

Justice means giving a person what he has coming. If a customer gets newspapers from a carrier, the customer ought to pay his bill. It's owed. It's due. The carrier has it coming. If a citizen breaks a law, the citizen will have to "pay her debt" to society. Obedience to law is what society requires; it is what society has coming. A disobedient citizen will then have to satisfy her debt some other way—by paying a fine, for instance, or by going to jail. She has it coming.

We all have a sense of justice. From the time we are small children we have an idea of what is right and fair and we speak of it, especially when it's to our advantage to do so! We sense that goods ought to be handed out in a fair way. We know that punishments ought to be deserved and ought to be measured to fit the offense. That's justice. It means giving a person what he has coming—no more and no less.

We receive many of our ideas about justice from Scripture. The Bible teaches that God is supremely just. For instance, he does not want rich and powerful people or nations to hog all the earth's goods. He wants a fair share to go to the weak and poor. Further, God hates sin. His justice requires that sin be punished and avenged. God punishes Cain, for example, because he hears the cry of his brother Abel, whom Cain has unjustly killed. Abel's shed blood cries out to be avenged. It cries out for satisfaction.

God's justice demands that when someone sins, someone must pay. From Genesis through Leviticus to Revelation, this truth is written in blood across the Bible. God cannot overlook sin. God will not go soft on sin. The axe must fall. Payment must be made. The blood of sacrifice must be shed. For when someone sins, someone must pay—even if it is not the sinner himself.

Why? Why must someone pay? The Bible never explains this so that we understand completely. Still, we can *feel* a sense of justice. We ourselves feel deeply that a cheater ought not to get away with cheating. We ourselves feel deeply that a neighborhood bully ought somehow to pay for his bullying. Why? Because it's right. Because it's just. Because only then is the debt paid, the wound healed, the emptiness filled up again.

Now think of God as a person to whom we owe obedience (like society, or like a parent). Then disobedience robs God of what he has coming. Disobedience is unjust. Disobedience creates, so to speak, an empty place in God that ought to be filled up again.

To satisfy God's justice is to offer what we owe. It means making amends, balancing things out on the scale of justice. It means filling God's empty place by returning the obedience that God has coming.

There is, however, one small problem. We owe but cannot pay. God has our obedience coming, but we can't deliver. God's justice requires satisfaction, but we can't come through with it. Our bill has come due, but we are bankrupt.

The Bible and the Christian church describe a remarkable solution to this problem. Already in the Old Testament sacrifices, God himself provides a way to satisfy his own justice. A sinner could sacrifice an animal to take her place. And the Bible says that the aroma of roast lamb is to God what a good meal is to a hungry eater: satisfaction. God's justice demands satisfaction, but God's mercy provides a substitute so that the sinner herself does not have to pay.

That is where the cross of Jesus Christ fits in. A sacrifice is made in order to satisfy God's justice. Our Savior is therefore a kind of priest, offering a sacrificial victim to God. But this time the victim is not a sheep or an ox. This time the victim is the priest himself who lies on a cross and thus turns it into an altar.

When someone sins, someone must pay. And the wages of sin is death, even for God.

Prayer

Lord God, for the wonderful way you find to meet your own demand, we give you thanks. You are a God of amazing grace. In Jesus' name, Amen.

REDEMPTION

Scripture

For you know that it was not with perishable things such as silver or gold that you were redeemed from the empty way of life handed down to you from your forefathers, but with the precious blood of Christ, a lamb without blemish or defect.

—1 Peter 1:18–19

Teachings

While justly angry,
God did not turn his back
on a world bent on destruction;
he turned his face to it in love.
With patience and tender care he set out
on the long road of redemption
to reclaim the lost as his people
and the world as his kingdom.

—Our World Belongs to God, 19

Until 1865 most American blacks in the South were sold or born into slavery. A *Time-Life* book tells about them.*
By age twelve most slaves had to begin a life of backbreaking field work. A work day was from "can see" to "can't see." If the moon was full, a slave might have to keep working the rows and hauling cotton till midnight. His diet included little more than fatty salt meat and a little corn. Clothing was cheap fabric called "Negro cloth." Housing consisted of drafty, dirty, one-room shacks, usually occupied by six to twelve people. Slaves were often sick; many had worms and rotting teeth. Unruly ones were sometimes viciously whipped by professional "slavebreakers." These paid thugs would then send the owner a bill listing each slave they had flogged and naming a cost per slave for this service.

Most slaves were sold at auction at least once in their lives. I suppose none of us can understand what a vile and degrading experience that was. White shoppers would sometimes make slave men and women hop or jump to see if they were lively. Like horses, slaves would have their teeth inspected and their rib cages poked. A few slaves turned out to be hard to sell because their backs were a mass of scars and old welts from a slavebreaker's rawhide whip.

Couples were separated, children forcibly removed from parents. Some slaves were treated better than others. But all were property, like animals, to be used or sold as their owners liked.

A few slaves managed to escape to the North by means of the Underground Railroad, a network of routes, rest places, and safe houses that led to freedom. A number of courageous blacks and whites tried to help the desperate fugitives make a good escape. But it was dangerous work. If

*Brother Against Brother: The War Begins

those who helped were caught, they could expect rough treatment. It cost a lot to free slaves.

Slave funerals were seldom sad. Often the relatives and friends of a dead slave would sing or dance, as if attending a wedding or graduation. Christian slaves longed for heavenly rest the way a thirst-crazed desert traveler craves liquid. When a slave entered his rest, those who were left would celebrate. After all, the only way most slaves could be set free was through death.

Come to think of it, there was one other way. Some slaves were set free in this life. They were freed by a person with a conscience, Northern or Southern, who bought them at an auction. After paying the price she set them free.

The name for this glorious work is *redemption*. Redemption is a liberation word. It means to rescue by ransom. That is, it means delivering someone from evil by paying the required price.

The Bible often speaks of liberation, ransom, and redemption. In the Old Testament God redeems his slave people "out of Egypt, out of the land of slavery." Later, God provides animal sacrifice as a redemption from sin: the animal is the ransom provided by God and then offered *to* God, so that the person offering it can be set free from guilt. In addition, psalmists sometimes pray to be redeemed from the hand of their enemies and from the power of death.

But, as we know, the Bible's great word about redemption is its word about Jesus Christ, our Savior. In a mysterious and powerful way, Jesus' life and death *redeem* us.

From what? Sometimes the Bible writers (such as Paul) speak of our slavery to sin. Sin has a stranglehold on us. In a frustrating and maddening way, sin is a kind of slave driver that first tempts and then brutally punishes us.

Sometimes the Bible speaks of redemption from the fear of death, or from the guilt of having broken God's law, or from the emptiness of an aimless life. Occasionally it speaks of the devil and the powers of this world as our slave drivers.

We do not fully understand redemption. But we do know this: the price paid at auction for us is not just money, not just silver and gold. Like a courageous member of the Underground Railroad, our Redeemer pays with his life. We are redeemed by the ransom payment of blood.

It costs a lot to redeem slaves.

Prayer
All praise and glory to you, O God, for setting us free through Jesus Christ our Lord. Amen.

DAY 4

RECONCILIATION

Scripture
"If only there were someone to arbitrate between us,
  to lay his hand upon us both."

—Job 9:33

Teachings
We find all comforts in his wounds
and have no need to seek or invent any other means
to reconcile ourselves with God
than this one and only sacrifice.

—Belgic Confession, Article 21

In Job 1 Satan appears one day in heaven. God and Satan begin to talk over how things are going on earth. "Say," says God, "I wonder if you've noticed my man Job. Have you seen how God-fearing he is? Have you noticed how perfectly he serves me and turns away from evil?"

Satan is unimpressed. "Sure," he says. "Sure, I've seen Job." Then Satan counterthrusts with a hard question: "Does Job serve God for nothing?"

"Look," says Satan, "You've *bought* Job's faith. You've made him rich. Every time he says the Apostles' Creed you send him a check. Of course he'll serve you. He's no fool. You think he doesn't know who writes the checks?

"But suppose we change the rules. Suppose you stretch out your hand and take away everything you've given him. He'll curse you to your face."

"You're on," says God. "I bet he won't."

So Job is thrown out onto the game board to be moved around by God's prosecutor, Satan. Satan is an accuser, a prosecuting attorney, a powerful adversary. God lets him out on a tether, just close enough to take some swings at Job but not close enough to kill him.

Job himself knows nothing of this. He's not in on any of it. All he knows is that the sun begins to set on his happiness. Job's world turns suddenly cold and dark and miserable. His possessions are stolen. Lightning strikes his sheep. His servants are slaughtered in a terrorist attack. Then, one day, a cyclone comes across the wilderness and the house falls in on Job's seven sons and three daughters. Finally Job himself is laid low with a disgusting sickness. Job sits on a pile of manure, nursing his oozing sores and cursing the day of his birth.

What does a person do when God seems to have become hostile? What does a person do when he can no longer make any sense out of what God permits to happen in the world? Job knows God exists—that's not the problem. But something has suddenly gone wrong with God. Some wire in God has gotten crossed. Some miniature circuit has gotten overloaded. Some terrifying personality change has come over God.

Job cannot understand it. He keeps wondering *why*. Why must he suffer so? How has he gone wrong with God? Why all this evil? Through all the banks of storm clouds Job keeps searching for one ray of light. He keeps wondering and storming and hunting for God.

The problem is that God is so silent, so invisible, so far away, so untouchable. If Job could only see God! If he could only somehow lay hold on God, maybe even talk to God!

But there you are. Job knows as well as you do that wishing doesn't make a thing true. And the fact is that God seems to have gone off duty. He seems unavailable for comment. There isn't any way to *get* to God, to get through to him.

But that's how it is. We have no line to God and he has none to us. There is nobody *between* us, says Job to himself.

An idea suddenly leaps into Job's mind: "If only there were someone to arbitrate between us, to lay his hand upon us both!" Job is thinking of a third party between God and humanity. This third party would be like a labor arbitrator, a person who gets a company and its workers reconciled during a strike. He would be a kind of umpire, a kind of mediator. He would be someone, says Job, "to lay his hand upon us both."

Who on earth could be an arbitrator? Where, for heaven's sake, could one find a mediator? Who could reconcile a fallen and hopeless human race with a high and awesome God? Who could represent humans by taking our case to God? And who could represent God by appearing among humans?

Someone, says Job, "to lay his hand upon us both." One nail-torn hand placed on a broken Job, sitting there on the manure pile. One mangled hand upon the King of heaven.

"If only there were someone to arbitrate between us, to lay his hand upon us both." God and humanity reconciled because of the coming of an arbitrator.

Could that ever happen?

Prayer
Our Father in heaven, we feel close to you today, at peace with you, only because Jesus, our Mediator, has laid his hand on us and on you. Thank you. In Jesus' name, Amen.

HOMEWORK

Vocabulary

41. atonement: the process by which Jesus Christ puts right what sin puts wrong. Christ's suffering and death are an atonement, a making amends, for sin.

42. sacrifice: the act of giving up something of value in order to get something of even greater value. Jesus sacrifices his life in order to win ours.

43. satisfaction: giving someone what he has coming, so as to "fill up an empty place" in him. Through his death Christ satisfies God's justice by obeying God perfectly, as we cannot, and by suffering the penalty for our disobedience.

44. redemption: to rescue someone by paying a ransom. Just as God redeemed Israel from the land of Egypt, so Jesus Christ redeems us from the slavery of sin and death by paying the ransom price of his lifeblood.

45. reconciliation: restoring peace and harmony to estranged parties. Jesus Christ brings peace and reconciliation by acting as arbitrator, or mediator, between God and humanity.

Questions

Day 1: In what way was Jesus' death on the cross a *sacrifice*?

Day 2: What does God's justice demand? What does God's mercy provide?

Day 3: Why does almost this entire reading talk about slavery? What's the point?

Day 4: How are we like Job? What does it mean to be reconciled to God?

Summary

Do *one* of the following:
a. Did any one or any part of this week's readings (including the Scripture passages and confessional statements) say something special to you or capture your attention in some way? If so, be ready to share your choice and the reasons for it with the class.
b. Write a brief statement of personal reaction to God's incredible way of paying for our sins (the atonement). If you prefer, find a Bible passage which expresses the way you feel.

12

JUSTIFICATION

JUSTIFICATION

Scripture

He was delivered over to death for our sins and was raised to life for our justification.
—Romans 4:25

Teachings

He carried God's judgement on our sin;
his sacrifice removes our guilt.
He walked out of the grave, the Lord of life!
He conquered sin and death.
We are set right with God,
we are given new life,
and called to walk with him
in freedom from sin's dominion.
—*Our World Belongs to God*, 27

Tom was a thief. Although he was just barely a teenager and hadn't been a thief for very long, Tom had become very good at thievery. He was smart, quick, and daring. He also happened to have the kind of job that gave him opportunities for theft.

Tom worked as a student assistant to the school custodian. He washed blackboards, swept floors, pushed desks back into neat, straight rows. He also raided students' lockers and teachers' desks, stealing small change and valuables. For, although Tom was never given a master key, he knew where one was kept. And he knew how to quickly use it and return it.

Over the weeks and months members of the school community grew more and more annoyed at their losses. Usually the missing amounts were small, but once the money from candy and ice cream sales at basketball games was stolen. That amounted to quite a lot of cash. Another time, an eighth grader left all her birthday money in her locker and found it gone on Monday when she returned.

Tom was meanwhile trying hard to get as much mileage out of his thefts as he could. He shopped for good clothes, hoping to impress his classmates with them. He also blew a lot of money on video games. And he tried to buy things for students he admired. Sometimes they would accept his gifts. Other times they'd just look at him strangely and walk away. In either case, Tom didn't seem to gain the friends he craved.

Tom knew he had a time bomb ticking in his life. One of these days he would be caught and it would blow him up. True, while he was actually in the middle of a risky theft, Tom didn't reflect on what he was doing. After all, his heart was racing as fast as his larcenous hands. But the nights—the nights were bad. The conscience that Tom had taught to shut up so it wouldn't shout at him began to whisper insistently at night. Some nights Tom could hardly get to sleep. Other nights he was troubled by nightmares of being pursued by people with guns and cuffs.

Then one Thursday he was caught. As he was going through Mr. Gunst's desk, Tom was startled by a voice. Mr. Gunst, the history teacher, had suddenly materialized behind him and was asking in a quiet voice what Tom was doing. Tom tried to imagine some innocent reasons why he would be searching Mr. Gunst's desk, but he couldn't think of any. He could tell from the tone of Mr. Gunst's voice that *he* couldn't think of any either.

So they talked.

Mr. Gunst was one of those teachers you didn't exactly like but you always respected. He never joked around with students; he was a firm man. But he was also fair.

At first Tom tried to lie about all the other thefts. But by now he was feeling tired and small and guilty. Besides, Mr. Gunst was remarkably hard to lie to. Tom ended up admitting everything. He even admitted the reason for his stealing: he told Mr. Gunst he felt unaccepted and out of the center of things and was trying to get in.

Mr. Gunst's attitude was interesting. He was firm about what Tom had done. It was plain wrong. Stealing could not be justified. Tom would have to make friends some other way, some right way. And somehow the stolen money would have to be repaid.

On the other hand—perhaps because Tom was so miserable and felt so wrong and guilty—Mr. Gunst was incredibly kind to Tom himself. He acted as if, although Tom had done something all wrong, Tom himself was all right. Mr. Gunst did not justify what Tom had done, but he did justify Tom. That is, he accepted Tom, forgave him for going through his desk, and tried to arrange things so that Tom could be reconciled with the school community.

In doing these things, Mr. Gunst acted like God.

Prayer

God, our heavenly Father, you are the one who hates sin but loves sinners. You are the one who is firm against wrong but kind to wrongdoers. Accept us, we pray, through the atoning work of Jesus Christ, in whom we pray. Amen.

DAY 2

FORGIVENESS

OF SINS

Scripture
. . . God was reconciling the world to himself in Christ, not counting men's sins against them. And he has committed to us the message of reconciliation.

—2 Corinthians 5:19

Teachings
Q. What do you believe
  concerning "the forgiveness of sins"?
A. I believe that God,
     because of Christ's atonement,
  will never hold against me
    any of my sins
    nor my sinful nature
       which I need to struggle against all my life.

  Rather, in his grace
     God grants me the righteousness of Christ
     to free me forever from judgment.

—Heidelberg Catechism Q & A 56

It was a scene much of the world saw and will never forget. One day in 1981 Pope John Paul II, one of the truly great popes of the twentieth century, was greeting people from his open car in St. Peter's Square in Rome. Suddenly he catapulted backward, collapsing into the arms of his security people. The Pope had been shot by a would-be assassin, Mehmet Ali Agca. The scene ended as the Popemobile moved away, helpers shielding the stricken John Paul.

Almost three years later there was another scene which most of the world saw and will never forget. It was a scene of grace. Pope John Paul II entered the prison cell where Mehmet Ali Agca was serving his life sentence. The two men talked. The Pope grasped Agca's arm. Speaking softly, John Paul forgave Agca for trying to kill him. Agca, a Muslim who was not familiar with Christian forgiveness, seemed confused. But at the end of the meeting Agca pressed the Pope's hand to his face, as if to express respect.

Forgiveness of sins is one of the main parts of justification. God never justifies sins—that is, he never excuses or accepts them. Someone has to pay for them. But God does justify sinners—that is, because of Christ's atonement, God excuses his sons and daughters from the punishment they deserve and accepts them as children he loves. Sin is unacceptable to God; sinners can be accepted.

Let's try to understand how this works. Look at it this way: sin is a problem to God as well as to us. Sin is like a short circuit that turns a computer program to garbage. It's like bad breath in a friendship or fleas in the family dog. Sin is something that stands between persons like a cactus stalk. God wants to receive and accept us, but sin is *in the way.*

We recall (lesson 9) that in his covenant of grace God promises to forgive our sins and make us clean. Like Tom in yesterday's story, or like Mehmet Ali Agca in the two scenes described today, we don't deserve to be forgiven. What we deserve, frankly, is punishment and trouble. And like Mr. Gunst and the Pope, God is no pushover. It is a deadly mistake to picture God as a sort of heavenly wimp. God is rock firm against sin and terrifyingly strong in hating and condemning it. Sin must be punished. Somebody must suffer for it.

The gracious solution to the problem, as we learned in lesson 11, is that the Son of God himself suffers and atones so that we might have forgiveness and peace with God. A name for this forgiveness and peace is *justification.* John Calvin thought justification was so important that he called it "the main hinge on which religion turns."

What, exactly, is justification? It can be described in many ways. It is that which makes us right with God. It is the act of God that makes peace between God and us, that reconciles us to God. But perhaps the best description of justification is that it is "God's acceptance of unacceptable people." Sin has made us unacceptable. But in a stunning move of grace God accepts us anyhow. Because of the mighty, painful work of Jesus Christ, God does a kind of gracious arithmetic to solve the problem of sin. He subtracts our sin from us; then he adds the righteousness of Jesus Christ in its place. God himself makes us acceptable to him. God himself gets rid of the stubborn problem that is in the way.

The subtracting part of the program is what I have been talking about in this reading: the forgiveness of sin. Sin is subtracted from us. It is taken away like a smaller number from a greater. And God bears no grudges. He never again holds our forgiven sin against us.

In fact, when you and I come mysteriously before God on the final judgment day, the person who presides—the person who holds our fate in his hands—is none other than the Lord Jesus Christ, who sacrificed himself for us.

Imagine that one day Mehmet Ali Agca comes before the prison parole board to see if he can finally be released. Whom do you suppose he would like to see sitting as judge at the head of the table?

Prayer

O God, forgive our sins and make us acceptable to you as your loved children. Through Jesus Christ, our Lord, Amen.

DAY 3

ALIEN

RIGHTEOUSNESS

Scripture

It is because of (God) that you are in Christ Jesus, who has become for us wisdom from God—that is, our righteousness, holiness and redemption.

—1 Corinthians 1:30

Teachings

Q. How are you right with God?

A. Only by true faith in Jesus Christ.
    Even though my conscience accuses me
      of having grievously sinned against all God's commandments
      and of never having kept any of them,
    and even though I am still inclined toward all evil,
    nevertheless,
      without my deserving it at all,
      out of sheer grace,
    God grants and credits to me
    the perfect satisfaction, righteousness, and holiness of Christ,
      as if I had never sinned nor been a sinner,
      as if I had been as perfectly obedient
        as Christ was obedient for me.

    All I need to do
    is to accept this gift of God with a believing heart.

—Heidelberg Catechism Q & A 60

The U.S. has a Declaration of Independence—a claim that the U.S. will no longer be a colony of Great Britain, but will now be a nation on its own. Ever since 1776 U.S. citizens have thought of this freedom as an improvement. Nations like to be independent. They like to make their own plans, choose their own friends, live the way they want. They like to be on their own.

So do individuals. But we have to wait for independence. We all started out as unborn persons. When we were in our mothers' wombs, we were totally dependent on them for our health and well-being—in fact, for life itself. If our mothers ate the right foods and drank the right liquids we thrived. If they ate junk, we suffered. If they got drunk, we got drunk. If they took certain drugs or caught certain diseases, it was as if we ourselves took those drugs or caught those diseases. We were totally dependent on them. That is, we depended on *aliens*.

But, of course, one day we were born. A physician snipped the umbilical cord and we began to breathe. People think of this as an improvement. We ought to put away childish things.

As we grow older, we do put them away. We learn to walk on our own two feet. We learn to feed ourselves (at first we only smear food around in the neighborhood of our mouths, but sooner or later we find exactly the right address). And as we become teenagers, we try for still more independence. We want increased freedom to spend time and money as we see fit. We want to make our own friends and some of our own decisions. We want to put away childish things. We want independence—and we should.

Up to a point.

As a matter of fact we never outgrow some dependencies. For example, as long as we live, we depend on God's creation for nourishing food and thirst-quenching drink. We cannot create these things; we can only gather and use them. Further, we depend on other people for friendship, fun, marriage, safety, and countless other things. We depend on the life and strength and gifts of others, of aliens.

This is especially true where righteousness is concerned. To be righteous is to be holy, just, and good. Because of original sin (and our own original copies of it) we are not very good at righteousness. We cannot create righteousness on our own; we can only gather and use the righteousness of another.

Justification is God's acceptance of unacceptable people. As we have seen, it includes the forgiveness of sins. But it also includes something else: the addition of alien righteousness. Something old is subtracted; something new is added. What is added is the righteousness of Jesus Christ.

Jesus loved his friends and treated them perfectly. He spent time and energy on unpopular people. He firmly resisted temptation. He criticized self-righteous people but accepted unrighteous people. He was willing to die rather than go against the will of God.

In justification all this is mysteriously transferred to us—as if *we* had acted in just the same way. Jesus' holiness is added, or granted, to us. This alien righteousness is like shopping with someone else's credit card. It is like getting past a checkpoint in someone else's uniform. It is like traveling on an alien passport. It is like being carried in the divine womb, blood-rich with the very life of God.

In fact, we now have perfect lives. We cannot *live* perfect lives, but if we repent of sin and trust our Lord, God sees Jesus' life when he looks at us.

Try to be independent of God, and you die. It is like a declaration of independence from oxygen. But depend on the alien righteousness of Jesus Christ, and you become more alive, more free, more splendid than you could ever imagine.

For the alien is our loving Savior.

Prayer

Lord Jesus Christ, enrich and purify us with your holy life and grace. Amen.

ACCEPTANCE

Scripture
Who will bring any charge against those whom God has chosen? It is God who justifies.

—Romans 8:33

Teachings
Q. What is your only comfort in life
    and in death?
A. That I am not my own,
  but belong—
    body and soul,
    in life and in death—
to my faithful Savior Jesus Christ.

—Heidelberg Catechism Q & A 1

All of us hunger for acceptance. It is one of the things we depend on for happiness. If people we admire accept us, we grow like a watered plant in sunshine. If people we admire reject us, we wither and die inside.

How can we tell that people accept us? We tell by their words and actions and even by the look in their eyes. If people use our names in a warm way, we feel accepted. If they invite us to join them for a game, or an overnight, or a party, or a prank, we feel accepted. If they are hurt by what we do but painfully forgive us for doing it, we feel accepted. If they look at us with care, with a light in their eyes that says we are important to them, we feel wonderfully accepted.

The hunger for acceptance is so deep and keen in most of us that we will do almost anything to get it. When we are teenagers, we will wear certain clothes, comb our hair in certain ways, use just the right language, and try for the friendship of particularly acceptable persons. We will do all these things rather than risk the pain of rejection. For if we taste rejection just once, we never want to taste it again. So we work and sweat and struggle and try for acceptance. We think we cannot accept ourselves unless we are acceptable to others.

It takes very strong and secure persons to live life the right way without worrying too much whether others will like and accept them. You have met people like this. They seem happy and friendly in the "wrong" clothes. They choose their friends because they like them, not because their friends are important. They seem relaxed, confident, outgoing. And they care about people who feel rejected.

Where do such people get this attitude and this approach to life? They get it from God. Like Mr. Gunst and Pope John Paul II, these people feel deeply accepted by God. They feel *justified.* They know their sins are forgiven and that when God looks at them he sees the perfect life of Jesus Christ.

A person like that also feels *free*. A person who knows she is accepted by God is free to accept others and to accept herself. She may still dress, talk, walk, and act a certain way peculiar to her group or school. But she doesn't worry about it or feel desperate about it. After all, she doesn't depend on these things to accept herself. She depends instead on God's love, on knowing that God treasures her so much that Jesus Christ died to set her free.

When God accepts us, we can accept ourselves.

A Spanish author, Miguel de Cervantes, tells a story that helps us understand acceptance. He tells about Don Quixote, a sad, awkward, brave, and silly knight. In one episode Don Quixote comes into a little village inn, where he meets the village prostitute. She *is* a prostitute. There can't be much doubt about that. After all, everybody in the village says she's a prostitute. And everybody treats her like a prostitute. Most important, when people look at her with scorn, she reads "whore" in their eyes.

But the strange and brave Don Quixote doesn't see a prostitute when he sees this young woman. He sees a noble lady. He tells her she is a great and noble lady. He treats her as if she is royalty. And most important, when he looks at her, she sees in his eyes the image of a great and respected person. When she sees this image in Don Quixote's eyes, she recognizes it as her real self.

So she starts acting like the image she recognizes. She stops acting like a prostitute and starts acting like a great and respected person. She becomes Don Quixote's noble lady.

This is what acceptance can do for unacceptable people. The God who comes for us in Jesus Christ is forever looking at people like you and me and saying not only with his lips and eyes but also with his life the words "son," "daughter," "noble lady," "my child." The same terrifying cross on Golgotha that tells us we needed someone to die for us also tells us that God thinks we were *worth* dying for.

If God accepts us, who are we to condemn ourselves?

Prayer

O God, for your great justifying love that accepts us we give you hearty thanks, through Jesus Christ, our Lord. Amen.

HOMEWORK

Vocabulary

46. justification: God's acceptance of unacceptable people. Justification includes the forgiving of our sins and the adding to us of Jesus' righteousness.

47. forgiveness of sins: the subtracting, or putting away, of sins so that they are no longer held against us. When God forgives our sins, we can be at peace with him.

48. alien righteousness: the holiness of another. We do not have our own holiness, so the holiness of another (an alien) must be given to us to make us acceptable to God. Jesus is the alien.

49. acceptance: the receiving and welcoming of another. Acceptance is the heart of justification. Accepted people often, then, begin to act acceptably.

Questions

This week would you please make up one good question and answer for each reading? Try to ask questions that bring out the main ideas in the readings (no true/false, yes/no questions, please). You may ask questions about the Bible passages and confessional statements as well as the readings, if you wish. Write out all your questions and answers and be sure to bring them to class next week.

13

FAITH

GRAFTING

Scripture

If some of the branches have been broken off, and you, though a wild olive shoot, have been grafted in among the others and now share in the nourishing sap from the olive root, do not boast over those branches.

—Romans 11:17–18a

Teachings

Q. Are all saved through Christ
   just as all were lost through Adam?
A. No.
   Only those are saved
   who by true faith
      are grafted into Christ
      and accept all his blessings.

—Heidelberg Catechism Q & A 20

G rafting is one of the most wonderful possibilities in creation. A person who has been badly burned in an accident can be saved from constant infection and excruciating pain by means of a skin graft. A strip of tissue from a healthy part of the body is surgically removed and transplanted to the burned area. There a surgeon carefully fastens the skin transplant to the surrounding tissue with special stitches. Gradually, if the graft "takes," skin from a healthy thigh or inner arm will begin to grow at the burned site.

Bones can be grafted too. In fact, sometimes a bone from one person is grafted onto the fresh end of someone else's bone. There are even bone banks that keep various bones on deposit till an injury or disease calls for them.

Perhaps most common of all grafts are those that people perform on plants. An expert described it to me the other day. A person slices a twig from one tree and carries it to another. There he cuts a V-notch, or "envelope," that can receive the new twig. The roughened end of the twig is inserted into the notch. The joint is then snugly sealed with grafting wax or tape to hold the graft securely and to keep out disease organisms. The joint will always be a little knobby and funny looking, but if the graft takes, nourishing food and water will soon run through the tree's "plumbing system" into the newly attached twig.

Why bother with grafts? Plant experts graft in order to produce more and better fruit. If a certain kind of tree (say, an apple tree) doesn't take root well or produce many new seeds, the expert can graft a twig from it onto the fast-growing, well-rooted, disease-resistant stem of another tree and get the best of both. One has fast growth and good roots; the other has the kind of fruit people want.

Interestingly, Romans 11 and the Heidelberg Catechism speak of human grafting. *Persons* can be grafted. You and I can be united to Jesus Christ in order to share in his nourishing food and drink. We can then produce the special fruit that God wants to harvest from each of us.

What is meant by this? How does it work?

You recall from our last lesson that justification means two things: it means that our sins are forgiven and that Jesus Christ's righteousness is added to us. But how do we actually *receive* his righteousness?

We receive it by faith. Faith is the grafting wax or tape that bonds us to Jesus Christ. He is the one with the fast growth and the good roots. We are the ones who, apart from him, are rootless and fruitless. Across the world God wants a vast orchard of fancy fruits: fairness, compassion, honest answers, kindness, and so on. Above all, he wants to see us blossom with love for him and for others. To get all these fruits, God has arranged to graft millions of his children into the one perfect vine, or stem. When faith attaches us to Christ, it is as if his rich blood is transfused into us, flowing through us like nourishing plant food and water. Love and other wonderful things then begin to bud and burst on all of us who are united to him. He is the vine; we are the grafted branches.

In fact, either we share in Christ's nourishing life or we wither. Either we are united to Jesus Christ by faith or else, day by day, we begin the terrible process of spiritual death.

How are we justified? By God's grace alone. How do we *receive* this gracious justification? Only through true faith that grafts us to Jesus Christ.

Prayer

Jesus, give us faith so that your goodness may flow into us. In your name, Amen.

DAY 2

BELIEF

Scripture

Now faith is being sure of what we hope for and certain of what we do not see.

—Hebrews 11:1

Teachings

Q. What then must a Christian believe?

A. Everything God promises us in the gospel.
That gospel is summarized for us
in the articles of our Christian faith—
a creed beyond doubt,
and confessed throughout the world.

—Heidelberg Catechism, Q & A 22

Many of us have passed through a supermarket checkout lane and seen those awful gossip papers that some people are willing to buy. The headings are difficult to ignore: "Boy, Two, Turns into Woman Overnight"; "Family of Wolves Raises Oriental Midget"; "Cigar-Smoking Dwarf Wins 'Pretty Baby' Contest."

Most of us do not believe such stuff. We know that some clever or greedy person is only trying to make money.

Disbelief can be valuable. It may save us from being fooled or cheated. Disbelief and suspicion may be our main protection against being abducted, for instance. As honest people sometimes say, if someone offers you something too good to be true, it probably is.

But disbelief can also cut us off from things that are true and from persons we desperately need. People told Columbus he was loony when he said he could get to the East by sailing west. He claimed that the earth was round; the disbelievers all knew perfectly well that it was flat. Bystanders nearly died laughing when those crazy Wright brothers said they would fly. Everyone knew God wanted humans to soar no higher than they could jump.

When Jesus acknowledged that he was the Christ, people told him he was a liar. They then expressed their disbelief with wads of spit and vicious head slaps. These people were standing in the presence of their only Savior. But in their disbelief they knew better. So they erased him.

Belief and disbelief are so important that our religion is often simply called "The Christian Faith." For it is faith that ties us to the person we desperately need and faith that receives his justifying gifts.

Faith includes two parts: one of them is belief; the other is trust. Today I want to talk some more about the first of these.

What is belief? Christian belief is the acceptance of the truth of the gospel. Christian belief means accepting as true the promises of God.

Christian belief, says Hebrews, "is being sure of what we hope for and certain of what we do not see."

What do we hope for? Some of the things we hope for never come. We hope for a B, but get a C. We hope for a cash gift, but get a woolen bathrobe. We hope for a goal, but settle for an assist.

But beyond these small hopes is a large one. Christian people hope for the triumph of right over wrong, of good over evil, of God over his enemies. In other words, we hope for the coming of the kingdom of God. All the promises of God, all the truth of the gospel, can be summed up in the coming of the kingdom.

We will learn much more about the kingdom later. For now it is enough to understand that the coming of the kingdom is the big thing we hope for and the main thing we are certain of, even though we cannot yet fully see it. By faith we believe that God's kingdom will come; by faith we also believe in Christ the King, who has come and is coming again.

Reverend Frederick Buechner, in *Telling the Truth*, illustrates this with an example from the *Wizard of Oz*. At the end of the Yellow Brick Road Dorothy and her friends are awestruck by "the great and terrible Oz," whose booming voice resounds throughout the castle. But in the end his stage props are removed and Oz turns out to be only a little bald guy in disguise. He offers help, but he has only human help to offer. Appearances are deceiving.

The promises of the gospel go just the other way. The gospel is Oz in reverse. For the gospel tells us that the unknown carpenter from Nazareth, seemingly helpless against the Roman thugs who pin him to a tree trunk, is actually God in disguise. Behind his human weaknesses, behind his humiliating torture and painful death, the Lord of life is powerfully at work, muscles rippling to save us. Appearances are deceiving.

You have to believe it to see it.

Prayer

O God, we are often fooled and cheated. But we do put our trust in the promises of the gospel because, O God, we believe in you. Amen.

TRUST

Scripture

"Do not let your hearts be troubled. Trust in God; trust also in me. In my Father's house are many rooms; if it were not so, I would have told you. I am going there to prepare a place for you."

—John 14:1–2

Teachings

Q. What is true faith?
A. True faith is

not only a knowledge and conviction
that everything God reveals in his Word is true;
it is also a deep-rooted assurance,
created in me by the Holy Spirit through the gospel,
that, out of sheer grace earned for us by Christ,
not only others, but I too,
have had my sins forgiven,
have been made forever right with God,
and have been granted salvation.

—Heidelberg Catechism Q & A 21

Faith includes two parts: belief and trust. We believe *that* Jesus Christ will return, for instance. But we believe *in* Jesus Christ himself. Again, we believe *that* God exists. But that is not enough. Even the devils believe that God exists, says James 2:19, and shudder at the thought! Besides believing *that* God exists we must also believe *in* God. To believe in a person is to trust him, depend on him, maybe be willing to risk ourselves for him. To believe in God, or in Jesus Christ, is to go further. It means to give ourselves into his safekeeping. It means to turn over, to hand over, our very self to this other person.

"Trust in God," says Jesus. "Trust also in me."

If we think for a moment, we can see how the two parts of faith, belief and trust, are connected. Suppose your basketball coach tells you to shoot more with your fingertips than with your palm. Or suppose your coach teaches you to dribble (a basketball; not saliva) with your head up. Neither of these things feels natural at first. You wouldn't be likely to believe that fingertip shooting and heads-up dribbling were the way to go unless you *trusted* your coach. If you trust someone, you tend to believe what he or she says.

Or suppose, on the other hand, that you are in a shopping mall and a stranger approaches. "Excuse me," says the stranger, "I'm Officer Smithski and I have to confirm your identity. Your name, please?" You blurt out your name without thinking. "Yes," says the stranger, "you are the person I've been sent to get. Your mother has been in an auto accident, and I've been dispatched to pick you up and take you to the hospital. She's been asking for you."

If you are alert, and if you have been warned of such abductors' tricks, you do not believe that your mother has been in an accident or that she is now in a hospital asking for you. You do not believe these things because you do not and cannot trust this stranger.

Disbelief often comes from mistrust, just as belief often comes from trust. If we trust God, then we believe what the Scriptures say, for example. They are, after all, God's Word. But the reverse is true too: trust often comes from belief. Thus, if you believe what the Scriptures say, you will tend to trust God. Belief and trust, in other words, usually reinforce each other.

Still, they are different things. And trust is often harder for us than belief. A gifted minister, Clarence Boomsma, used to tell students a story that helps us understand the difference between belief and trust. This true story is about a man named Blondin, who was a famous high-wire performer years ago. Blondin once proposed a remarkable feat. He announced that he would walk a tightrope stretched across Niagara Falls.

On the fateful day huge crowds gathered on both sides of the falls. Sporting men bet large sums on Blondin's chances. High above the deadly torrent the great performer started slowly along the thin wire. Foot by agonizing foot, leaning against the wind, Blondin made his way across the whole length of tightwire. In fact, he later made a crossing with bushel baskets tied to his feet.

Then Blondin came up with an even more outrageous stunt. He announced that he would attempt a crossing with a man riding on his back. Bigger crowds gathered; larger sums were bet. Blondin set out with his precious cargo. As he inched along, several of the men who had bet strongly against him began to fear that he might succeed. So they reached for the guy ropes that braced the main wire and cut one of them. Halfway across the span Blondin at once felt the wire beneath him beginning to sway dangerously. And Blondin began to *run* to the far side, his human freight bouncing along on his back! Once more he succeeded. He actually made it!

But now let me ask you the two questions Rev. Boomsma used to ask. Do you *believe* that Blondin could do this? Suppose you do. Then you are like the spectators. Even the big bettors believed it and trembled.

But now the harder question: would you have *trusted* Blondin enough to get on his back?

Prayer

O Lord Christ, it is easy for us to say we believe what you have said and done. But give us also the trust that lets us place ourselves in your hands. Amen.

DAY 4

CHOICE

Scripture

"You did not choose me, but I chose you and appointed you to go and bear fruit—fruit that will last . . . . If you belonged to the world, it would love you as its own. As it is, you do not belong to the world, but I have chosen you out of the world. That is why the world hates you."

—John 16–19

Teachings

Q. It is by faith alone
   that we share in Christ and all his blessings:
   where then does that faith come from?

A. The Holy Spirit produces it in our hearts
      by the preaching of the holy gospel,
   and confirms it
      through our use of the holy sacraments.

—Heidelberg Catechism Q & A 65

Some choices cannot be avoided. If you are holding a twin-dip, peanut-butter-and-double-fudge-chocolate ice cream cone in bright sunlight on a hot day, you have to decide whether to gulp it down or let it melt. You *have* to choose. You cannot refuse to decide. For that refusal is itself a decision—one soon dripping with melted ice cream.

The same goes for a city gardener who refuses to decide whether to let his garden go to weeds. The same goes for a confused sailor who has one foot on a dock and the other in a departing catamaran. In each of these cases, if you do not choose, the choice will be made for you. And you may not like the result very well.

When we reach our early teens, we begin to understand how much the shape and happiness of life depend on our choices. True, some of our choices are small and innocent. Will we wear jeans or sweats? Ride or walk? Swim freestyle or backstroke? Small matters.

But some choices are very serious. They have to do with who or what will control us. A rock star may decide, for instance, to turn his brain to oatmeal by sniffing, smoking, or shooting certain drugs. In some cases a drug-ridden person can choose to get help before the damage is permanent. But sometimes an addiction that begins with a free choice to experiment ends up robbing a person of the power to choose anything *but* drugs. That's how frightening an addiction can be. It starts with a choice and ends with slavery. A person ends up mastered by chemicals.

Your most important choice is the choice of your master. You cannot refuse to choose: the refusal is itself a choice. For someone or something *will* master you. It might be God or it might be the devil. It might be your own changing moods or feelings. It might be the opinion of your friends. If you say "I refuse to choose," you will then be mastered by whoever and whatever happens to come along. Instead of having one master, good or bad, you will have many. There are people like that. They change masters as often as a square dancer changes partners.

To be a person grafted into Jesus Christ by belief and trust is to choose your master. It is to choose the only master who will never disappoint you. Instead of yourself, instead of evil, instead of friends or feelings or fondness for foolishness, you turn in faith to Jesus Christ and his promises.

You may do this very gradually. You may, year by year, *find* yourself believing in him. Or it may happen quite rapidly some winter week when things have broken down and friends have failed. You find one night that your prayers seem especially important to you. A part of the Bible suddenly speaks to you. You are strangely ready to do a painful thing that you know is right—confessing sin, for instance. A sermon one Sunday seems aimed at you like a shot to the heart.

In the midst of such things you turn to face Jesus Christ, your Master. "O Lord," you stammer, "now I give myself to you." And then, in one of the great and beautiful mysteries of faith, you discover something startling. You discover that it is not really you who has been doing the choosing. He has.

"You did not choose me," says Jesus. "I chose you."

How? By images and feelings and Bible stories that seeped into us when we were tiny. By the sight of our parents on their knees in prayer. By a children's sermon that one day reached in and would not let go. By the life of a person we admire. By a great joy or a shattering tragedy. Above all, by the silent, powerful work in us of the Holy Spirit. God has his ways. We cannot avoid him. God knows a thousand combinations that will unlock the treasure house in each of us where God has stored his goods.

God chooses us to choose him. God's choice is called *election*. Ours is called *faith*. Both are a sheer gift.

Prayer

O Lord, we don't deserve it, but we hear you calling our names. Thank you for choosing us to choose you. Thank you for your wonderful gift of saving faith. In our Savior's name, Amen.

HOMEWORK

Vocabulary

1. union with Christ: the bonding or attaching of persons to Christ. All of us are united to Christ by being members of his church, but the union is finally secure only when we are personally grafted to Christ by true faith.

2. faith: the bond to Christ from our side. Faith includes belief in the promises of God and trust in Jesus Christ. Faith *receives* justification.

3. election: God's choice of us for the gift of saving faith.

Questions

Day 1: Did the grafting idea help you understand your relationship to Christ? Why or why not?

Day 2: What's the most important thing Christians hope for? What's meant by the last line in the reading?

Day 3: What are the two parts of faith and how are they different?

Day 4: Explain Jesus' words: "You did not choose me, but I chose you."

Summary

Talk with a parent about how the Holy Spirit has worked and is working in your life to help you receive God's gifts through faith.

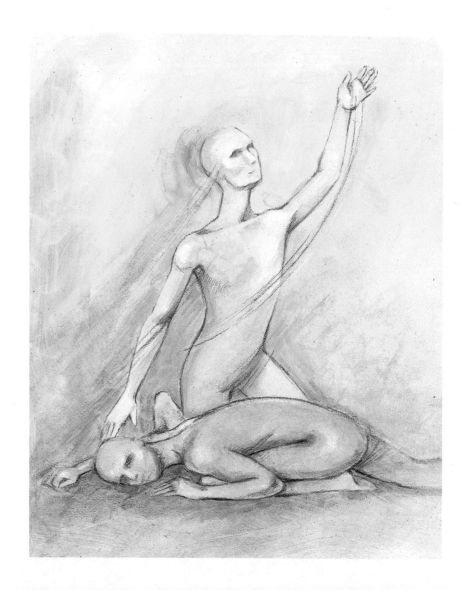

14

REPENTANCE

TURNING

Scripture

"Repent, then, and turn to God, so that your sins may be wiped out, that times of refreshing may come from the Lord."

—Acts 3:19

Teachings

Q. What is involved
   in genuine repentance or conversion?
A. Two things:
      the dying-away of the old self,
      and the coming-to-life of the new.

—Heidelberg Catechism Q & A 88

An absentminded driver turns the wrong way onto a one-way street. He tools along for a hundred feet and then sees two lanes of cars coming straight at his hood ornament. He slams on the brake pedal, flips the gear selector into reverse, lurches backwards into a driveway, waits for traffic to pass, and then drives off in the opposite direction.

A novice hiker tries a shortcut through a patch of woods. She keeps bearing left, as she thinks she should, but the path disappears, the woods get thicker, and the hiker begins to feel waves of panic washing over her. So she turns around and heads out the way she came in.

A father watches his prodigal son stride off down the road to a far city. Day after day the father walks out to the gate and peers down that road. He keeps watching and aching and hoping. He keeps praying that if his son is lost in the far city, he will not lose the memory of his home. And one day, perhaps years later, shading his eyes against the late afternoon sun, the father spies a figure in the distance. The approaching figure droops and hesitates, but there is no mistaking who it is. Overwhelmed with need, arms extended like a finishing sprinter, the father rushes toward the son he wants home.

The son and the hiker and the driver all repent. Repentance is more than simply turning a corner or turning over a new page. To repent is to stop in your tracks, pivot one hundred eighty degrees, and head back. To repent is to *turn completely around*. Sometimes it happens quickly; sometimes it takes years.

Most of us have heard of repentance. We may have the feeling that it is somewhat unpleasant. We are wrong. It is entirely unpleasant. Repentance is no fun at all. And yet we have to do it. In fact, as the great Christian writer C. S. Lewis once said, repentance is a special problem to us because only bad people need to do it and only good people *can* do it.

What is this turning and why can't we forget about it if it's so unpleasant?

Repentance—or *conversion*, as it is often called—is the complete turnaround of our lives. Because of original sin we have a tendency to do wrong—to lie, to envy, to think of ourselves as the best thing since button-down collars, and so on. We also tend to avoid doing what's right—working hard, for example, or encouraging a person we don't like very well. We are like a small outboard fishing boat headed downstream toward a ruinous waterfall. Our tendency is to let the stream carry us. That's easiest, especially if we don't know or don't care about the danger. We tend to go with the flow.

Repentance in such a situation is a hard and delicate move. We have to see our danger, shift into reverse, plow stern-first backwards till we get upstream to quieter water. Then we have to turn carefully around and head against the current.

These descriptions of repentance are all pictures. They tell what repentance (conversion) is *like*. Repentance is like a U-turn in traffic. It is like a hiker's retreat or a runaway's homecoming. Repentance is like an outboard backing upstream, full-speed astern.

There is, as a matter of fact, one more thing that repentance, or conversion, is like. It is like dying and rising. It is as if an old person in us—one that cheats and struts—is killed off and a fresh new person—one that is clean and straight—is born. Repentance is the conversion, the turning, of a person from old to new, from death to life. Repentance is like being born again.

What does this mean in detail? As we shall see, it means feeling the pain of those we hurt. It means running away from evil. It means taking delight in what's right. It means starting to think of ourselves as being driven by a new engine, by the power of the Holy Spirit.

Why do we have to do these things? Because without them we will drown or crash or get lost or die in some far-off pig pen.

Without repentance we will be without God.

Prayer
O God, we are bad enough to need to repent. By your Spirit make us good enough so that we *can* repent. Through Jesus Christ, our Lord, Amen.

DAY 2

DYING-AWAY

Scripture
Godly sorrow brings repentance that leads to salvation and leaves no regret, but worldly sorrow brings death.
—2 Corinthians 7:10

Teachings
Q. What is the dying-away of the old self?
A. It is to be genuinely sorry for sin,
   to hate it more and more,
   and to run away from it.

—Heidelberg Catechism Q & A 89

People say it all the time.
You get a wrong number because of your machine-gun speed with touch-tone buttons. "Sorry," you say to the Mafia hit man who answers. You walk down the aisle of your bus and accidentally conk someone on the head with your bug display. "Sorry," you say. You reach for the dinner rolls and drag your cuff through your brother's mashed potatoes, opening up a chute for beef gravy to flood the rest of his plate. "Sorry."

These are all apologies. They are small sorrows for small errors. They are the oil that cuts down friction in the turning of life's little wheels. Politeness means saying you're sorry.

So does repentance. But a repentant person who uses these words means something far more serious by them than does the person who is only being polite. In his book *Forgive and Forget* Lewis Smedes, a fine Christian writer, has helped us understand this.

Suppose, for instance, that another student has suspended himself by his knees from a chinning bar. You think it would be fun to swing him like a hanging side of beef. So you give him a shove. Suddenly he flips off the bar and lands on the back of his head. He doesn't move. The principal calls an ambulance which speeds the injured student to Emergency. Eventually he recovers, but meanwhile he suffers through several weeks of blurred vision, headaches, and time lost from school.

An apology is not quite good enough. You need to do more. You need to feel the other person's pain. You need to feel sadness and concern. You need good grief. After all, you hurt someone. You may want to bring the person a gift, trying somehow to make it up to him. You will want the person to know how bad you feel and how deeply you wish you hadn't pushed him. Finally, you make a determined covenant with yourself never to try something like that again.

You repent.

Our whole life needs repentance. The old self we are born with is tempted to push and shove. It likes to stand in the winner's circle while crowds roar and bands play. It wants deliciously to chew on a juicy morsel of gossip that will bring another person down. And it shrinks from the honest praise that will build another person up.

To tell the truth, the old self in us shrinks from God. We know God is there. There are times, like some late night on a camping trip, that we have almost felt the breath of God. But because we want to drive our own life, run our own show, hoist our own flag, we find that God becomes a kind of embarrassment to us. We ignore God. We neglect Jesus Christ. We do not pray unless we have to. We daydream through church services. Though we are radiant, pulsing images of God, we try to become instead images of some human jock, or clown, or queen, or star, or fool.

Repentance (conversion) means turning away from all this. It means feeling the pain of those we hurt or ignore. It means feeling the pain and fearing the anger of the God of the universe. Repentance includes a softening of our hearts and a turning towards the Father who waits by the gate for us to come home. He is the only person in the world who can open a door and welcome us *inside.*

To repent is to muscle aside familiar habits. You have to beat down old attitudes. You have to try to kill somebody—the old self with all its warts and ways. This is hard work. Old selves die hard. You might put out a contract on your old self but find that it takes a long time to get up the nerve to go through with the act itself. It is humiliating to be your own hit man.

But it can be done. Over time repentance works. God is at work in this painful, holy suicide. Like the last notes of a filthy song, like the freight-train rumble of a killer tornado, like the roar of a lynch mob, the old self slowly dies away.

It can still be heard from time to time. But each time its voice begins to sound more and more like the voice of a stranger.

Prayer
O God, you are the holy one whom we have ignored. Forgive us, we pray. Kill off everything in us that crowds you out. Amen.

DAY 3

DYING-AWAY CONTINUED:

FIGHT OR FLIGHT

Scripture
But you, man of God, flee from all this, and pursue righteousness, godliness, faith, love, endurance and gentleness. Fight the good fight of the faith.

—1 Timothy 6:11–12

Teachings
Q. What is the dying-away of the old self?
A. It is to be genuinely sorry for sin,
    to hate it more and more,
    and to run away from it.

—Heidelberg Catechism Q & A 89

Animals are like humans. They will respond to a threat either by facing it or by running away from it. They fight or flee. Hunters know that a startled deer, for instance, will run. A deer hears the crackling of underbrush, turns its tail up so that the white underside shows, and bounds off. That is, a deer usually responds to a threat by hightailing it out of danger. But an injured animal, particularly a cornered one, responds to danger by becoming dangerous itself. It may attack. Savvy hunters know this and take precautions. They tell each other tales of men being slashed or gored by the sharp antlers of wounded bucks.

Humans are like animals. Homeowners that are tormented by repeated vandalism will stay up at night in the dark with a telephone or even a shotgun. *Some* do that; others simply move out of the neighborhood. Fight or flight. Similarly, a person who is unfairly criticized might face and speak up to the critic. Or she might just walk away and seek a place to pout. Fight or flight.

Look at the quotation from the catechism at the top of this page. Repentance includes dying-away. Dying-away, in turn, includes sorrow for sin (which we thought about last time) and two other things—namely, hating sin and running away from it.

Let's think of these as fight and flight. Part of dying-away means hating sin enough to want to fight and kill it. Somebody wrecks a family by causing a divorce. A Christian will *hate* that sin, even if he loves the sinner. Somebody is tempted again and again to brag about imaginary accomplishments. The bragging and lying regularly get him in trouble with his friends. He comes to hate that sin. He wants to attack and kill it before it does more damage. Or suppose a person likes to bully smaller and weaker people. As he begins to turn toward God, he begins to hate his own bullying. He wants to root out this tendency in himself. For this (and all sin) is an enemy that corrupts and destroys.

Part of repentance is coming to *feel* a hatred of sin and its power to hurt. Repentant people especially hate and fight the sin they have some control over. They level their biggest guns at their own sin.

But sometimes the right response to the temptation of sin is to run away from it. Suppose you are alone on a dark street late at night. Three young gentlemen swinging bicycle chains start walking toward you. You'll feel like a fool if you run, but the truth is that only a fool would stand and fight against those odds.

It is the same way with some sins. We are not strong enough, or wise enough, or old enough to fight some of them—and we know it. These may be sins that are especially tempting to us, sins we especially fear, or sins that are brought to us as temptations by others. Suppose, for example, that a group wants to play a truly humiliating prank on a weak or unpopular person. You cannot stop them. You are afraid even to try. Perhaps you ought to have more courage. Maybe someday you will. But, for now, you can at least walk out. You can hightail it out of there. If someone accuses you of being afraid, the right answer would be, "Yes, I am. I'm afraid of what this will do to Herman (or whoever). And I also don't like what it's going to do to you and me."

The fact is that sin is frightening. Fools will pretend that it isn't—just as fools will play with live grenades. More mature people have the same healthy fear of sin that they have of a wounded wild animal. They do not snuggle up to it.

You have your choice with sin: fight or flight. Dying-away "is to be genuinely sorry for sin, to hate it more and more, and to run away from it."

We have to die before we can be born again.

Prayer
Lord, give us the courage to fight sin when we can. Give us the wisdom to run away from it when we have to. Amen.

DAY 4

COMING-TO-LIFE

Scripture

Restore to me the joy of your salvation
and grant me a willing spirit, to sustain me.

—Psalm 51:12

Teachings

Q. What is the coming-to-life of the new self?
A. It is wholehearted joy in God through Christ
and a delight to do every kind of good
as God wants us to.

—Heidelberg Catechism Q & A 90

Many of us know what it's like to feel a stab of joy when reading fantasy. A writer named Frederick Buechner (BEEKner) talks about the reasons for that feeling in one of his books.

In fantasies we read of places different from our own: a far-off country, or a deep forest, or a dark and fearful castle. A person from ordinary life, often a child, enters one of these strange places. She may wander into the forest or come upon the castle at the end of a yellow-brick road. She may step into a wardrobe to hide from friends and find herself moving clear through it to an icy land ruled by an evil queen whose face is as white as death.

Fantasies often include danger. There are wicked fairies and envious stepsisters. There may be a great and terrible wizard. There are forks in the path where a wrong choice means lostness or death. There are witches who cackle and drool over plump children. Above all, there are deceptions. Things are not as they appear. A gingerbread house is really a trap. A beautiful queen is a disguised witch. A great and terrible wizard is only a hairless little man with a microphone. Or a lion, in the end, appears to be someone like God.

Fantasy almost always includes a "turn" too. After wild events and frustrating setbacks, after confusions and threats and dangers and battles, things take a turn for good. A sleeping beauty awakens. An ugly duckling is transformed into a stunning white swan. Children who had been treated terribly by a cruel stepmother are rescued by their kind father. Cinderella's "wicked sisters with their big feet and fancy ways . . . repent in the end and are forgiven." The children and animals in *The Lion, the Witch, and the Wardrobe* celebrate and sing for joy because Aslan has conquered.

We rejoice with them. J. R. R. Tolkien (the man who wrote *The Lord of the Rings*) says that when the turn comes, we feel "a catch of the breath, a beat and lifting of the heart." In fact, many of us feel like weeping—but not for grief. We cry for joy at the triumph of good. We weep because this triumph has a beauty as sharp as a northern wind.

Something old and deep in us is born again when we read of Aslan or

178

of Mrs. Whatsit or of the Velveteen Rabbit. Christians are especially open to these things because the coming-to-life of the new self in repentance includes "wholehearted joy in God through Christ." There is that stab of joy again. I think we can begin to understand it when we think of the gospel *as fantasy come true.*

The gospel is the story of a son coming home from a far country. It is the story of a sheep rescued from a dark and fearful wilderness by the strong arms of a fierce shepherd. It is the story of children released from prison, of demons unmasked, of the crushing of lethal snakes, and of the triumph of the Lamb of God. It is the story of all heaven breaking loose, the stars singing together and the sons of God shouting for joy.

For things are not as they seem. There is a turn. The dying Jesus, nerves stretched over nails, rises to kill death and to live for good. It happens this time not in a fantasy, but in the Bible; not in fantasy land, but in Israel; not once upon a time, but on the first day of one week about A.D. 29. The Son of God awakens.

For us the stab of joy, the catch of the breath, is not only for our dead Lord who comes alive. It is also for ourselves. For in our baptism and in our repentance we die and rise *with* him, rejoicing in the triumph of God, a triumph with beauty as sharp as a northern wind. Once more, as when Adam awoke and when Jesus arose—once more God blows into us the breath of life.

Repentance is the dying-away of the old self and the coming-to-life of the new.

Prayer
Breathe into us, breath of God, the new life of repentance. Let there be a turn for us, so that you may triumph and all heaven may rejoice. Through Jesus Christ, our Lord, Amen.

HOMEWORK

Vocabulary

53. repentance: the complete turning around of our lives. Repentance is like dying and then being born again. Repentance is sometimes called *conversion.*

54. dying-away: the killing of the old self. Our old self is the person we are by sin, original and actual. Dying-away includes fighting sin and fleeing from it.

55. coming-to-life: the arising of the new self. The new self is the person we are by justification, faith, and repentance. The new self is Christlike and full of joy.

Questions

Day 1: Mention three things that repenting is *like.*

Day 2: How is repenting different from just saying "sorry" to God? Why is repenting difficult and unpleasant?

Day 3: Give an example of (a) a sin young people could probably fight against, (b) a sin young people should flee from.

Day 4: How is the gospel like a fantasy-come-true? How is it unlike a fantasy?

Summary

Discuss this question with your parents: Should people be able to point to a specific hour in their lives in which they repented (were converted)? Why or why not? Jot down a brief answer.

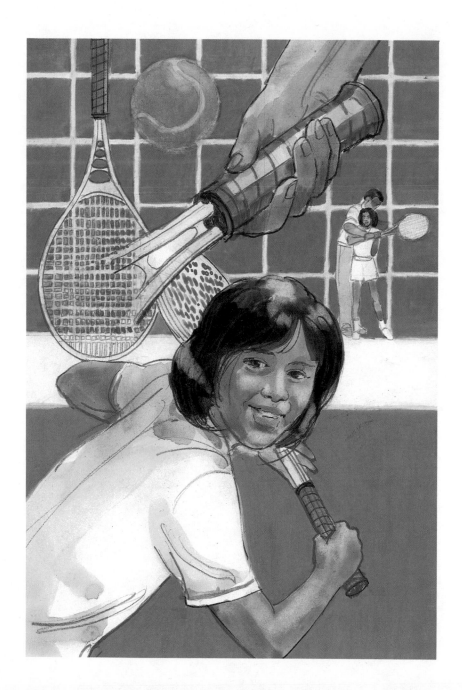

15

SANCTIFICATION

SANCTIFICATION

Scripture
So then, just as you received Christ Jesus as Lord, continue to live in him, rooted and built up in him, strengthened in the faith as you were taught, and overflowing with thankfulness.

—Colossians 2:6–7

Teachings
We believe that . . . true faith . . .
  makes (us) . . . new . . .
causing (us) to live the "new life"
  and freeing (us) from the slavery of sin.

—Belgic Confession, Article 24

Things can belong to a person in more than one way. A public library, for instance, belongs to all the citizens of a town or city. But only some of them actually use the library. They consult its reference works, copy articles from its magazines, browse through its stacks, borrow its books, tapes, and records. These smart people "make the library their own" in a way that others do not. The library really belongs to those who use it.

The same goes for sports equipment and musical instruments. An older brother might give you a used set of golf clubs or a trumpet, but if you never learn how to hit a straight iron shot or play a scale, you do not really possess these gifts. Such things must be used before they fully belong to you.

Something like that is true in our Christian faith. In justification God forgives our sins and credits us with the righteousness of Christ. We receive these gifts, as we know, by faith and repentance.

But how can we use them? How can we actually begin to live like Christ and think like Christ? How can we learn to treat our friends as valuable persons made in the image of God instead of as stepladders for our own ambitions? How can we learn to spend time with shy or boring persons? How can we become readier to die rather than go against what we know is the will of God? That is, how can the righteousness of Jesus Christ get injected into our bloodstreams so that it circulates through every part of our lives? How can the righteousness of Christ actually start to *belong* to us?

The answer lies in what Christians call *sanctification*. Justification is like the gift of golf clubs or a trumpet. Sanctification is like the long process of learning to play well.

Even in this process much must be done by God. Just as a musician has to be given a talent and an instrument and good lessons, so God must justify us and fill us with faith and show us the example of Christ, our Master. In addition, the Holy Spirit must energize us with breath and new life before we can blow a single note.

But there's also something we must do. Perhaps you have noticed that in the Bible we are sometimes treated as children and sometimes as adults. We must be childlike in our faith—mouths and hands and hearts wide open to receive nourishing life and breath from the Holy Spirit. But as adults we are to do what *we* can in sanctification. Christians who have been grafted into Christ by faith and who have died and risen with Christ in repentance are then told to go to work. We are told to fight the good fight, run the race, finish the course. We must put off old habits and put on new ones. We are to strive, sow, reap, follow, obey, take up our crosses. In other words, we are to become holy.

That may seem disappointing. We may think of holiness as boring or weak.

But if so, we are mistaken. In protecting Jews from Nazis, people in the Second World War were doing something dangerous—and holy. In fighting to liberate blacks in the U.S., Martin Luther King, Jr., was doing something risky—and holy. In struggling to obey his Father when he felt like backing out, Jesus, our Lord, was doing something painfully difficult—but holy.

To be holy is to be like Jesus Christ. Sanctification is the long process—partly painful, partly joyous—of learning to live well. That is, sanctification is the process of learning how to live like the holy Christ.

Look back at the Bible text for today. "Just as you received Christ Jesus as Lord," says Paul, now "continue to live in him."

Receiving a gift is one thing. Learning how to use and live with our gift is another. Only then will the gift really belong to us.

Prayer
Give us new life, O God. But then teach us to live as new persons. Through Jesus Christ, our Lord, Amen.

DAY 2

MOTIVES OF THE

CHRISTIAN LIFE

Scripture

I am the vine; you are the branches. If a man remains in me and I in him, he will bear much fruit; apart from me you can do nothing.

—John 15:5

Teachings

It is impossible
    for those grafted into Christ by true faith
not to produce fruits of gratitude.

—Heidelberg Catechism, Answer 64

Q. What do we do that is good?
A. Only that which
    arises out of true faith.

—Heidelberg Catechism Q & A 91

The other night my family and I watched an old Perry Mason murder mystery on TV. A woman had been accused of murdering her boss. She had had an opportunity to do it. She had the murder weapon. What was missing, as Perry Mason observed, was a motive.

What did he mean?

A motive is anything that drives or moves us to do or say something. For instance, a thief may be motivated by greed. That is, greed moves her to steal. A murderer may be motivated by envy. That is, a murderer may hate and want another person's success so much that he feels driven to kill him. People do not usually act at random. There is something *behind* what they do or say. Ordinarily, bad motives such as greed or envy produce bad deeds. Ordinarily, good motives produce good deeds.

What are some motives behind good deeds? Or, to ask the question another way, what are motives for holiness? (After all, good deeds, as we shall see, are only one part of holiness.)

There are three main motives behind the Christian life of holiness. Especially three main things drive us forward in sanctification.

One of these we learned way back in lesson 1. There we learned about our *desire for God*. We hunger and thirst for God even when we don't know it. And just as hunger for food motivates us to eat, so hunger for God drives us to do good and to be holy. Why? Because acting like God is a way to get close to God. You have seen people imitate sports heroes or film stars. You have watched a small child try to act like an older brother. These people are using imitation to try to get close to someone, to share his or her life. So it is with us and God.

Another motive for holiness is *gratitude,* or *thankfulness.* Suppose a person you admire takes an interest in you. This person asks about you, wants to spend time with you, tries to build up your strengths. You feel pleasure and appreciation in all of this. You are grateful for this person's interest and want to show it.

But suppose that in an emergency the person you admire actually saves your life in some spectacular way. You might feel gratitude toward him or her for the rest of your life.

Gratitude is a main motive in the Christian life. Our lives have been saved by the powerful rescue work of Jesus Christ. This must always be in the back of our minds. We could have been wrecked. Instead we have been accepted and loved. We ought to be grateful to God for the rest of our lives.

But there is one more motive. In striving for holiness, a Christian is motivated by *faith*. Faith tells me I belong to Jesus Christ and am justified. I really do need faith to believe this. After all, it sometimes seems as if I am making little progress in repentance. If I had to judge by how I act, I might doubt my justification.

But suppose I do actually believe I am a saved child of God. Suppose I trust Jesus Christ for rescue. Then this belief and trust make me try to *act* like a saved person. Faith drives me to act in accordance with who I am.

You recall Don Quixote's noble lady. She thought she was only a whore. But when she began to trust Don Quixote, she began to act like a noble lady. For he accepted her and called her noble. And faith made her act in accordance with the new person that she was in the eyes of her savior.

It is like that with us. By faith we believe God when he calls us his saved children in the Bible, in our baptism, and in the eyes of our loved ones. We believe this even when we don't feel very close to God and have not been acting very much like God's children. We must keep reminding ourselves who we are. We must remember who accepts us and calls us noble. We must then begin to act once again in accordance with the new person that we are in the eyes of our Savior.

Prayer
O God, make us want to be close to you. Then build up our gratitude and faith so that we may be driven to act in Christlike ways. Amen.

DAY 3

THE STUFF

OF SANCTIFICATION

Scripture
Turn from evil and do good;
   then you will always live securely.   —Psalm 37:27

For physical training is of some value, but godliness has value for all things,
holding promise for both the present life and the life to come. —1 Timothy 4:8

Teachings
Q. What is the coming-to-life of the new self?
A. It is wholehearted joy in God through Christ
   and a delight to do every kind of good
      as God wants us to.

—Heidelberg Catechism Q & A 90

In lesson 7 we learned that original sin includes guilt and corruption. These are humanity's oldest and deepest problems. We have now come far enough in our study to understand the solution to them.

Justification is God's solution to the problem of guilt. To people who have broken God's law and deserve punishment God brings instead forgiveness and alien righteousness.

Sanctification is God's solution to the problem of corruption. Corruption, you recall, is the seeping power of sin. Corruption is like an overflowing sewer that pollutes all we think, say, and do. Sanctification is the gradual process of getting unpolluted. In sanctification God goes to work with us to clean the grime off and to polish us up as God's images.

It begins when we are old enough to feel really sorry about our sin. Soon we gain enough experience of sin's destruction to hate it and to want to get away from it. Then, perhaps suddenly one summer, or gradually over a period of years, our faith in God's forgiving love sharpens and our joy in God himself deepens. All of this, we know, is repentance, or conversion.

Sanctification is the word we use when we think of conversion stretched out across a whole life. After all, it takes a long time to unlearn habits that are old and deep. The righteousness for which Christians hunger and thirst is not fast food. It needs time to simmer into something rich and savory.

Let's think of another comparison. An athlete trains. He or she will eat right, get to bed on time, and take on the daily discipline of practice. Certain muscle groups will be worked in thousands of repetitions till they have mass and flexibility. Certain moves will be practiced again and again till they become second nature: a one-on-one fake, for example, or an overhead smash, or a flip turn.

Each time the athlete trains, he gets a little better. Each time she works out, some sloppy old habit dies a little and some disciplined new one begins to come to life. That is, each training session causes a tiny conversion. But it is only after many seasons of such training that a person can perform his skills by second nature. The mini-conversions repeated thousands of times add up to the change of one's life. A duffer becomes a disciplined athlete.

The Christian life is almost exactly like that. We have to be *trained* in godliness, or holiness, till it becomes second nature. Each time we pray; every time we resist a temptation, or bring a gift to a lonesome person, or make ourselves think of the needs of others—each time we do these things our old self dies a little and our new self comes more to life. Add up all these mini-conversions across years of training and you have a spiritual athlete. A flabby and clumsy Christian becomes a trim and graceful one. A polluted person gets sanctified. Sanctification is lifelong conversion.

We know its motives. We also know that in sanctification the Holy Spirit must decontaminate us who have been radioactive because of sin. So what must *we* do?

We must do good. Besides joy in God, the life of holiness includes "a delight to do every kind of good as God wants us to." The content, the "stuff," the material of the new life is doing good.

I know of course that some Christians are not terribly keen on doing good. They think it's too hard or too boring. Some sneer at "do-gooders." Others do good—but sullenly, as if it's a joyless chore.

These folks are out of shape. They have broken training. They have forgotten what athletes know: you need discipline to be free. Trained people have fun. It takes hard work to be able to *play* well.

Doing good is the very stuff of the Christian life. We are not saved by doing it; we are saved *to* do it. We are saved to go into training and do our stuff.

Prayer

O God, coach us and train us to do good and to do it well. Make us fit to serve you and your other children. For Jesus' sake, Amen.

REFLECTORS

Scripture

"Let your light shine before men, that they may see your good deeds and praise your Father in heaven."

—Matthew 5:16

Teachings

Q. What do we do that is good?
A. Only that which
     arises out of true faith,
     conforms to God's law,
     and is done for his glory;
and not that which is based
     on what we think is right
     or on established human tradition.

—Heidelberg Catechism Q & A 91

Anybody can see *reflectors* at night. Joggers wear reflecting tape on their shoes and shirts. Bike pedals and wheels show us moving circles of reflected light. Lane dividers, roadside mileage indicators, traffic signs, guard rails, bridge piers, the eyes of deer and raccoon—all these things reflect. Even the moon acts as a giant reflector of the hidden light of the sun.

A reflector is something that returns, or bends back, energy from a source. Wall tiles, for example, can act as reflectors of sound. If you sing in the shower, the sound waves of your voice hit hard surfaces and come bouncing back to you. "Bathroom baritones" like to make and hear those reflected sounds. Other family members do not.

The main thing about reflectors, whether they return sound or light, is that they do not produce energy themselves. The light must come from an auto's headlamps, or from the sun, or from some other power source. Sound waves must come from your larynx, or your radio, or your alto saxophone. A reflector does not produce energy. It only deflects or returns it.

But reflectors can do something else to light or sound energy. They can transform it. They can change its color or focus, for instance. Depending on the color of the reflector, light from auto headlamps can come back to you green or red instead of yellow. A spherical mirror (like the sideview mirrors on some cars, or the "shoplifter mirrors" in stores) can focus light so that a particular part of what's reflected can be seen especially well.

Christians are reflectors of God's glory. In sanctification we become clean mirrors, or polished images, of the glory of God.

What is glory, and how do we reflect it?

Glory really means two things. One of them is "light." A sunset, for instance, may be described as "glorious" because it is brilliant, because it lights up the whole western sky.

One thing we mean, therefore, when we talk of the glory of God is that God appears dazzling to us: hot and pure and brilliant. All over the Bible we read of persons meeting God and comparing the experience to walking into the center of the sun.

The other meaning of glory is something like "weightiness" or "worthiness." A glorious person is one who is centered, weighty, important. You cannot push such a person around. He has, so to speak, a low center of gravity. He is a kind of heavyweight. He is a person of important reputation. The glory of Solomon or the glory of ancient Greece, for instance, had to do with the weightiness of their reputation for wisdom.

The Christian life of sanctification has three main parts. One part is its motives: desire, gratitude, faith. Another is the content, or stuff, of holiness: doing good. The third is its purpose, or goal. What are we trying to *achieve* by doing good? What's the point?

The point, or purpose, is to glorify God. But how could mere humans glorify God? We are not like the sun in energy. Surely we do not all have dazzling reputations.

True. But we can reflect. Powerful energy from God—energy like dazzling light—can come from God and be reflected back to him from human beings. When this happens, we "color," or transform, such energy as reflectors always do. Energy from God goes back to him colored by the personalities of millions of God's children.

One more, almost unbelievable, thing. God's reputation is actually made greater when we act like Christ. By doing good we have the power to *focus* the reputation of God so that people can see it especially well and be awed. As Jesus said, "Let your light shine before men, that they may see your good deeds and praise (glorify) your Father in heaven."

A saint, said C. S. Lewis, is a person who makes God believable. A saint—a sanctified person—is a good reflector.

Prayer

Polish and clean us, O God, so that we may reflect your light and make your reputation great. Through Jesus Christ, our Lord, Amen.

HOMEWORK

Vocabulary

56. sanctification: the lifelong conversion by which Christians become gradually holier—that is, more like Jesus Christ. Sanctification is the solution to the problem of pollution. We want to live the life of holiness because of our desire for God, our gratitude to him, and our faith in him.

57. glory of God: the light of God and his weighty reputation. Christians glorify God by reflecting his energy back to him in good deeds. These actually increase God's reputation among humans. To glorify God is the goal of the Christian life.

Questions

Day 1: In your own words, what does *sanctification* mean? Who does it? How does it differ from *justification*?

Day 2: Why should we want to live a life of holiness (What three things drive us forward in sanctification)?

Day 3: How is sanctification like athletic training? And what's the connection between sanctification and conversion?

Day 4: How are we—as Christians being sanctified—like reflectors?

Summary

Ask any three adult Christians what the goal of the Christian life is. Write down their answers.

16

THE

   LAW

      OF

        GOD

DAY 1

INSTRUCTIONS

FOR NEW DRIVERS

Scripture
And God spoke all these words: "I am the Lord your God, who brought you out of Egypt, out of the land of slavery. You shall have no other gods before me."

—Exodus 20:1–3

Teachings
Q. What do we do that is good?
A. Only that which
    arises out of true faith,
    conforms to God's law,
    and is done for his glory;
and not that which is based
    on what we think is right
    or on established human tradition.

—Heidelberg Catechism Q & A 91

About three months after the Lord God rescued Hebrew slaves out of Egypt, he gave them his law.* Of course the Israelites had known law before. They had been up against the Egyptian law of bricks and straw, a law for slaves. But now they were free. And the same God who had freed them, the same God who had originally *created* them—this God gave them a set of instructions for the new life of liberty.

It happened at Mt. Sinai. Out of the fire and smoke and the mystery of his glory, God spoke. Moses went up the mountain to listen. Up and down he went. But when Moses came down a final time, he had with him God's instructions: a set of Ten Commandments as well as smaller rules that explained them.

These and other requirements from the rest of the Bible together make up the law of God. The law of God is a statement of what God wants from us. He wants us to do justice and love kindness and walk humbly with him. He wants us to love him above all and our neighbor as ourselves. That is, God wants his people to *do good*.

But what is good? What do we do that is good? Whatever is motivated by desire for God, by gratitude, and by faith. Whatever has the reflection of God's glory as its goal. These are things we have already learned. Let's now add a third item: what's good is whatever is in accord with God's law. The law is a kind of recipe for the right stuff of the Christian life.

Let's think of a comparison. When people get to be a certain age (sixteen in my state), they may apply for a driver's license. Most teenagers can hardly wait. Beyond the sheer fun of driving, the reason, of course, is

*Much of the material in the readings for this week depends on the insights of Lewis Smedes in *Mere Morality.*

that the person who can drive is free. When you learn to drive, you can zip into town or across town. You can visit somebody two towns away. You can go to a drive-in bank, to a restaurant, or to church. You can pick up friends and cart them around. When you learn to drive, you are free.

But as you learn in driver's education, you need guidance in order to use your new freedom well. You need a set of instructions for your new life.

First, you need an owner's manual for the car you drive. The manufacturer may have designed the engine to run on diesel fuel, for instance. You may personally prefer to fill the tank with leftover kerosene, but then the car won't run. It's wise to know that before trying it. In general, you need to know how your car operates and how to operate it that way.

Second, you need to learn a set of traffic laws so that you can pass your driver's exam and get along with other drivers out on the road. Laws for stopping, turning, yielding, and merging are instructions allowing a whole townful of people to drive at the same time.

The law of God is something like instructions for new drivers. Part of it tells us how to run our own cars: You shall have no other gods before me. Do not make an image to worship it. Do not swear. Keep the Sabbath. These first four commandments (the "first table" of the law) are summed up in the first great commandment: You shall love God above all.

The first great commandment is a kind of owner's manual. It tells us that we were designed by our manufacturer to run on love for him.

Another part of the law is like traffic regulations. It tells us how to get along with other drivers: Do not kill. Do not commit adultery. Do not steal. Do not bear false witness. Do not covet. These last six commandments (the "second table" of the law) are summed up in the second great commandment: You shall love your neighbor as yourself.

The law of God is a set of instructions for all of us new drivers who find ourselves in possession of a new life of liberty.

Prayer

Thank you, O God, for the great freedom we have because of Jesus Christ's powerful work. And thank you for your law, which helps us run the lives you give us and helps us get along with others. Through Jesus Christ, our Lord, Amen.

DAY 2

A LAW

OF JUSTICE

Scripture
He has showed you, O man, what is good.
  And what does the Lord require of you?
To act justly and to love mercy
  and to walk humbly with your God.

—Micah 6:8

Teachings
Eager to see injustice ended,
we expect the Day of the Lord.
And we are confident
that the light which shines in the present darkness
will fill the earth when Christ appears.

—Our World Belongs to God, 6

The family of a murder victim troops grimly into court on the day the killer is to be sentenced. The wife of a man who has run off with another woman makes an appointment with a lawyer. A bank manager forces an embezzler to pay back every cent he stole. A judge punishes a witness for perjury. A government takes away some of the earnings of rich people and distributes the money to poor people. A panel awards first prize to the best entry in a photo contest. God disciplines his people for their idolatry.

What do all these cases have in common? What thread runs through them all? In all these cases persons are seeking or doing *justice*.

Justice means giving others what they have coming. For example, we owe God our worship and total obedience. As our Maker and Savior, God has a right to these things. Justice means giving God what he has coming. As we saw in lesson 9, we have covenant obligations to God. Justice requires that we fulfill them.

The Ten Commandments tell us how. They are a set of instructions for the new life of justice. The first four commandments tell us what justice toward God amounts to. First, God alone has a right to our worship: we must have no gods before him. Second, human beings are the only images of God that have God's patent on them: we must make no other images of him. Third, God has a right to our reverence: we must not abuse his name. Fourth, God has a right to our celebration of his great acts in the creation and exodus: we must not abuse his holy day.

The owner's manual tells us that God has these things coming from us. If we offer them, we are doing justice. If we withhold them, we deserve a penalty. Penalties for unjust acts are themselves just. For when we are disobedient, we have punishment coming.

The second table of the law is a recipe for doing justice to other human beings. As persons in the image of God, others have a right to our respect. They have a right to be treated fairly—to be given a fair share of the earth's food, for instance. If they are our parents or governors, they also have a right to our obedience (fifth commandment). Other people have a right to many additional things.

For example, '(sixth commandment) others have a right to life: we may not murder. They have a right (seventh) to loyalty and promise-keeping in marriage: we may not commit adultery. They have a right (eighth) to keep some private property: we may not steal. They have a right (ninth) to the truth: we may not falsely accuse them. In fact, (tenth) all our desires for God, property, and persons should be shaped by God's law.

We can now see how the second table of the law is like a set of traffic regulations. These commandments tell us how millions of people can live together in justice. They tell us what rights others have and what obligation we, therefore, have to respect those rights.

The Bible also tells us of God's penalties for those who act unjustly, those who trample on the rights of others. God is jealous of his own rights as God (third commandment). But he is also jealous of the rights of his children—especially the widows, the orphans, and the poor. The great Old Testament prophets tell us about this.

Judges, courts, and prize panels all deal with rights and justice. But God's justice is blended with love and thus goes beyond them. If you look, for example, at the little rules (Ex. 21–23) that follow the Ten Commandments, you will find some special provisions. For instance, it is unlawful to charge interest on a loan to a needy person (22:25). It is unlawful to keep a person's overcoat overnight (22:26). Why? Because such acts lack compassion. Further, if you are a farmer, you must harvest in a way that leaves food for the poor. Why? Because the poor need extra help.

God's laws are a recipe for justice. Beyond that they are a recipe for love. When you put justice and love together, you have what we call "doing good."

Prayer
O God, help us to see you and others as persons to whom we owe justice. Then give us the will and the strength to do what is right and just. In Jesus' name, Amen.

DAY 3

A LAW

OF LOVE

Scripture

Jesus replied: " 'Love the Lord your God with all your heart and with all your soul and with all your mind.' This is the first and greatest commandment. And the second is like it: 'Love your neighbor as yourself.' "

—Matthew 22:37–39

Teachings

In marriage and family
we serve God
by reflecting his covenant love
in life-long loyalty,
and by teaching his ways,
so that children may know Jesus as their Lord
and learn to use their gifts in a life of joyful service. —*Our World Belongs to God*, 49

People are more likely to *talk* about love than to understand it or do it. People talk about love all the time. They mention books or movies they love. They confess to being in love with another person. Kids claim to love peanut butter. In the U.S. patriots place one hand over their heart and sing, "God bless America, land that I love." Romantic poets begin poems with such words as this: "How do I love thee? Let me count the ways."

All this talk about different kinds of love can be misleading, because, really, all these variations can be boiled down into two kinds of love: need-love and gift-love. Need-love is the kind of love we feel when we think we cannot get along without another person. We *need* this person to fill us, to complete us, to make us feel whole and happy. The classic case of need-love is romance—what a man and woman feel for each other when they fall in love.

Gift-love, on the other hand, is almost the opposite. Gift-love is the kind of love we feel when we want to bring something of value to another just to make *that* person whole or complete or happy. Need-love cares about its own needs; gift-love cares about the needs of others. Need-love is empty and wants to be full; gift-love is full to overflowing and wants to fill someone else who may be empty. Need-love wants to receive; gift-love wants to give. Need-love is a powerful yearning for others; it wants others to adorn us with something they have. Gift-love is the power of caring for others and of wanting to adorn them with something we have.

Healthy relationships have some of each. In fact, both kinds of love come from God. Take need-love: we are *created* to need others. It is not good for us to be alone. When a person hungers and thirsts for God, or for family, or for a person of the opposite sex, this hungering is an appetite that God made. And whatever God makes us want is good.

Gift-love also comes from God. In creation God makes room for others and welcomes them into life. In incarnation God sends his only Son as a Christmas gift to the world. In atonement God gives up his only Son as a sacrifice for sinners. God's love is the original gift-love. Ours is a human copy.

But how important a copy it is! Our gift-love is so important, in fact, that Jesus summarizes the whole law of God by means of it. We are to love God above all; we are to love our neighbor as ourselves. The Ten Commandments tell us how.

How do we love God above all? By giving God what he has coming—our obedience, our loyalty, our very selves. In our relationship to God justice and gift-love are the same thing. We owe all that we have and all that we are to God. We cannot give more than this.

But to other human beings we *can* give more than we owe. The last six commandments tell us how. To love others means two things: it means being just to them; it also means caring for them and wanting to adorn them with something we have. Love goes beyond justice.

Think of three examples. The sixth commandment says I must not murder. Justice means respecting my neighbor's right to life. The priest and Levite who passed by a wounded stranger in the ditch acted justly (Luke 10). They did not harm him. But the Samaritan showed love. He cared for the stranger. He gifted the stranger with time, energy, and money.

Justice keeps me from stealing (eighth commandment). Love goes beyond justice by giving money to those in need. Justice keeps me from telling a damaging lie (ninth commandment). Love goes beyond justice by leading me to tell people the truth in a way that is tender toward their feelings.

Need-love comes naturally. You do not have to tell people to fall in love. They just do. But gift-love must be learned. That is why God commands it.

Prayer

O God, you have given so much to us. Now help us learn the gift-love that returns good to you and to others. In Jesus' name, Amen.

DAY 4

A LAW

OF LIBERTY

Scripture
I will always obey your law,
  for ever and ever.
I will walk about in freedom,
  for I have sought out your precepts.

—Psalm 119:44–45

Teachings
Looking for life without God, we find only death;
grasping for freedom outside his law,
we trap ourselves in Satan's snares;
pursuing pleasure, we lose the gift of joy.   —*Our World Belongs to God*, 15

T oday we are going to learn a paradox. A paradox is a statement that looks as if it contradicts itself but really doesn't. The Bible is full of paradoxes. For example, Jesus once said, "Whoever wants to save his life will lose it, but whoever loses his life for me will find it" (Matt. 16:25).

Jesus means that if you try to hang on to earthly money, power, or popularity—if you want to "save your life" in these ways—you will be cold toward your real Savior. Your life will end in ruin, ashes, and hell. But if you give up the idea that earthly things can save you—if you are willing to be a loser in this world—you may find yourself open toward your real Savior. Your life will end up in glory, in heaven, and in unspeakable joy. Losers are winners.

The text for today states a paradox. It says that if we obey God's laws, or statutes, or precepts, we shall be free. For God's laws are statutes of liberty.

It sounds paradoxical. How can laws make us free? Don't they do just the opposite? Don't laws hem us in, cramp our style, reduce our options? Doesn't obedience to God's law make us slaves to God?

In a way, yes. The whole Bible declares that we are to be slaves, or servants, of Jesus Christ. We are to do what he wants, not what we want. We are to obey God rather than ourselves.

But just here is the paradox. For the truth is that we are never so free as when we are obeying God. Perfect slavery to God means perfect freedom for us.

How can this be so?

Let's think again of some comparisons. In the lesson on sanctification I said something every athlete knows: it takes discipline to be free. The same could be said for musicians, drug addicts, and even trees.

An athlete trains. A basketball player, for instance, learns not only the rules of his game but also the rules for getting the most out of his body. If he trains long enough, he will have dozens of options on the court. He can go left or right. He can shoulder-fake or head-fake. He can stop and pop a jump shot or power-move straight to the hoop. He is free to do any of these things. He is free because he is disciplined by rules and practice.

But he doesn't think of these rules in the middle of a game. That's because the rules have all become second nature to him by now. All he wants to do in a game is to play.

A musician practices. When you hear a great concert artist perform, you are impressed with her freedom. She looks as if she could play her piece backward if she felt like it. She soars. She is free because she is disciplined by the basic rules of her art.

But she doesn't think of these rules in the middle of a concert. That's because the rules have all become second nature to her. All she wants to do in a concert is to play.

Think of a sapling. When a tree is young and tender, you have to stake it with guy ropes. You do this to protect the tree from strong winds and to "train" the sapling to grow straight. But one day you can remove the stakes and ropes. Why? Because the tree has matured. It now grows straight and tall by second nature. And the tree is free to bend any way it wants because it has been well-trained.

Drug addicts who have been saved by Jesus Christ will tell you that when they were doing dope, they were slaves. They will also tell you that by obeying God's law they have become free at last. They are free *from* drugs: they are free *for* life and joy.

Isn't it odd? Why are we never so free as when we are obeying God? The reason is that God made us. He knows how we work. God also saved us. He knows what gives us joy. The law is intended, like guy ropes or training rules, to teach us to do what's right and to do it by second nature.

Then we no longer have to think of the law at every step. For we are free.

Prayer
You, O Lord, are the one who turns slavery into freedom. You are the one who makes us free at last. Thank you for your law of liberty. Amen.

HOMEWORK

Vocabulary

58. law of God: the statement of what God wants from us. The law of God is a training guide for the new life of liberty.

59. justice: what persons have coming. The first table of the law tells us what God has coming from us. The second table tells us what other humans have coming.

60. need-love: a powerful yearning for others. Need-love wants others to adorn us with something they have. Need-love is created by God and comes naturally to us.

61. gift-love: the power of caring for others. Gift-love wants to adorn others with something we have. Gift-love is created by God but has to be learned by us.

62. freedom: the removal of things that drag us down and the opening up to joyful life in God. According to the Bible, we are never so free as when we are slaves of God.

Questions

Day 1: How is the law of God like a set of instructions for all of us new drivers who find ourselves in possession of a new life of liberty?

Day 2: What things does God justly expect from us (first table of the law)? What things should others justly expect from us (second table of the law)?

Day 3: Describe one way in which you could show more than justice to another person.

Day 4: Explain: "We are never so free as when we are obeying God."

Summary

Ask your mother or father to name one rule they want you to observe and to explain *why* they have made that rule.

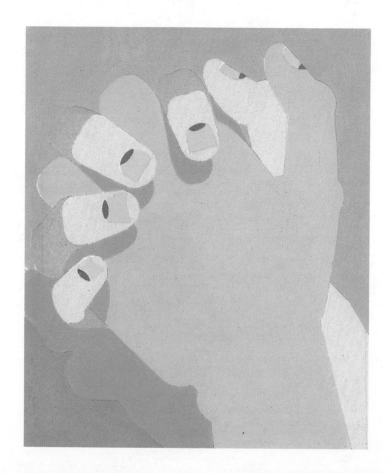

17

PRAYER

THANKSGIVING

Scripture

Be joyful always; pray continually; give thanks in all circumstances, for this is God's will for you in Christ Jesus.
—1 Thessalonians 5:16–18

Teachings

Q. Why do Christians need to pray?
A. Because prayer is the most important part
   of the thankfulness God requires of us.

—Heidelberg Catechism Q & A 116

It's one of the first prayers a small child learns. Over some days and weeks a parent teaches the words. Gradually the child learns them and puts the sentences together. The family sits around a table, savoring the blended aromas of a six-pound, golden-brown roasting chicken with pan gravy, buttered corn, fresh bread, garden salad with bacon dressing, and other good things. The child speaks: "God is great. God is good. Let us thank him for this food. Amen."

The child is taking her place with godly people around the world and across the centuries. Christians thank God for food received, thus distinguishing themselves from animals and TV families who simply graze.

But Christians are thankful to God for many things besides food. We thank God in the morning that we have awakened in our right minds. We thank God in the evening that we may fold our bodies between the covers and shut down our minds while God himself stays awake and on duty. If we are alert, we thank God for a sister to play and quarrel with; for parents who care about us more than they can say; for the breakup of winter and the promise of tennis and baseball in spring. If we have our wits about us, we thank God for teachers who test us, for good neighbors who trust us, for our church that turns us toward God. We thank God for friends who understand and accept us.

In a quiet mood, we may give thanks for a stand of trees we like, or for a hill or valley where we seem to belong. We may thank God for a red fern that grows in a special place, or for a red-boned coon hound that bawls in a deep voice against the trees and across the fields.

But there is much more. If we have started to come alive to Jesus Christ, we go further in our thanks. For we know in thunder and in stillness, in sickness and in rosy health, in good complexion and bad, that we are loved by him. We know that when we are weary or strong, guilty or innocent, popular or temporarily out to lunch—we know we have been loved to the point of death. The supreme thanksgiving of Christians is for the mighty suffering of Jesus, our Savior.

Prayer is a way of saying our thanks for all these things. Besides doing good out of gratitude, we also *say* what's good, especially when God has done it. Prayer is any attempt to address God. Thanksgiving is our attempt to address God out of gratitude.

Why do it? Surely we don't give thanks just to keep the gifts coming. People may try this with their grandparents, but even grandparents aren't fooled by it. Neither do we give thanks as a way of paying God back—as if we were to say, "We like gifts. God likes thanks. Even-Steven."

No. We give thanks to God because it is *fitting* to do so. Just as fans cheer a spectacular shot, just as grieving relatives cling to each other, just as people rest after work, so all of us give thanks to God for his gifts. It is right and proper and appropriate. It fits.

There is a side benefit. When we pray our thanksgiving, we ourselves feel somehow rich and complete. We notice how *many* wonderful things we have from God, and how good they really are, and how good God is. A grateful person is happy. An ungrateful person is miserable. It's as simple as that.

According to the catechism, prayer is the chief part of thanksgiving. But thanksgiving, we may add, is also one of the chief parts of prayer.

Prayer

For daily food, O God, we thank you. For our family and teachers and friends, we thank you. For sports and games and interesting things to read and beautiful places to be, we thank you. For your rescue that saves us, for you, O God, we give you hearty thanks. Through Jesus Christ, our Lord, Amen.

CONFESSION

Scripture

Have mercy on me, O God,
   according to your unfailing love;
according to your great compassion
   blot out my transgressions.
Wash away all my iniquity
   and cleanse me from my sin.

For I know my transgressions,
   and my sin is always before me.

—Psalm 51:1–3

Teachings

Q. What does the fifth request mean?
A. *Forgive us our debts,*
   as we also have forgiven our debtors means,

   Because of Christ's blood,
   do not hold against us, poor sinners that we are,
      any of the sins we do
      or the evil that constantly clings to us.

   Forgive us just as we are fully determined,
      as evidence of your grace in us,
   to forgive our neighbors.

—Heidelberg Catechism Q & A 126

Ned was the sort of guy who could never admit he was wrong. For instance, he would needle his brother Leroy mercilessly till Leroy got irritated and told him to stop. This always offended Ned. "You telling me to stop?" he'd ask. "You trying to tell *me* what to do, boy?" Then Ned would try to smack old Leroy right in the chops. So Leroy would shove him. War would rage through the room till a parent appeared to break it up. When questioned, Ned would claim that the fight had started when Leroy had suddenly shoved him for no reason at all.

In school, Ned would claim that he had handed in missing assignments and that his teacher must have lost them. If Ned's test answers were exactly the same as those of a top student at the next desk, Ned always insisted he hadn't cheated. In fact, he would suggest that maybe the other student was trying to copy from *him.* When Ned borrowed money or sports equipment or tapes from friends so foolish as to lend anything to him, Ned often forgot to return them. When reminded, he would protest that his friends were picking on him.

People like Ned are exasperating. They protect themselves with layer upon layer of lies that are all wound and twisted around each other. You can't tell where one lie ends and another begins. Trying to reach out and take a firm hold on Ned is like trying to take hold of a large mound of spaghetti.

The uncomfortable truth is that there is some of Ned in all of us. We all deceive ourselves about who we are and what we do and what we have failed to do. Probably no one of us is truly honest with himself. It's too painful. For the same reason, few of us are completely honest with God. For in order to be totally honest with God we have to be honest with ourselves. And that is just what we would like to avoid.

And yet we must face up to our need for such honesty. We cannot be spiritually healthy without it. We are like alcoholics in this way. At meetings of Alcoholics Anonymous members of the group stand up to speak one at a time. Each begins the same way. She mentions her first name and then admits her condition: "My name is Mary. I am an alcoholic." When an alcoholic tells his story at a meeting, he is never allowed to get away with excuses or denials. That's because alcoholics know that nobody can hope for help or healing without frankly admitting his weakness. Confession is the first important step toward wholeness and health.

It is the same for all of us. Besides thanksgiving, our prayers in church and by ourselves must include *confession*. To confess in prayer before God is to own up to who we are: "My name is Ned. I am a liar." To confess is to admit what we have done and what we have failed to do: "O God, I have purposely deceived people who have a right to the truth. O God, I had a chance to stop a damaging lie about another person, and I failed to do it."

Confession is painful. It digs beneath our surface, throws off our masks and disguises, and lifts up the truth. The truth includes not only our sin but also our dependence on God for health, and breath, and life itself. Confession includes mentioning our weaknesses.

Confession is like cleansing a wound. It hurts to do it thoroughly. But if you go ahead and clean it, the wound may heal without getting infected. It is part of the dying-away of the old self and the coming-to-life of the new.

Prayer
Have mercy on me, O God,
according to your unfailing love;
according to your great compassion
blot out my transgressions.
Wash away all my iniquity
and cleanse me from my sin.

For I know my transgressions,
and my sin is always before me. Amen.

DAY 3

INTERCESSION

Scripture

Jesus said, "Father, forgive them, for they do not know what they are doing."

—Luke 23:34

Then he fell on his knees and cried out, "Lord, do not hold this sin against them." When he had said this, he fell asleep.

—Acts 7:60

Teachings

God tells us
> to love our neighbors as ourselves,
> to be patient, peace-loving, gentle,
>   merciful, and friendly to them,
> to protect them from harm as much as we can,
> and to do good even to our enemies.

—Heidelberg Catechism Answer 107

Someone has thought of a way to teach us to pray for others. You look at your hand. The thumb is closest to you. It therefore reminds you to pray for people who are close to you. We pray for family members, for instance. We bring before God a parent who is having trouble at work, perhaps, or a sister who feels left out of things.

Your index finger is used to point. It therefore reminds you of people in authority. We must pray for teachers, police, bus drivers, crossing guards.

Your middle finger is highest. It reminds all of us to pray for presidents, prime ministers, governors, mayors—for all who are in *high* authority.

The ring finger is weakest, as all pianists know. It reminds us to pray for weak people—for people crushed by poverty or ignorance or sickness or cruel governments. Weak people can be found in our own schools and neighborhoods. They can be found in some of our own families. These may be people Jesus calls "the least of my brothers." He says that they especially need our help and care. He even says that helping them counts as helping him.

Finally, there is the little finger. It comes last and reminds us, at last, to pray for ourselves.

Four out of five of these prayers are for other people. We call them *intercessions.* To intercede is to act as a "go-between," standing between a neighbor and God. In such prayers we play the part of priests, speaking on behalf of, or for the sake of, another person.

You can find intercessory prayers throughout the Bible. Moses pleads for the children of Israel. Job prays for his friends. Paul intercedes for his young churches. Our Lord pleads for the very people who are killing him: "Father, forgive them, for they do not know what they are doing." Stephen the martyr imitates Jesus in this.

Intercessions are wonderful prayers because they have a sort of double effect. When God hears and answers an intercessory prayer for good, our neighbor is blessed. Church ministers pray for such blessings every week in congregational prayers. We pray that God will comfort a grieving person, heal a sick person, save the life of somebody in grave danger. So one good effect of an intercessory prayer is that God may help a neighbor.

The other effect, strange to say, is that an intercessory prayer helps *us*. When we set aside our own concerns and lift before God the needs of somebody else, *we* are improved. For example, our anger can be softened by praying for the persons who anger us. Our pride is reduced when we make ourselves focus on the hurts and struggles of others. Our envy shrinks when we pray our gratitude to God for gifts given to someone else.

Look at your hand. Four out of five fingers remind us to pray for others. That is, they remind us to love.

Prayer

O God, we pray today for members of our own families: give them faith. We pray for our teachers: give them strength and patience. We pray for our national leaders: give them wisdom and justice. We pray for people who are weakened by sickness or poverty: lift them up. We pray at last for ourselves, O God: teach us how to love. Through Jesus Christ, who loved even his enemies, Amen.

PETITION

Scripture
"Ask and it will be given to you; seek and you will find; knock and the door will be opened to you."

—Matthew 7:7

Teachings
Q. Why do Christians need to pray?
A. Because prayer is the most important part
    of the thankfulness God requires of us.
    And also because God gives his grace and Holy Spirit
    only to those who pray continually and groan inwardly,
        asking God for these gifts
        and thanking him for them.

—Heidelberg Catechism Q & A 116

A petition is a solemn request. Somebody gets an idea about a plan or event that needs to be pushed forward or held back and draws up a petition about it. The petitioner may want to save whales from harpoons or babies from abortion. She may want a governor to permit casino gambling or to forbid it. People sometimes petition a government to release a prisoner. In a petition we ask someone in power to *act*.

You or your parents may be asked to sign a particular petition. Many others are asked as well. Finally the petition, signed by thousands of people, is delivered to the right person, and everybody waits to see what happens. Sometimes we get what we petition for; sometimes not.

In prayer we petition God. Along with thanksgiving, confession, and intercession, we include solemn requests for God to act. We may ask God to do something for a neighbor—to heal an injury, for example, or to protect our neighbor in her travels. Then our petition really amounts to an intercession. But at other times we pray for the whole world. When we pray as our Lord taught us, for instance, we say, "Your kingdom come, your will be done on earth as it is in heaven." These are petitions for God to move his great world plan forward.

Sometimes we pray for ourselves. These are our little-finger prayers. We ask God for comfort when we are humiliated, for forgiveness when we are guilty, or for a friend when we are lonely. We may pray in faith for a place on a team, for a newspaper route, for a decent performance on a test, or for two red-boned coon hounds to hunt with. Some children, God help them, must pray for foster parents to care for them.

We pray for all kinds of things. But almost at once we face a problem with petitionary prayer. Jesus promises, "Whatever you ask for in prayer, believe that you have received it, and it will be yours" (Mark 11:24). The problem is that sometimes we receive something very different from what we asked for. Sometimes we seem to receive nothing at all. And we wonder what is going on.

A famous passage in Mark Twain's *Huckleberry Finn* describes this problem in a memorable way. In this passage Huck is getting "civilized"; Miss Watson is trying to teach him to pray:

> Miss Watson, she took me in the closet and prayed, but nothing come of it. She told me to pray every day, and whatever I asked for, I would get it. But it warn't so. I tried it. Once I got a fishline, but no hooks. It warn't any good to me without hooks. I tried for the hooks three or four times, but somehow I couldn't make it work. By and by, one day, I asked Miss Watson to try for me, but she said I was a fool. She never told me why, and I couldn't make it out no way. I set down one time back in the woods and had a long think about it. I says to myself, if a body can get anything they pray for, why don't Deacon Winn get back the money he lost on pork? Why can't the widow get back her silver snuffbox that was stole? Why can't Miss Watson fat up? No, I says to myself, there ain't nothing in it.

What must we say to this? *Is* there anything in it?

Yes, there is. But what we can say about God's response to our petitions is not easy and not at all complete. We can say this: probably God does not give us what we ask sometimes because we ask him to do something wrong. Suppose someone prays, "Smash my enemy to smithereens, O God." We can see why that petition might be turned down. Or perhaps we ask God for something that would harm us: "Reward me with a motorcycle and a subscription to *Playboy,* O Lord." No. Or suppose that two teams both pray to win. Not even God can grant both requests at the same time.

We can understand why God sometimes denies our requests. Our requests might be wrong, or dangerous, or impossible to grant. But at other times what we ask for seems to be perfectly good and right. We ask that someone's life be saved, for instance, or that separated parents be re-united. Suppose we then get only terrible silence from God or the sound of a door being slammed.

Why? Why would that happen? To tell the truth, nobody knows. We believe that God has his reasons, but we cannot claim to know what those reasons are. All we can do at such times is to cling to the God we do not understand.

Prayer

O God, help us trust you even when we cannot understand what you are doing. For Jesus' sake, Amen.

HOMEWORK

Vocabulary

63. prayer: any attempt to address God. Our prayers include thanksgiving, confession, intercessions, and petitions.

64. thanksgiving: a kind of prayer that flows out of gratitude. We are thankful for many things, but especially for the mighty work of Jesus Christ, our Savior.

65. confession: a kind of prayer in which we own up to who we are, what we have done, and what we have failed to do. In confession we also admit our dependence and our weaknesses.

66. intercession: a kind of prayer in which we play the role of a priest by pleading the case of someone else. Our intercessions are helpful not only to others but also to us who pray them.

67. petition: a kind of prayer in which we make a solemn request of God. Petitions may be for others (intercessions), for the whole world, or for ourselves. Denied petitions sometimes raise a problem in our minds.

Questions

This week, instead of writing out answers to questions, please do the following:

Day 1: Take a little time out of your busy schedule today to thank God for his gifts—big and small—to you.

Day 2: Take time today to offer a sincere prayer of personal confession to God.

Day 3: Use your hand (as explained in the reading) as a guide to your own prayer of intercession.

Day 4: Talk to God about the big and small things you need.

Summary

Talk to your parents (or to someone else in your family) about a time when they offered a prayer that meant a great deal to them. Ask how God answered their prayer.

IV

CHURCH

AND

KINGDOM

18

THE

CHURCH

THE CHURCH

Scripture

You are a chosen people, a royal priesthood, a holy nation, a people belonging to God, that you may declare the praises of him who called you out of darkness into his wonderful light.

—1 Peter 2:9

Teachings

I believe in . . . the holy catholic church.

—Apostles' Creed

In the middle of a busy workday in New York City, a woman walks up the steps of a cathedral and enters the hush of the great sanctuary. There she kneels to pray to the God who alone can keep her sane in a mad world. In the middle of a silent night in Chicago, three refugees from a Latin American country slip into a church in which they seek refuge and protection. At the end of a long and bitter war, the bells in a thousand churches clang and peal to celebrate the return of peace. At the beginning of their new life together, a man and a woman step into the sunshine from a building in which they have promised to love each other till death. On a regular Sunday in North America, millions of people stream in and out of church.

What is the church, and why does it matter?

The word *church* can simply mean a particular building that is used for worship, weddings, and refuge. When someone says "Our church burned down last year," this person is speaking of a structure of wood or brick.

But *church* can also refer to what goes on in such a building. When people whose church burned down gather for worship in a gymnasium, they can still speak of "going to church." They do not mean they are heading over to the gym. They mean they are getting ready to attend public worship.

Church can refer to a building. It can refer, too, to what God's people do when they gather. But the word *church* also has a wider, more important meaning: when we stand up to say the Apostles' Creed, we confess that we believe in "the holy catholic church."

When we use *church* in this sense, we are referring to a certain group of *people*. This group or community is the most important meaning of *church*. The church is the community of all those who truly believe in Jesus Christ: it is believers as well as their children. The church is the group of people who are justified and sanctified. These are people with faith and repentance. Among them you can find prayer and reverence for the law of God. In fact, all the Christian "things of the faith" that we have been learning for weeks—all these things happen in and to the church. That is, they happen in and to people who belong to Jesus Christ.

Let's reflect on this for a moment. We often think of the church in too small a way. We think of it as the group we worship with on Sundays. But that's like looking east from Miami Beach and calling the twenty miles of water you see "the Atlantic Ocean." So it is. But the Atlantic is more—much more—than the little stretch of sea you say you can see.

So with the church. The church of Jesus Christ is incredibly vast and colorful. It includes high-tech Japanese Christians from Tokyo and dignified African tribal chiefs from the bush country of Kenya. It includes high-powered businesswomen from the boardrooms of great corporations and scared young fishermen from tiny villages in Portugal. The church contains ripe old Christians who have believed the gospel for seventy years and infants so young they do not yet believe anything at all.

The church stretches not only across continents and seas and occupations and races but also back across time. Martin Luther belonged to the same community as you and I do. So did C. S. Lewis and Bach and Calvin and Augustine and Paul and even Abraham and Sarah. All these belong to the same church we do because all of us belong to the same Lord. As Abraham was called out of his country to serve God in a new land, as Paul was called out of his blindness to serve the Lord he had savagely persecuted, so you and I are called out of the darkness and into the light. We are called out of a fallen world and into the warmth of the Christian community. In fact, the word *church* in the New Testament really means "those who are called out."

The key question for each of us is whether we will answer this call. On this our growth, and the growth of God's work in the world, depends.

Prayer

O God, we belong to a great and mighty community. Help us to see how large and old and deep it is. And help us to answer when you call. Through Jesus Christ our Lord, Amen.

DAY 2

A HOLY

CHURCH

Scripture
It is written: "Be holy, because I am holy."

—1 Peter 1:16

Teachings
The church is a gathering
of forgiven sinners,
called to be holy,
dedicated to service. . . .
Knowing our own weakness and failures,
we bring good news to all sinners
with understanding of their condition,
and with hope in God.

—Our World Belongs to God, 42

The church is God's gift to sinners. It is like a mother for orphans, or an ark in a flood, or a hospital in an epidemic, or a wayside inn on the road from Jerusalem to Jericho. In the community of the church those who have been hurt may be comforted. People can be inoculated against certain types of sin. Those who have been drowning in their own misery can be pulled aboard. All of us may be nourished and fed by the Word of God and the sacraments.

At least that is how things are supposed to go. In the church we are supposed to learn sanctification so that our sin may be gradually scoured away and our pollution controlled. Then we are supposed to go back into the flood to pull other swimmers into the ark, or out onto the robber-infested roads to carry other wounded travelers to the wayside inn. Christians, who are called out of the world, are then sent back into it with their new equipment and training.

Because a holy God wants us to become holy, we are to come together in the church. Because God then wants to set us apart for rescue work in the world, we are to be trained in compassion and strong love. Being holy means not only being good but also doing good. This is what the church is for. We believe in the *holy* catholic church.

Is it hard to believe that the church is holy in these ways? Is this so hard to believe that we have to keep saying it over and over every week in the Apostles' Creed?

A lot depends on where we look. In some parts of the great universal church we can find striking holiness. It can make us feel at the same time humble before God and proud to be Christians. For example, some Christians visit prisoners once a week. It's hard work. After all, some prisoners are dangerous people. Some prefer four-letter words. But others are hungry for the gospel of Jesus Christ. Many deeply appreciate the care and concern that a visitor may bring.

Other Christians minister in other ways. They may try to bring joy to a lonesome old person or friendship to someone whose mind has gone dark. Every day across the world Christians struggle to teach peasants to farm, or adults to read, or beginners to pray. Wise and strong Christians assist pregnant teens. Streetwise believers spend time helping drug abusers get unhooked. Some Christians even lead protests against tyrannical governments. We look at all this and much more. Then we say, "I believe in the holy catholic church."

Christian teenagers here and there have gotten the idea. I once read of a high school student who had leukemia. He became very sick—not only from the disease but also from the cure. The killer chemicals that doctors aimed at his cancer made him retch and throw up. What was to him even worse, the chemicals caused his hair to fall out in clumps. Being sick was bad enough, but the thought of returning to school bald filled him with horror and dread.

But he did it. He went to school on the day he was expected back. Walking timidly into his first class, he was astonished to see a whole group of his friends with their hair shaved down to their scalp! Their shaved heads told him they cared about him and wanted to share his burden. Those bald heads that day became reflectors of the glory of God.

The church can be like that! It can show a beauty of holiness that makes you gasp.

Why is it, then, that in some Christian communities sleek and handsome people are celebrated while uglies and losers are thrown away? Why in some churches are wealthy people respected and poor people ignored? Why in some schools are sports heroes turned into teenage gods for whom hundreds cheer—even if their god is cocky, ignorant, and profane?

Is this holiness? Or is it a small reminder of hell?

Prayer

O God, we are going to have to keep on saying it. We have to keep *saying* we believe in the holy catholic church. Let your slow miracle turn us into the holy people we believe we could be. Through Jesus Christ, our Lord, Amen.

DAY 3

A CATHOLIC

CHURCH

Scripture
Make every effort to keep the unity of the Spirit through the bond of peace. There is one body and one Spirit . . . one Lord, one faith, one baptism; one God and Father of all, who is over all and through all and in all.

—Ephesians 4:3–6

Teachings
We grieve that the church
which shares one Spirit, one faith, one hope,
and spans all time, place, race, and language
has become a broken communion in a broken world.

—*Our World Belongs to God,* 43

Ordinary letters have ordinary addresses. You write a person's name, street and number, city, state or province, postal code, and, if necessary, country. That's it. That should be enough to get the letter properly delivered.

But suppose one day you are really thinking big. In order to avoid all misunderstanding, you address your letter as follows:

Mr. Homer Klankenfelder
1665 Pennybrook Lane
Grand Rapids, Michigan 49508
U.S.A.
North America
Northern Hemisphere
Earth
The Solar System
The Milky Way
The Universe

You can see, of course, that each item in the address fits into the next larger one. You move from smaller to larger, from more specific things to more general ones. You don't want just any old Klankenfelder; you want Homer himself. You don't want just any number on Pennybrook; you specify 1665. You want the 08 postal district out of all districts, Grand Rapids out of all cities, Michigan instead of Minnesota, and so on.

It's good to know what you want and to say so on your envelope. Your chances for hitting the target with a letter addressed simply to Homer, the Universe, would be slim.

The church is structured in a similar way, smaller to larger. If you are a baptized person, you belong to a particular congregation—call it Church of the Servant. Your congregation belongs to a denomination—say, the Christian Reformed Church. This denomination belongs to a group of churches that follow Calvin's Reformation teachings more than Luther's.

This group is called Reformed churches. Reformed and Lutheran churches are Protestant instead of Roman Catholic or Greek Orthodox. But all Protestants, Catholics, and Orthodox belong to Christianity instead of Hinduism or Mohammedanism.

Your church address, then, might look like this:

Vanessa Klankenfelder
Church of the Servant
Christian Reformed Denomination
Reformed Churches
Protestantism
Christianity in the Twentieth Century
The Universal Church

Now you can see what we mean when we say, "I believe in the holy catholic church." We are saying that all true believers in all congregations and denominations and branches of the Reformation; all true Protestant and Catholic and Greek Orthodox Christians of all times and places—all these add up to a church, one church. We call it "catholic," meaning universal. We believe it is the "one body" that Paul describes in Ephesians. This is a metaphor. Just as a human body is made up of many parts and limbs, so the universal church is like a body of which Jesus Christ is head.

In this body your congregation is a square millimeter of northwest thumbnail, left hand.

"I believe in the holy catholic church," we say. We need to *believe* there is only one universal church, for it is hard to see unless you look for it. And we need to join with other Christians in doing Christ's work in the world. All the parts of the body, however different, are intended to fit and work together.

Of course, the part of the church we know best is our own congregation. Here we are baptized and taught. Here we listen and sing and give. Here we have pancake suppers, retreats, and Christmas programs.

C. S. Lewis once used a helpful picture. The universal church is like a great hall. Along the hall are doors to rooms. Everybody in the hall is a true believer in Jesus Christ. But it is when you leave the hall and enter a room that you can have fires and chairs and meals.

Naturally, we may like our own room best. We are used to it. But it is not polite to run down the rooms of others. What would be the point? What would be the point when so many people are not yet even in the hall?

Prayer
Thank you, Lord, for giving us a place in your church. Amen.

DAY 4

THE MARKS

OF THE TRUE CHURCH

Scripture

The Spirit clearly says that in later times some will abandon the faith and follow deceiving spirits and things taught by demons. Such teachings come through hypocritical liars.

—1 Timothy 4:1–2

For myself I feel certain that you, my brothers, have real Christian character and experience, and that you are capable of keeping one another on the right road.

—Romans 15:14 (Phillips)

Teachings

The Spirit empowers each member
to take part in the ministry of all,
so that hurts are healed
and all may rejoice
in the life and growth of the fellowship.

—*Our World Belongs to God,* 41

P eople go out to eat a lot more than they used to. People used to have restaurant meals only at special times, such as the day before a wedding. But now, especially in families where two parents work outside the home, people eat out more often.

People care about restaurant quality. For instance, they want food to be fresh: lettuce ought to be crisp; bread should be soft and fragrant. People want restaurants and their workers to be clean: if a restaurant worker handles money and then immediately palms your hamburger, you can lose your appetite. People also want service that is reasonably fast and always courteous: rude waiters don't last long in restaurants (except in Paris, where they thrive!). Finally, people expect fair value in food for their money.

These are all *marks* of a good restaurant: fresh food, cleanliness, courteous service, fair value. They are qualities, or characteristics, that will show up in any well-managed place to eat.

The Christian church also has marks. Across the world one can find millions of Christians and hundreds of thousands of congregations. Where, among all these, do you find the church true to its nature? Where do you find the church doing what it's supposed to do? Where is the church obedient to Jesus Christ, its head? In other words, what are the *marks* of the true church?

The church is true to its nature wherever it faithfully preaches the Word of God, offers sacraments in a pure way, and keeps up the discipline of the group. Good preaching, sacraments, and discipline are the marks of the true church.

Let's take each of these in turn. What makes preaching good? It ought to be interesting. And you ought to be able to understand a sermon. In addition, a well-preached sermon might make you laugh, or wonder, or feel like weeping. It will *get* to you. You may also learn something new from it. Over time, good preaching can actually change your life in important ways.

But these things, necessary as they are, do not finally make preaching good. For the most important thing has been left out—namely, that a sermon ought to become a carrier of the Word of God. God ought to *speak* to you and me in a sermon. That's why ministers study Hebrew and Greek. That's why preachers choose a text from the Bible rather than from *Sports Illustrated.* A minister who preaches faithfully is God's voice to us. This voice tells us of sin and salvation. It speaks of forgiveness and compassion, hope and courage for dark days. This voice brings the gospel of Jesus Christ.

Faithful biblical preaching is a mark of the true church. So is proper offering of the sacraments. I'll say more about these in our next lesson. For now, recall that whenever a child is baptized, people make promises within the whole gathered congregation. A minister doesn't just go to a shopping mall and start baptizing every kid within reach. Parents of children who are baptized must be believers. People must make promises within the covenant of grace and in the gathering of the church. Sacraments must be done right.

Finally, group discipline is a third mark of the true church. We have already learned something about the need for training in sanctification. We have to become spiritual athletes, training out sloppy habits and adding trim, dynamic spiritual muscle.

This is true not only for individual Christians but also for the whole church. The church is like an army in basic training, or a baseball team in spring training, or an orchestra in rehearsal. Ministers and consistory members act like player-coaches, reminding us of the Ten Commandments and other training rules. They keep motivating us to do better in the Christian life and to reach our goal for the season. Once in a while they suspend someone for missing practice too often. All this is church discipline.

But we also discipline *each other* with encouragement and warning and support. We try to keep each other "on the right road."

Good preaching, sacraments, and discipline are marks of the church that people have talked about for centuries. If you look back at the reading for day 2, can you think of some others?

Prayer
Keep your church strong, O God, and give us high marks so that we can truly be the living body of Christ in this world. Amen.

HOMEWORK

Vocabulary
68. church: the group of people who have been "called out" of the world for true faith in Jesus Christ. Even though the members of this group—across the world and across the centuries—are often different from each other, they still belong to only *one* group.

69. holiness of the church: the sanctification of the church in doing good and becoming more Christlike. To say that the church is holy also means that it is set apart for doing rescue work in the world.

70. catholic church: the church in its biggest, most universal form. The catholic church is like a great hall. Denominations and congregations are like rooms off this hall.

71. marks of the true church: the qualities you can find in the church when it is true to its nature and obedient to Christ. These include good preaching, sacraments, and discipline.

Questions
Day 1: In what three ways do we use the term *church*? Which is the most important? Why?

Day 2: Jot down two or three ways in which your congregation expresses its holiness.

Day 3: Why do we say the church is *catholic*?

Day 4: What are the marks of a true church? Check the reading for day 2 and add a couple of other "marks." Then explain what good it does to know the marks of a true church (check 1 Tim. 4:1–2 for one reason).

Summary
Talk to your parents about the *strengths* they see in your congregation. List those strengths on your paper.

19

THE

SACRAMENTS

RITUAL

Scripture

Whenever you eat this bread and drink this cup, you proclaim the Lord's death until he comes.

—1 Corinthians 11:26

Teachings

We believe that our good God,
mindful of our crudeness and weakness,
has ordained sacraments for us
  to seal his promises in us,
  to pledge his good will and grace toward us,
  and also to nourish and sustain our faith.

—Belgic Confession, Article 33

Rituals tie life together and help persons act out deep feelings or important promises. Some rituals are so common we hardly notice them. You meet somebody new, for instance, or greet your pastor after a service. Each of you extends one hand. You then clasp them and begin to wave the locked pair of hands briskly up and down for a few seconds. Then you stop.

It's a ritual. It's a piece of behavior that "acts out" a greeting or a feeling of friendship.

Hands are often important in rituals. A person swearing an oath in court, for example, raises his right hand or places his left hand on a Bible or both. These rituals act out promises to tell the truth. People getting married join hands while repeating their vows. Then each places a ring on the other's hand. These rituals act out their promise to be faithful for life. Boxers touch gloves. Basketball and baseball players do high fives. Ministers lay hands on new ministers who are just beginning their work. Army officers salute. Patriots place their hands over their hearts.

Rituals say things with actions. They say such things as "My country is important to me" or "I respect your authority" or "I promise to tell the truth, the whole truth, and nothing but the truth—so help me, God."

Some rituals say even more than that. This is true not only of wedding and funeral rituals but also of the two most important rituals of Protestant worship, the sacraments of baptism and the Lord's supper. What really goes on in these rituals? Why do we do them and what do they mean?

To understand sacraments we will need a comparison. U.S. citizens celebrate Independence Day on the Fourth of July. People set off fireworks and shoot cannons. Some dress up in eighteenth-century costumes and pretend to sign the Declaration of Independence all over again. At certain ceremonies citizens take the solemn vow of loyalty by placing their hands over their hearts and saying, "I pledge allegiance to the flag of the United States of America. . . ."

Fourth-of-July observances in the U.S. are ritual celebrations of a past event—colonial victory in the war for independence. But they are more than that too. Besides acting out the main events by signing documents or shooting off cannons, people also try to *include* themselves or *identify* themselves with the history and nation begun by the Declaration of Independence. They do this by parading, by waving flags, by pledging allegiance, and by singing "The Star-Spangled Banner." By these acts such people are saying, "We are the people who come from the war of independence. We are the people of that event and of all that it means." They are saying, "This is our event and our nation and our history. I am a part of these things. They are part of *my* history, even though I wasn't born till much later."

Fourth-of-July rituals celebrate a past event and identify people with the history that began back then. Such people feel as if they *belong* to this history and this event.

Church sacraments are something like that but are far more important. By dipping in water, by breaking bread and pouring out wine, we "act out" the central event of our Christian existence. That is, we act out the saving death and resurrection of Jesus Christ, the event that won our independence from sin and Satan. In sacraments we identify ourselves as the people of this double event and of all that it means.

We do this by gathering as the church, the covenant people of God. We reenact the main event to recall it to God and to ourselves, to give thanks for the gift it brings, and to pledge our allegiance to the Lord of this event.

We are saying, "We are the people of the war for redemption. This victory has made us who we are. We belong to this history and this Christ."

Ritual sacraments tie life together for us—because they tie us to Jesus Christ.

Prayer
Thank you, O God, for the gift of sacraments. Thank you that we belong to you and to your Christ and to each other. Amen.

DAY 2

SIGNS

AND SEALS

Scripture
If we have been united with him in his death, we will certainly also be united with him in his resurrection.
—Romans 6:5

Teachings
Q. What are sacraments?
A. Sacraments are holy signs and seals for us to see.
  They were instituted by God so that
    by our use of them
  he might make us understand more clearly
    the promise of the gospel,
  and might put his seal on that promise.

  And this is God's gospel promise:
to forgive our sins and give us eternal life
  by grace alone
  because of Christ's one sacrifice
  finished on the cross.
—Heidelberg Catechism Q & A 66

Human life is full of signs. You know the obvious ones: a metal rectangle with a number painted on it indicates the legal speed limit on a street or highway. A billboard displays a huge photo of a succulent, crosshatched, medium-rare, charbroiled steak—a sign of the good food you can expect at a particular restaurant.

When you get off the highway, you find other signs. A trousered figure on a door indicates a men's room; a skirted figure, a women's room. If you see 4/4 printed into a staff of music, you know that in that composition each measure will have four beats, and quarter notes will be worth a beat apiece. The composer *signs* this information by simply writing a pair of vertical 4's.

A sign *points to* or *indicates* something. A traffic arrow points out which way to turn. A first crocus in March indicates the coming of spring. A thumb jerked out to one side indicates either that the signer wants a ride or else that he has just called a base runner out. Your name written by your own hand indicates your identity: only you sign your name just that way.

Without signs many things would drag on a lot longer, and life would seem much poorer and less interesting. For signs have great power. Making the sign of the cross, for instance, reminds millions of Roman Catholics of the central event in the life of Jesus Christ. The straight-armed Nazi salute told millions of Germans that Hitler was god.

Sometimes a sign becomes a seal. Your signature doodled all over your history notebook is a sign of your identity (and maybe your boredom), but it doesn't mean much more than that. However, if you sign a $50 IOU, you are sealing your promise to pay back this amount. A wedding kiss indicates love between a bride and a groom, but it also seals their wedding promises; it confirms their covenant with each other. A handshake after a business deal is not only a ritual sign of human politeness or trust; it is also a seal on the deal.

A seal *confirms* or *certifies* something—often an agreement or a promise.

Sacraments sign and seal our closeness to Jesus Christ. You may recall that we call this closeness "union with Christ." It is like the union between a grafted twig and a well-rooted receiving plant. Or it is like the covenant union between a man and a woman in marriage.

How do sacraments sign and seal? In many ways. When we gather within the covenant community for the Lord's supper, for instance, we break bread and pour out wine. We are then acting out the crucifixion of Christ that atones for our sin. The breaking and pouring are a *sign* of this terrible and splendid event. When Christians then eat the bread and drink the wine, they are indicating that they want to get as close to Jesus Christ as they possibly can. In a reverent, spiritual way, they want to *take him in* to the center of their lives. These Christians are acting out, or signing, their union with Christ—and actually making the union stronger at the same time.

But these signs, like a signature or a handshake or a kiss, also become seals. For with these sacramental gifts God confirms that his promises of salvation are good. They can be trusted. God *binds* himself to us with these rituals. A sacrament is in fact a binder. That is what the word *sacrament* means.

But when we take and use the sacraments, we also bind ourselves to God. We seal our obedience and faith as if with a signature, or a handshake, or a kiss.

Sacraments are church rituals in which we act out the central events of Christ's life and in which our union with Christ is signed and sealed.

Prayer

Thank you for showing us through simple things like water, bread, and wine that we can trust your promises of salvation. Let us see and believe through Christ. Amen.

DAY 3

HOLY

BAPTISM

Scripture
. . . having been buried with him in baptism and raised with him through your faith in the power of God, who raised him from the dead.

—Colossians 2:12

Teachings
Q. Should infants, too, be baptized?
A. Yes.
Infants as well as adults
    are in God's covenant and are his people.
They, no less than adults, are promised
    the forgiveness of sin through Christ's blood
    and the Holy Spirit who produces faith.

—Heidelberg Catechism Q & A 74

During a Sunday-morning church service two parents walk up to the baptismal font. They are carrying their eight-week-old daughter. In a solemn ritual, the parents confess their faith and promise to raise their child as a Christian. The congregation then promises to help care for this child's instruction in the Christian faith. Meanwhile, the minister states God's promise to surround this child with love.

Then, several times, the minister dips his hand into the font and drips water onto the child's head. The child flinches. The minister says words from Matthew 28:19: "I baptize you in the name of the Father and of the Son and of the Holy Spirit. Amen." In some congregations, a minister then takes the child in his arms and blesses her, as Jesus used to do. In most congregations the ritual is concluded with a hymn about children.

We have all witnessed this event many times. What is going on during baptism, and why does it matter?

Children are not baptized at a kitchen sink. The event happens before a worshiping congregation. Why? Because baptism is a ritual of the whole church, not just of children and their parents.

Let me explain this further. Baptism signs and seals union with Christ. As Christ went down into death and rose up into life, so a child in baptism gets washed by going down into water and coming back up. Baptism acts out Christ's death and resurrection.

I admit that sprinkling a child isn't a very good sign of this. Dipping would be far better. But, then, most of our churches aren't equipped to dip.

Baptism is a sign of the events of Christ and of our union with Christ. For by acting out the Christ events, we say, "We are the people of the cross and resurrection and of all that they mean." They mean washing away of sin. They mean justification and sanctification. They mean faith and law and prayer. They mean compassion for unpopular people and stunning mercy for leukemia victims. We place ourselves, identify ourselves, include ourselves within this history and these meanings of it.

But especially we place ourselves within the people that have come from that history. Baptism is a church ritual because in it we say that a new person has been accepted into the holy catholic church and into one of the rooms off its main hall. In this room Jesus Christ will be worshiped and the people will be shaped into spiritual athletes and will become good reflectors of the glory of God.

Of course, an infant cannot place *herself* within this history of these people. She's too young, too weak, too helpless, too ignorant. But that's just when God wants us accepted. That's just the point of infant baptism and the grace that flows in it. God reaches for us and marks us as his children and as heirs of his fortune *when we don't even know what's going on!* When our minds are still being formed and our movements are still random—*then* God grasps us and says "my child."

In infant baptism God promises that we will be included in the history and people of Jesus Christ. The gospel of Christ will be taught to us, preached for us, learned by us. Parents and others will try to be models of what it means to live like Christ. People will show us how to pray, how to give, how to treat others with kindness even when we don't feel like it.

In other words, people around us will try to make Christian history *our* history, the Christian community *our* community. Baptism is the start. In your baptism God says "my child."

What everyone is waiting for is the day, years later, when you walk back into the same church on your own two feet. You stand before the same worshiping community that witnessed your baptism. And to the God who years ago said "my child," you now say "my God."

Prayer

O God, you are the one who marks us when we are small and weak. Now that we are growing stronger and more mature, let us turn to you and call you Father. Through Jesus Christ, our Lord, Amen.

DAY 4

THE LORD'S

SUPPER

Scripture

And he took bread, gave thanks and broke it, and gave it to them, saying, "This is my body given for you; do this in remembrance of me."

In the same way, after the supper he took the cup, saying, "This cup is the new covenant in my blood, which is poured out for you."

—Luke 22:19–20

Teachings

Q. What does it mean
   to eat the crucified body of Christ
   and to drink his poured-out blood?
A. It means
   to accept with a believing heart
      the entire suffering and death of Christ
   and by believing
      to receive forgiveness of sins and eternal life.

But it means more.
Through the Holy Spirit, who lives both in Christ and in us,
we are united more and more to Christ's blessed body.
   And so, although he is in heaven and we are on earth,
   we are flesh of his flesh and bone of his bone.
   And we forever live on and are governed by one Spirit,
      as members of our body are by one soul. —Heidelberg Catechism Q & A 76

Everyone knows you have to eat and drink to live. A person can last only a few days without water; then the tongue blackens and swells to fill the mouth like a gag. A person can last only a few weeks without food; the body lives off stored fat for a time but then begins to consume its own muscle tissue and bloat with gas. Death from hunger or thirst is unimaginably slow and painful.

Yet, in the short time it takes to read this meditation, a number of people across the world will die in these ways. That is why we have relief agencies. Fear of starvation is one obvious reason we ourselves eat and drink: we don't want to die.

Eating and drinking not only nourish us, however; they also nourish others. When we share a meal with others, we are saying we don't want *them* to die. We want them to flourish and thrive and be alive with us. We want the same food and drink that nourish us to nourish them.

That is one reason people eat together. Of course, sometimes you have to grab a bite by yourself. But people usually try to avoid that kind of self-serve filling of their tank. It's lonesome and boring. There's no chance to share food and good talk with others.

To avoid such loneliness people make a ritual of meals. Christians surround their meals with prayers and songs and readings and unhurried conversations. They serve and pass and offer each other good things to eat and drink. They may even use cleanup time to discuss something interesting.

Christians and others also celebrate important events with meals. The festive Lord's day gets celebrated with special Sunday dinners or brunches. Part of Christmas and Easter and Thanksgiving is spent in leisurely meals with people we care about. People eat together after weddings. It is a way for bride and groom to share their happiness with others. People often, eat together even after a funeral. It is a way of saying to bereaved people, "We are the ones who share this sadness with you."

Eating and drinking, in other words, are not only for nourishing bodies, but also for nourishing *fellowship.*

The Lord's supper is a meal of this kind. In this ritual meal we act out the death of our Lord by spilling wine into a cup and breaking a loaf into pieces. Then, by eating and drinking, we identify ourselves as people of this event and of all that it means. And by taking nourishing bread and refreshing wine into the center of our bodies, we sign and seal union with Christ.

But I think we can now see that in the Lord's supper we are also doing something else. We are nourishing the body of the Lord, the church. We are sharing the gifts of food and drink as a way of building up our fellowship together.

All confessing members lift the cup and take in a piece of broken bread. But they also serve and offer and pass these good things to other Christians. They are saying, "We don't want *your* faith to die. We want you to flourish and thrive and be alive to Jesus Christ with us. Here, take and eat. Here, take and drink this cup."

We say these things because everyone knows you have to eat and drink in order to live together. Whites say these things to blacks, Koreans to Japanese, women to men, adults to teenagers, poor to rich. We are trying to pass on the grace of Jesus.

Prayer

Thank you, Lord, for your supper. Thank you for reminding us of your death for our sins; thank you for binding us close to you and to each other. Amen.

HOMEWORK

Vocabulary

72. ritual: a pattern of motions and words that "acts out" some deep feeling or important belief or promise. Rituals say things deeper in meaning than we see at first. The two most important Protestant church rituals are the sacraments of baptism and the Lord's supper.

73. sacrament: a sacred ritual, a sign and seal, by which God binds himself to us and we bind ourselves to God.

74. sign: a pointer or indicator. Breaking bread and pouring wine are signs of the death of Christ. Dipping a person in and out of the water (or sprinkling a person) is a sign of the death and resurrection of Christ.

75. seal: something that confirms or certifies. The sacraments sign and seal our union with Christ.

76. holy baptism: the church ritual in which a believer or the child of a believer is sprinkled with or dipped in water. Baptism identifies us as members of the people of God.

77. the Lord's supper (holy communion): the church sacrament in which confessing believers ritually eat bread and drink wine. This sacrament binds us not only to Christ but also to each other. That is, it nourishes the whole church.

Questions

Day 1: List several of your own examples of rituals from sports or everyday life. Why do we say that the sacraments are church *rituals*?

Day 2: What's the difference between a sign and a seal? In your own words, what do baptism and the Lord's supper sign and seal?

Day 3: What do God, the child's parents, and the congregation promise every infant at baptism?

Day 4: In your own words tell what benefits you could expect to receive as a result of taking communion.

Summary

Do *one* of the following:

If you were baptized as an infant, talk with your parents about this. Ask them what your baptism has meant to them over the years. Summarize their comments.

Explain the connection between baptism and profession of faith.

20

THE

KINGDOM

OF

GOD

DAY 1

THE RETURN

OF THE KING

Scripture
"The time has come," he said. "The kingdom of God is near. Repent and believe the good news!"
—Mark 1:14–15

Teachings
The rule of Jesus Christ covers the whole world.
To follow this Lord is
to serve him everywhere,
without fitting in,
as light in the darkness,
as salt in a spoiling world.
—Our World Belongs to God, 45

The universe is at war. We cannot see all the fighting or measure it. But it goes on every day. Beyond the wars everyone knows—civil wars and world wars, rebellions and revolutions, terrorist attacks and border skirmishes—beyond all these the whole universe itself is at war with God.

The war began before the dawn of human history in a revolt so mysterious and unthinkable that the Bible only whispers of it. A powerful nonhuman creature, one made by God and loved by God, rebelled against God the King and challenged others to join him. This "evil one" set up a rival kingdom whose inhabitants prefer darkness to light, cruelty to tenderness, deception to truth.

We call this evil power "Satan" or "the devil" because the Bible does. We do not have a great deal of information on him. We don't even know how to interpret much of what the Bible says about him.

But we do know this: the evil one is a rebel. And we know that his rebellion has spread like a disease into the human race. In this rebellion and in its spread, war has been declared against God, the King of the universe.

Where do we see signs of this war?

We see them in the fall of humanity, as the great deceiver turns human beings into great pretenders. We see signs of war in teenagers who steal from their classmates, and in Mehmet Ali Agca, who tries to gun down the Pope. We see them in four youths who try to rob a single, gun-packing citizen on a New York subway. We see signs of war and rumors of war in cheating and invitations to cheat, in lying and temptations to lie. We see signs of war, in short, wherever we see sin and the misery that follows from it.

All the Bible, all Christianity, all world history is the story of this universal war between sin and holiness, evil and good, the kingdom of darkness and the kingdom of light. The warring, you see, is not just on the side of the rebels. God the King doesn't simply hand over his world to them. God doesn't just give up on his rebel children and say, "To hell with you." For the universe belongs to God. Our world belongs to God. He wants it back. And he has taken certain steps to *get* it back.

The Bible traces these steps. God makes a covenant with Abraham and seals it with Moses and the law. God rules his people Israel through kings and prophets and judges and priests. Later God establishes a new people, the church, among whom the gospel may be preached, sacraments celebrated, people shaped to look and act like God.

For the whole universe is God's kingly realm. And all these things—covenant, prophets, law, church, sacraments—are the tools of God's kingly reign. They are all part of what could be called God's reelection campaign. God wants the whole world to acknowledge again that he is King and that our world belongs to him.

Why? Is God so weak and insecure that he needs lots of praise and acknowledgment to build him up? No. God wants us to recognize his kingship because it's true: he *is* King; our world *does* belong to him. And he wants to protect us from falling under the rule of other kings who will sooner or later destroy us.

The gospels tell us the most important part of this story. They tell us the turning point. The turning point in the universal war is revealed when a man from Nazareth leaves his home, moves out into Galilee, and begins to preach. "Repent," he says. "Lay down your arms. For the kingdom of God is at hand."

C. S. Lewis once put it like this: The world has become enemy-occupied territory. It has become the kingdom of the evil one. "Christianity is the story of how the rightful king has landed, you might say landed in disguise."

Now is the time for sabotaging the kingdom of darkness and reelecting the King of light.

Prayer

O God, you are not only our Father but also our King. O Christ, you are not only our Savior but also our Lord. Praise be both to you and to the Holy Spirit. Amen.

DAY 2

SABOTAGE AND

REELECTION

Scripture
Then the end will come, when he hands over the kingdom to God the Father after he has destroyed all dominion, authority and power. For he must reign until he has put all enemies under his feet. The last enemy to be destroyed is death.

—1 Corinthians 15:24–26

Teachings
We serve Christ . . .
(in) sexuality . . .
in marriage and family . . .
in education . . .
in our work, even in dull routine . . .
(in) rest and leisure . . .
    (in) science and technology . . .
    in politics . . .
For this world belongs to God.

—*Our World Belongs to God*, selections from 49–54

We think of our religion as a devotional thing. When we pray or sing hymns or read the Bible—*then* we are being religious. When we have devotions, we are acting like Christians. When we attend church and observe the sacraments, we are being faithful.

So we are. But the Christian faith is much bigger than these things, and being religious includes much more. After all, the whole universe belongs to God the King and Jesus the Lord. A thoughtful Christian once put it like this: Of every square inch in the universe, Jesus Christ says, "It is mine." In every square inch we therefore need a campaign to sabotage the kingdom of the evil one and reelect God the King.

What does this mean?

Let's look at some examples from various areas of human life. In *medicine and health care* Christians fight against drug abuse, including alcoholism, and try to help its victims with tough love. In the kingdom of darkness, athletes, rock stars, and film actors sometimes celebrate the high life of drug abuse till it wrecks or kills them. But in the kingdom of God, one's body is a temple of the Holy Spirit. God lives in us: we must keep his house clean.

In *earthkeeping* Christians fight against abuse of nature. Christians and others reclaim the earth with skillful animal care and with expert soil, water, and forest management. In the kingdom of darkness, people strip and rape the earth for profit. They foul clean air and pollute pure water. They neglect and abuse animals. But in the kingdom of God, the earth and its fullness are treated with respect. For they come from the hand of God.

In *sexuality* Christians fight against the attitude that women are men's inferior servants. Christians see men and women as equal partners—

serving God together and trying to build each other up. Christians also fight against the use of sex to trap, humiliate, or make money off people. In the kingdom of darkness, sexual partners are disposable tissues and bones. In the kingdom of light, sexuality is for imaging God in love and trust. It is a gift of such power and beauty that it is protected by the covenant of marriage.

In *education* Christians fight against the idea that learning is just for getting jobs and making money. In the kingdom of darkness, learning happens without the light of God's Word to shine on it. Learning is used to make people powerful but not to make them wise. But in God's kingdom, education is for deepening our wonder at the greatness of God and his world. It also prepares us to serve wisely all across the kingdom of God itself.

In *politics* Christians fight against the use of power to frighten other nations or to take advantage of the weak citizens of one's own nation. In the kingdom of darkness, citizens ride over elderly and poor people, children and minorities, and all those who don't matter except when they vote. But in the kingdom of God, governments protect the freedoms and rights of all citizens—and even make extra allowances for those who are disadvantaged.

Our religion, you see, is not just for devotions and worship. We also serve God when we take care of our bodies, care for animals and plant trees, respect the dignity of the other sex, learn a math lesson well, serve the poor and elderly—and do all of this because we are citizens of the kingdom of God. For all these acts and many more are ways of sabotaging the kingdom of darkness and reelecting the King of light.

After all, our world belongs to God.

Prayer
Make us, O God, good citizens of your kingdom. Even through us let your kingdom come and your will be done on earth as it is in heaven. Amen.

DAY 3

THE UPSIDE-DOWN

KINGDOM

Scripture
"Blessed are the meek,
   for they will inherit the earth."

—Matthew 5:5

Teachings
Our hope for a new earth is not tied
to what humans can do,
for we believe that one day
every challenge to God's rule
and every resistance to his will shall be crushed.   —*Our World Belongs to God*, 56

In one of her Mrs. Piggle-Wiggle stories, Betty MacDonald presents an upside-down house. Children come to visit this amazing place. Floors stretch overhead; ceilings lie underfoot. The piano that hangs from the floor above is very hard to get at; a person has to dangle from a trapeze in order to play it. Couches and chairs are also suspended from the floor overhead. This makes sitting in them extremely awkward. If someone wants to open a cupboard, or go to the bathroom, or even heat up some hot chocolate on the stove, he or she has to stop and think about the right approach. Nothing is, after all, quite where you expect it. Surprises wait for anyone who is careless.

The kingdom of God is like this house. Things in it seem upside-down. For instance, in our world it's pretty clear who the great people are. They are the people with power. Such people are presidents, prime ministers, tycoons. They fly in private jets and give orders over telephones in the backseat of their stretch limousines. They sneeze and the world reaches for a handkerchief. They order someone to jump and on the way up the person shouts, "How high?" These are the great people.

One day the disciples of Jesus Christ began to argue with each other about who would be the greatest. Jesus took a little child and had the child stand beside him. "Like this," said Jesus. "Try to be more like this." Then he said, "For he who is *least* among you all—he is the greatest" (Luke 9:48). That's what the kingdom of God is like.

In our world it's pretty clear who the rich people are. They're the ones with money. They dine in swanky restaurants and sail in yachts that cost $1,000 per foot. They dine; we eat. They sail; we row. The houses of the rich are large, their debts small. Their wallets are fat, their bodies thin. They vacation in places where every desire is fulfilled and every itch gets scratched. They are the rich.

In his Sermon on the Mount Jesus gathers disciples around him and begins to preach: "Blessed are you who are poor," he says, "for yours is the kingdom of God. . . . But woe to you who are rich, for you have already received your comfort" (Luke 6:20,24).

In our world it's pretty clear what you ought to do to enemies. You clean their clock, fix their wagon, take 'em to the cleaners, string 'em up and hang 'em out to dry. You do it to others before they do it to you.

Jesus says, "But I tell you . . . love your enemies, do good to those who hate you . . . pray for those who mistreat you. . . . Do to others as you would have them do to you" (Luke 6:27–31). This is, incidentally, just what Martin Luther King, Jr. did in his great civil-rights movement. It drove racists crazy.

So it goes. In the kingdom of darkness, loving enemies, shunning riches, trying to be great in service—these things are for suckers. In the kingdom of light, they are signs that one has been with Jesus Christ.

It's all a kind of upside-down house. The worldly-wise with Ph.D.'s turn out to be fools in the kingdom of God—unless they know how to be saved. Blue bloods are simply passed by—unless they are washed in the blood of the Lamb. The person who wants to save his life will lose it, but the one who flings his life away into the service of Christ—that person will *find* his life and find it abundantly.

Somehow it seems all wrong. It's all upside-down by the world's standards.

Or do you think it's the world that is upside-down and the kingdom of God that is really right-side up?

Prayer

O God, we have wanted to live right-side up in your upside-down kingdom, and it hasn't worked. Change our values so that they become more like those of Jesus Christ, your Son. Amen.

DAY 4

THE SECRET OF

THE KINGDOM

Scripture

He told them another parable: "The kingdom of heaven is like a mustard seed, which a man took and planted in his field. Though it is the smallest of all your seeds, yet when it grows, it is the largest of garden plants and becomes a tree, so that the birds of the air come and perch in its branches."

—Matthew 13:31–32

Teachings

Q. What does the second request mean?
A. *Your kingdom come* means,

Rule us by your Word and Spirit in such a way
that more and more we submit to you.

Keep your church strong, and add to it.

Destroy the devil's work;
destroy every force which revolts against you
and every conspiracy against your Word.

Do this until your kingdom is so complete and perfect
that in it you are
all in all.

—Heidelberg Catechism Q & A 123

At the heart of the Christian religion is the claim that God is the cosmic King and Jesus Christ the Lord of the whole universe. The world belongs to God.

Sometimes it is hard to believe. A pastor tells about a time during World War II when he was minister of a church in Germany. One night he came to meet his Bible class. They were going to discuss one of Jesus' magnificent sayings: "All power in heaven and earth has been given to me." For this discussion of Christ's great power only three people showed up—two very old women and one trembling old man.

Outside the church Hitler's storm troopers marched. Crowds cheered and searchlights crisscrossed. Bands and banners and salutes and marching orders all said, "Hitler is king. All power in heaven and on earth has been given to Hitler."

Inside the church two very old women and one trembling old man tried to believe instead in the power of Christ. It must have been uphill work. For everything they could hear and see said to them, "There is no king but Hitler."

Christians today sometimes struggle with the same problem. Cities seem to move through each noisy day without thinking of Christ. Cocktail parties glitter, nightlife fades into dawn. The big universities hum, the great stadiums roar, the factories belch and smoke and cough. All the busy people in all the busy places work and eat and play and rest. Then they do it all over again. How many of them know that Christ is Lord? How many know the kingdom of God is coming? How many care?

Jesus' disciples were already worried about the kingdom's progress way back at the beginning. They believed Jesus was the promised Messiah. They believed he would make things right in the land and turn people back toward God. But progress seemed so small and so slow.

Every once in a while the disciples would ask about it. "Lord," they would say. "Lord, if it isn't too much to ask, when *will* you restore the kingdom?"

The disciples had their doubts. Of course, they knew Jesus had done some good things. But it didn't seem like enough! Shaping up a few ragged beggars—that wouldn't budge King Herod. Healing some sick folks, or befriending a whore, or having dinner with a little weasel like Zacchaeus—that wouldn't shake up a man like Caesar!

Looking at the Roman army and the Roman tax system and all the arrogant Roman power, the disciples must have struggled hard to believe that Jesus was King. Everything they could hear and see told them there was no king but Caesar.

For such doubts Jesus tells one of the secrets of the kingdom. The kingdom of God, he says, is like a mustard seed. A man reaches with two fingers into his seed pouch and draws out a tiny seed. The seed is so small you can hardly see it. But the man sows this seed into the ground. Slowly, over the months and years, the dead seed grows into a ten-foot shrub.

The kingdom is like that. At the time of sowing, progress may look small and slow. But one day there is the tree.

That is God's way in history with his kingdom. Who would have thought God could make a great nation out of Abraham and Sarah—two barren people old enough to be on medicare? Who could have known what God would do with one man named Luther—a monk who nailed some protests to the door of a church and thus launched the Protestant Reformation? Who would have thought that a weary black woman, Rosa Parks, could start a movement that would help millions of people? Yet one day in 1955 when Rosa refused to give up her bus seat to a white man, the U.S. civil-rights movement was born.

On Good Friday who could have predicted what God would do with the dead body of Jesus, our Lord—a seed sowed in the ground for three days? Only somebody who knows the secret of the kingdom.

Prayer
O God, thank you for doing great things through small beginnings. Amen.

HOMEWORK

Vocabulary

78. the kingdom of God: God's reign over his universal realm. Covenant, prophets, priests, human kings, and the church are all tools, or instruments, of the kingdom of God. Like a mustard seed, the kingdom starts out small but grows and grows. The things that kingdom people cherish and value—like humility, forgiveness, kindess—seem "upside-down" to people of the world.

Questions

Day 1: What universal war does this reading describe? What steps has God taken to reclaim his world? What's the turning point in this war?

Day 2: What does it mean to be religious?

Day 3: Mention some things Christians do which show that the kingdom of God is an "upside-down" kingdom.

Day 4: Explain the secret of the kingdom found in Matthew 13:31–32.

Summary

Carefully complete the following statement, giving at least three specific responses:

> I can be an active kingdom member by . . .

LAST

THINGS

21

THE

CONSUMMATION

DAY 1

THE SECOND

COMING

Scripture
For the Lord himself will come down from heaven, with a loud command, with the voice of the archangel and with the trumpet call of God.

—1 Thessalonians 4:16

Teachings
He ascended to heaven,
and is seated at the right hand of God the Father almighty.
From there he will come . . .

—Apostles' Creed

P redicting the future can be big business. People try to make money from it. People bet, for example, on who will win the World Series or the Super Bowl. They lay wagers on boxing matches and horse races. People predict who will win these contests and by how much. Then they stake money on their predictions.

People predict other sorts of things too. They try to guess, for instance, whether stocks and bonds will rise or fall in price. They stake money on whether oats and soybeans will gain or decrease. These money-backed predictions are sometimes called "futures."

People also try to predict the future when they're deciding whether to train for one occupation or another. For example, most folks today doubt there's much future in stagecoach repair or crossbow manufacturing.

Some people spend their whole lives studying signs and trends of the future and making guesses about it. Those who gaze into crystal balls are called fortune-tellers. Those who have degrees and write books are called "futurologists." Those who appear on the local TV news are known as weather forecasters.

But one problem plagues all these people. Bettors, investors, fortune-tellers, and other predictors of the future all suffer from one drawback. Nobody *knows* the future. We can predict, of course. We can make educated guesses. We can even form intelligent opinions backed up by pretty good evidence. Still, we don't really know. Except for death coming sometime—except for death, taxes, and a poor year for the Chicago Cubs—we can never be sure. We never know exactly what's coming.

But we do know *who's* coming. Christians know that in the future lies the third great event of history. We have had two of them so far: the creation and the first coming of Jesus Christ, our Savior. What we are waiting for is his second coming. In this great supernatural event history will come to its climax, God will triumph completely over sin and misery, and the new age of peace in a new heaven and new earth will begin.

We call the second coming, together with the events attached to it, the *consummation.* We mean the "summing up," the "completing," of all history. We mean the end of the human story as we now have it.

Christians do not know very many details about the second coming. The Bible says that Jesus will return "on the clouds of heaven." The Bible talks of shouts and the sounds of trumpets. It says Jesus will reappear with angels "in blazing fire." But we don't know how much of this language ought to be understood literally. Neither do we know how Jesus could reappear to a whole globe simultaneously. Nor whether people will know right away who he is. Finally, we don't know just when this remarkable event will occur.

Certain Christians do attempt to figure it out. They work up charts and timetables and calculations. At various times in history small bands of Christians have been so sure of their predictions that they have staked everything on them—quitting their jobs, pulling out of school, selling all their furniture. But the times they pinpointed have always come and gone without the return of our Lord. As a matter of fact, the Bible tells us, in effect, that the time of the second coming is none of our business. We are simply to watch and be alert (Mark 13:35–36). We are to do our work and look forward in trust.

We know who's coming. We don't know just when or how. But the fact of our Lord's return does shape our future. We know that life has a goal. We know that work and play and good relationships have purpose. No kindness, no prayer, no small act of friendship is lost. It all counts. For these things are signs of the coming of the kingdom of God.

And the coming of the kingdom will be complete with the second coming of the King.

Prayer
Give us trust, O God, that our future is with you and with Christ. Let us look forward with hope to the coming of Christ, the Lord of history. In his name, Amen.

DAY 2

RESURRECTION

OF THE BODY

Scripture

Listen, I tell you a mystery: We will not all sleep, but we will all be changed—in a flash, in the twinkling of an eye, at the last trumpet. For the trumpet will sound, the dead will be raised imperishable, and we will be changed.

—1 Corinthians 15:51–52

Teachings

I believe . . . the resurrection of the body.

—Apostles' Creed

Q. How does Christ's resurrection
   benefit us?
A. First, by his resurrection he has overcome death,
      so that he might make us share in the righteousness
      he won for us by his death.

   Second, by his power we too
      are already now resurrected to a new life.

   Third, Christ's resurrection
      is a guarantee of our glorious resurrection.

—Heidelberg Catechism Q & A 45

People do it morning, noon, and night. They fix their faces. They moisturize dry skin. They apply a liquid-base "foundation" to even out facial skin color and cover up small blemishes. Then they rub in a cheek color and brush on a blush powder—as if they want to look continually embarrassed.

Lips get color-coated by brush, fingers, or tube. Teeth get whitened, gaps in them cleaned and flossed. Hair gets washed, rinsed, set, combed, and brushed.

Eyes get a fuller treatment. People use one pencil to outline eyelids and another to shape and darken eyebrows. Neither pencil comes with an eraser. Then they seize a small wand loaded with a substance called mascara. The mascara is applied as the wand is passed through each eyelash in order to color, separate, and thicken it. Finally, a colored powder is brushed around generally in the area under the brow.

The result is impressive. Nobody can miss the eyes on these folks. They stand out like small twin lighthouses.

People fix their faces because, of course, faces draw more attention than, say, backs or elbows. That, in turn, is because one's face is a communications center. We not only speak, taste, and smell but also give a lot of signs from this part of our bodies. Flared nostrils and tight lips can reveal anger, for instance. Broad smiles and twinkling eyes can show joy or mischief. Sagging jowls can indicate old age. Eye shape, nose shape, lip shape, muscle firmness, skin color and clarity—such things can signal a person's race, age, health, occupation, and emotional condition. Sometimes a person's face even reflects whether she is kind or mean. In other words, you can tell something about who a person *is* just by looking at her face.

Christians believe faces and bodies are important. They are closely connected with who we are. But bodies, including faces, ought not to become idols, the way they sometimes do on TV.

Christians actually take a place in between those who worship bodies and those who despise them. We all know body worshipers. They're the ones who mistakenly believe they ought to spend most of each day in some body shop—fixing, shaping, painting. They're convinced they have to be pretty or handsome to be happy. Not so. Most people, in fact, are neither pretty nor handsome by TV standards. They just look like themselves. They just look like who they are. And they get along fine.

On the other hand, some people lack respect for bodies. They neglect or abuse their own bodies. They may think sex isn't nice—just because it's done with bodies. Or they foolishly believe that work done inside one's head is more important than work done with one's hands. All this is a mistake.

Bodies are important. God made them. Jesus Christ became incarnate in one of them. And we ourselves are souls, or selves, that are *embodied*. True, when we die, we can be with Christ till his second coming without our bodies. But this is an incomplete and unnatural kind of existence for us.

One of the clearest signs that bodies are natural to us is that at the second coming we shall be resurrected like Jesus Christ. That is, we shall have renewed bodies like his.

This is marvelous enough for those of us who are healthy. But think what it means for those of us whose bodies now need repair. Think what it means for a person with cerebral palsy or muscular dystrophy or blindness. Think what it means for those who have been spine-injured in accidents.

The gospel promises that we shall have bodies like Christ's. As C. S. Lewis once said, if the body you are now driving is a junker, take heart. One day God will give you a new one.

Prayer

O God, we believe in the resurrection of the body. Today let this be a strong help to anybody we know whose body badly needs your miracle of resurrection. Through Jesus Christ, our Lord, Amen.

DAY 3

THE LAST

JUDGMENT

Scripture

"When the Son of Man comes in his glory, and all the angels with him, he will sit on his throne in heavenly glory. All the nations will be gathered before him, and he will separate the people one from another as a shepherd separates the sheep from the goats. He will put the sheep on his right and the goats on his left." —Matthew 25:31–33

Teachings

From there he will come to judge the living and the dead. —Apostles' Creed

Then "the books" (that is, the consciences) will be opened,
and the dead will be judged
   according to the things they did in the world,
   whether good or evil. —Belgic Confession, Article 37

At the end of history our Lord shall return. We do not know just how or when he will come. But we do know he is coming. We also know two things that will happen. One is the resurrection of our bodies. The other is the last judgment.

What is a judgment? A judgment is a determination that a thing is good or bad, or that an act is right or wrong. In some cases, as we know, *persons* are judged to be right or wrong, good or bad, guilty or innocent.

Of course, we think at once of courts. A man or woman wearing a robe enters a courtroom and mounts the bench. This person, when no jury is present, makes judgments of guilt. He has the power to find you guilty of riding a moped without a license or of vandalizing someone's mailbox.

Other people make judgments too. Teachers judge whether your math answer is right or wrong and whether your performance on a history exam is good or fair. Contest judges determine who played an instrument best or who submitted the winning pencil drawing or photograph. Umpires judge whether an infield throw beat a runner to first base and whether a pitcher is guilty of a balk.

You yourself make judgments every day. You judge safe distances on a bike. You judge whether clothing fits right and whether it's appropriate for a party. You determine what books and music as well as which friends you want.

A judgment is a determination, or assessment, of some act or thing or person. We deal with judgments all the time.

The trouble is that human judgments are flawed. Sometimes they are plain wrong or even wicked. More often they are partly slanted by our own prejudices.

Most courtroom judges, for example, are honest and wise. But a few can be bribed to help criminals go free. Most teachers are skillful and caring. But a poor teacher might have it in for you just because he didn't like your older brother. Contest judges can be prejudiced. Umpires sometimes need a visit to an optometrist. You and I sometimes make wrong judgments about distances, clothing, friends, books, and music.

The Bible says that at the end of history there will be a perfect judgment, a last judgment, a final judgment. All those who are then raised from the dead, plus those who are still alive at the second coming—billions of people—will be judged. The judges will be Jesus Christ and God the Father. The God of the universe and the King of history will judge.

This time there will be no slipups, no bribes, no prejudices, no slanted judgments. In this final, perfect judgment the loose ends of the world will be tied up and the friends and enemies of Jesus Christ exposed. The sheer truth of all history will be publicly revealed.

We don't know exactly how it will go. There are great mysteries here. But the Bible makes one thing clear: people will be judged according to whether they have done good or evil. Compassion, kindness, fairness, and other things will count for good, especially when done to "the least" of Jesus Christ's brothers and sisters. Hard-heartedness, meanness, cruelty, and dishonesty will count for evil, especially when done to the least, the poorest, the most vulnerable.

Of course, we are not *saved* by our good works. We are saved by grace and through faith. But we are judged according to works. For works are the evidence of faith. People sometimes have more faith than they think. Their works show this. And sometimes people have less faith than they think. Their lack of works shows this.

In other words, we can expect surprises at the last judgment.

Prayer
O God, strengthen our faith. Help us today to do some good work to the least of Christ's brothers and sisters. Help us spend this day in such a way that at the last judgment we need not be ashamed of it. Through Jesus Christ, our Lord, Amen.

DAY 4

THE LIFE

EVERLASTING

Scripture

"Then the King will say to those on his right, 'Come, you who are blessed by my Father; take your inheritance, the kingdom prepared for you since the creation of the world.' . . . Then he will say to those on his left, 'Depart from me, you who are cursed, into the eternal fire prepared for the devil and his angels.' "

—Matthew 25:34,41

Teachings

I believe . . . the life everlasting . . .

—Apostles' Creed

Q. How does the article
   concerning "life everlasting"
   comfort you?
A. Even as I already now
      experience in my heart
      the beginning of eternal joy,
   so after this life I will have
      perfect blessedness such as
         no eye has seen,
         no ear has heard,
         no human heart has ever imagined:
      a blessedness in which to praise God eternally. —Heidelberg Catechism Q & A 58

Christians believe that Jesus Christ is coming. We believe he is coming to judge the living and the dead. We also believe in the resurrection of the body and the life everlasting.

Because life everlasting comes in two kinds, the final judgment divides humanity into two groups. In his parable our Lord calls these groups the sheep and the goats. The goats receive everlasting punishment, the sheep everlasting bliss. The goats get to join the devil and his friends for eternity; the sheep join the friends of God. Goats are resurrected for what amounts to everlasting death; sheep are raised to everlasting life. To the goats God shows his dark justice, to the sheep the brightness of his mercy. For, you see, the sheep are naturally no better than the goats. Their good works have come from faith and from the warm glow of the Holy Spirit working within them. And both faith and the Spirit are sheer gifts from God.

Let me admit that the whole arrangement feels uncomfortable. Anyone who thinks about it very long will have questions. Many Christians wonder whether we properly understand our Lord about everlasting life and death.

Still, here it is in the Bible. We must do the best we can with it. Leaving behind our questions and agonies about everlasting punishment, let's think for a bit about everlasting life with God.

Let's be honest. You probably do not think of everlasting life very often or even want it very badly. The idea of "going to heaven," or living with God, seems strange, remote, not very inviting.

Why? Why is that so even for some grown-ups who have been Christians all their lives?

Two reasons occur to me. First, if God has blessed you with a loving family, good health, plenty of food and clothing, and a good friend or two, you *already* have some of the benefits of life with God. These are gifts of the King. These are inheritances of the kingdom. If, in addition, you are reading the Scriptures, trying to obey Christ, praying as honestly as you can—if you are doing these things, you are already living with God in a way. So perhaps you cannot see that heaven would be much of an improvement.

Things are very different, of course, if you are sick or poor or badly hurt by the cruelties of others. Then you may want the life everlasting very much. You hunger and thirst like Oliver Twist, who longed for God to fill his emptiness and show him the love and acceptance he did not feel from others.

There is a second reason that heaven often seems so remote: none of us fully understand what the joys of the life everlasting will be like.

I am writing these lines right now in Cambridge, England. Until we arrived a week ago, neither my family members nor I had ever visited England. Some of us didn't even want to make the trip. After all, when you live abroad for some time, you leave behind good friends, familiar places, and everyday ways of doing things. These losses can make a trip abroad seem uninviting.

Before we left, we consulted with some people who had lived in England. We asked them questions. They told us what we could expect in England, what life would be like. They described wonderful things to see and do here. That helped. It made living abroad sound more like an adventure than an inconvenience.

But we have no one to consult with about life everlasting—no one who's been there. We have no one to talk with personally who can answer our questions. We do not therefore really understand the joys of everlasting life, even after reading what the Bible says.

C. S. Lewis once used a helpful comparison. We don't know what we're missing, he said. We are like a small child who insists on staying in his sandbox because he cannot imagine what is meant by the offer of a day on the beach.

The life everlasting is like a day on the beach—a day that never ends.

Prayer
Thank you, O God, for the resurrection of the body and the life everlasting. Even in the middle of living this life, make the life to come more real for us. In Jesus' name, Amen.

HOMEWORK

Vocabulary

79. second coming: the event at the end of history in which Jesus Christ returns in a special way to earth. In the second coming history comes to its climax.

80. the consummation: the second coming and the events attached to it: the resurrection of the dead, the last judgment, and the beginning of everlasting life.

81. resurrection of the body: a consummation event in which, at the second coming, dead people are reunited with their bodies. Those who belong to Christ shall have bodies like his.

82. the last judgment: a consummation event in which all the people of history are judged by God the Father and Jesus Christ according to whether they have done good or evil. Though many of our works may be judged evil, we face as judge the same Christ who died to save us.

83. everlasting life: the eternal state of those who are judged. Some face everlasting punishment; others—because of the mercy of God—are given everlasting bliss.

Questions

Day 1: What do we know about Christ's return? What are some things we don't know?

Day 2: When will our bodies be resurrected? Where are we in the meantime? (See Phil. 1:21–23)

Day 3: Who will be judged? By whom? According to what? Should Christians fear the final judgment? Why or why not?

Day 4: Describe the two forms of life everlasting. Why might heaven not sound so inviting right now?

Summary

Please write one question of your own that this week's readings raised in your mind.

22

THE NEW
HEAVEN
AND
EARTH

DAY 1

THE NEW HEAVEN

AND NEW EARTH

Scripture

Then I saw a new heaven and a new earth, for the first heaven and the first earth had passed away, and there was no longer any sea. I saw the Holy City, the new Jerusalem, coming down out of heaven from God, prepared as a bride beautifully dressed for her husband. And I heard a loud voice from the throne saying, "Now the dwelling of God is with men, and he will live with them. They will be his people, and God himself will be with them and be their God."

—Revelation 21:1–3

Teachings

With the whole creation
we wait for the purifying fire of judgment.
For then we will see the Lord face to face.

—*Our World Belongs to God*, 58

Art museums often reserve one of their galleries for special exhibits. In this gallery artworks from other museums across the world are displayed. Every so often the exhibit changes. The paintings hanging in the exhibit gallery are removed and new ones hung in their places. And, of course, the gallery then looks remarkably different.

Our own imagination is like one of these galleries. In it hang various pictures—pictures of home and country and family and friends and school and even ourselves. Every so often the pictures have to be changed. Suppose, for instance, that some wonderful person tells you how interesting and likable you are. Your self-image changes. You pull down the old portrait of yourself and replace it with one of your likable and interesting self. On the other hand, suppose someone you thought was wonderful does something really cheap and mean. You would sadly remove the old perfect portrait of this person and replace it with one that includes a mean streak.

Many of us have a small gallery of pictures of heaven. We have, perhaps, a few pictures of angels and clouds and harps. Maybe God and Christ on thrones are pictured in our gallery. Possibly we imagine gleaming gold streets and a population of heavenly residents quite a lot like ourselves. We have pictures of churchgoing and hymn singing and resting. All of it is airy and high up and, to tell the truth, somewhat boring and unreal to us.

It's time to change the exhibit, to replace these pictures with others. For the Bible, especially in Revelation 21 and Isaiah 60, includes some pictures that are very different from those in our galleries. I have just read a remarkable little book about heaven by Richard Mouw. It's called *When the Kings Come Marching In*. In these readings I want to take some of Dr. Mouw's ideas and pass them on to you.

When our Lord returns, he will judge those who are living and also those who have just been resurrected. Then begins the life everlasting. But where will that life take place?

We usually think of heaven as up, way up. We think of spirits with airy bodies floating about on cumulus clouds. These pictures must come down. For in Revelation 21 John suggests that the new heaven and new earth will be right here where we now live. Heaven descends to earth, *this* earth. This earth will be purified and renewed so that heaven can be on-site where we now live.

Think what this means. It means Banff will be part of heaven, and Rocky Mountain National Park. Toronto, especially Ontario Place, will be included. So will Miami and Montreal, Paterson and Vancouver. There is an outside chance for Grand Rapids.

Of course, things will have to be purified and changed. It's hard to imagine smog and sleet and floods and urban decay in the new heaven and new earth. But it is this present earth that will be invaded by heaven— these forests, these mountains, this city and that one, these streams and rivers, lakes and lagoons.

Into this renewed earth, into the heavenly city on earth, into the new Jerusalem will come some familiar things, all of them changed to match God's perfect portraits of them. Whole nations will march in, not just individuals. Symphonies and bands will be as much a part of the throng as choirs. Not just pastors, but kings and presidents and ex-dictators and prime ministers will march in. Revelation 21 tells us there will be no temple. I guess that means no church. But sports will probably be plentiful in the new earth, for we will have new, free, powerful bodies. The new earth will be filled with friends and old enemies and humble apologies.

Above all, Jesus Christ will be there. And everyone will be drawn to him as if by a magnet, for he is the center of the new heaven and new earth. Whatever pictures change in the gallery of our minds, his portrait must remain.

Prayer
O God, give us eager, longing hearts for the reality of your new heaven and new earth, through Jesus Christ, our Lord. Amen.

DAY 2

THE REFILLING

OF THE EARTH

Scripture
"Then you will look and be radiant,
    your heart will throb and swell with joy;
the wealth on the seas will be brought to you,
    to you the riches of the nations will come.
Herds of camels will cover your land,
    young camels of Midian and Ephah.
And all from Sheba will come,
    bearing gold and incense
    and proclaiming the praise of the Lord."

—Isaiah 60:5–6

Teachings
God will be all in all,
righteousness and peace will flourish,
everything will be made new,
and every eye will see at last
that our world belongs to God!

—*Our World Belongs to God*, 58

When God made the earth, he told people to fill it. We read of this in Genesis 1:28. God blessed the man and woman and said to them, "Be fruitful and increase in number; fill the earth and subdue it. Rule over it."

As Dr. Mouw says, God did not mean just that Adam and Eve ought to make a lot of babies and fill the earth with them. God meant that human beings were to produce *culture* and fill the earth with it.

What is culture?

Human culture is the sum of what humans produce and of the ways in which they are organized for life together. When humans are organized economically, for instance, they produce goods and services such as electric clippers and haircuts. When humans are organized politically, they produce judges and presidents and lawmakers—together with their judgments and vetoes and laws. When humans are organized artistically, they produce artworks and galleries to show them in. And so on.

Add all this (and much more) together and you have human culture. Culture is civilization plus its goods and services.

God wanted the first humans to order the garden, to tame and manage it. He wanted them and their children to produce goods and services so that people could live, and even live well, together. God wanted culture.

As we know, the fall intervened. And in the fall culture got twisted by sin. For instance, people discovered that if they could make a plow for splitting the earth, they could also make a sword for splitting a head. The same hand that turned out a pruning shears for trimming a rose bush could also, with a few new turns, fashion a spear for impaling an enemy.

270

Nowadays twisted culture fills the earth. Great scientists use their excellent minds to dream up megadestructive intercontinental ballistic missiles. Filmmakers put a good face on divorce or godlessness. Some politicians try to become dictators, and some doctors get more interested in wealth than in healing. Some ministers preach sermons that are popular but not true.

What's more, people take pride in their bad or dangerous culture. Nations boast of their destructive might. Schools brag about their prestige. Racists pride themselves on their color. People everywhere accept with open arms and minds the products of a bad culture—products such as pornography, dope, gambling casinos, abortion mills, and terrorist training centers.

The earth is full all right. But it's full of—well, it's full of trash as well as treasure.

Isaiah 60 says that the new heaven and new earth will be refilled. Isaiah uses ancient pictures, of course. He says the ships of Tarshish will sail into God's city. Herds of camels (the ships of the desert), flocks of sheep and rams, lumber from Lebanon and gold from Sheba—all these things will come into the holy city of the future. That is, the wealth of the seas and the riches of the nations *outside* Israel will all be gathered into the city of God.

Why? What's the point? These are, after all, products of pagan culture, of twisted culture. They are products of wealth and might that have made pagan nations proud.

The point is that the earth—*and* its fullness—is the Lord's. God means to reclaim the fullness that is his. God means to transform all this fullness, to refill the earth, so that culture can serve him and his people the way it was intended to do way back at the beginning.

In this great refilling, spears will be turned back into pruning shears and swords into garden rakes. ICBM silos will be transformed into training tanks for scuba divers and switchblades into steak knives. Artists and teachers, business people and attorneys, animal trainers and filmmakers—all will use their skills and products to make great God's name and to serve his people.

Can you think of a good use for old grenade launchers?

Prayer
O Lord, the earth is yours and all its fullness. Let us already seek good uses for the culture we know and have. In Jesus' name, Amen.

THE MARCH OF

KINGS AND NATIONS

Scripture
"Your gates will always stand open,
   they will never be shut, day or night,
so that men may bring you the wealth of the nations—
   their kings led in triumphal procession.
. . . You will drink the milk of nations
   and be nursed at royal breasts.
Then you will know that I, the Lord, am your Savior,
   your Redeemer, the Mighty One of Jacob."

—Isaiah 60:11,16

Teachings
He will heal our hurts,
end our wars,
and make the crooked straight.
Then we will join in the new song
to the Lamb without blemish
who made us a kingdom and priests.

—*Our World Belongs to God,* 58

At the end God will refill the earth. The new heaven and new earth will be filled with the pure culture of art and education, science and technology, law and commerce. Animals and animal trainers will be part of the new earth. So will gardens and garden keepers. Possibly so will computers and computer programmers. What used to be a source of human pride will become instead a reflector of the glory of God. For the earth is the Lord's and its fullness.

Isaiah mentions in particular two kinds of culture, both political. He mentions kings and nations.

Why kings? Why will kings come marching in?

In his book Dr. Mouw offers three reasons. First, in ancient times a king was not just a ruler. He also represented his nation's whole culture. A king provided for arts and learning. (That is why some colleges have been named "King's College.") A king sponsored business, law, and medicine. In fact, a nation's cultural treasures were, in a sense, all on deposit in its national ruler. When kings come marching in, therefore, so do their cultural deposits. They are part of the "filling" for the new heaven and new earth.

Second, Isaiah says that when kings come into the new earth, they will not head the parade. Instead, they will be "led in triumphal procession." They will be followers rather than leaders. The tables will be turned on unjust kings. Those who once dominated people will now have to meekly follow their victims into the new city. Those kings and queens who once tortured people or crushed them will now have to bow low before them.

For in the new heavens and new earth, rulers will have to *account for* their use of the political power that God lent them.

Should we think of Nero bowing before the Christians he torched? Shall Hitler be led by Anne Frank? How about slaves leading slave drivers?

Perhaps. In any case the purpose of this turning of the tables is not mere revenge. The purpose instead is a public demonstration of the justice of God. History's wrongs must be righted. The truth must come out. Oppressors must be made to face their victims and repent.

Think what this will be like if both parties are Christian believers. Catholics and Protestants, heretics and orthodox, masters and slaves—all must face each other before the Lord they both confess.

Third, Isaiah mentions kings because he wants us to know that in the new heaven and new earth politicians will serve people instead of using them. Rulers will nourish people instead of sucking them dry. Isaiah uses a strange and striking image for this. He says people in the new city will be "nursed at royal breasts." The point is that the mother-kings who rule will be people who nurture. They will be like our Lord himself, who wanted to gather his people as a hen gathers her chicks.

Perhaps it seems unfamiliar to think of politics in heaven. But that is what Isaiah says. Even political discussions and debates might be part of life there. But this time all politics will be perfectly managed by him who is King of kings and Lord of lords.

Finally, Isaiah says that nations will come into God's city. Not just individuals, but whole peoples will stream into the holy city. What's the idea?

The idea is that God takes pleasure in the sheer *kinds* of people he has made and rescued. Red and yellow, black and white—all are precious in his sight, and all have their place in the new Jerusalem. Ethnic groups can bring in their ethnic treasures without sinful pride. Races may offer their gifts to God without racism. For as surely as Pentecost opens the door to people of every tongue and tribe, so the gates of heaven will swing wide for the multicolor procession of God's people.

When the kings and nations come marching in—this will be a parade not to miss.

Prayer

O Lord, you are the King of kings and the Lord of lords. You are the one in whom all treasures are hid. We praise and thank you for your greatness. Amen.

DAY 4

SEEKING THE

CITY OF LIGHT

Scripture

"Arise, shine, for your light has come,
    and the glory of the Lord rises upon you."

—Isaiah 60:1

For here we do not have an enduring city, but we are looking for the city that is to come.

—Hebrews 13:14

Teachings
Even as I already now
    experience in my heart
    the beginning of eternal joy,
so after this life I will have
    perfect blessedness such as
        no eye has seen,
        no ear has heard,
        no human heart has ever imagined:
    a blessedness in which to praise God eternally. —Heidelberg Catechism, Answer 58

A hundred years ago in Sweden a county doctor came out to a farmhouse one night to help deliver a child. As the woman labored on the kitchen table, her husband assisted the doctor by holding up a gas lamp to illuminate the makeshift delivery room. After a time of courageous labor, the mother produced a fine baby boy. Then, to the surprise of both parents, the doctor announced that a second child was on the way. The mother, it turned out, had been carrying twins. And indeed, before long the mother delivered a lovely daughter.

The father was already shaken by this unexpected turn of events, so you can imagine his astonishment when he heard the doctor say, "Hold everything. I think there's a third. I think there are triplets."

At this, the father began to move out of the room. "Hold it!" called the doctor. "Come back here with that lamp."

"O no," said the father. "It's the *light* that attracts them."

Something does indeed attract us to light. Keepers of great churches and other buildings know this. They know how to illuminate a magnificent building at night so that people can hardly keep their eyes off it. Other lights also attract. Lost miners or cave explorers, for example, long for the light at the end of a tunnel. Insomniacs yearn for morning light. Long-distance bikers lean forward in their saddle toward the bright lights that signal a village and the inviting end of a long day's trek.

We all crave light because something in us fears and mistrusts the dark. Darkness seems to be a cover for danger and disease. Darkness can make us feel depressed. And darkness makes it hard for us to find our way.

Ancient people shared our dislike of the dark. In fact, since their methods of illumination were primitive and weak, they were probably more afraid of the dark than we are. Their candles and torchlights, for instance, provided some illumination, but also cast fearful, flickering shadows on the walls of a cave or city.

We can understand, then, why Isaiah 60 says that the city of God is full of light. Light represents safety in darkness. Light represents health against disease, guidance instead of lostness, warmth instead of the coldness of outer darkness. Indeed, in the new heaven and new earth, says Revelation 21, there will be no more night at all.

Why? Think back to what we learned in lesson 15 about glorifying God. The glory of the Lord has to do with light and it has to do with worthiness. *Glory* means both "brilliance" and "good reputation."

The new heaven and new earth will be a city of light because it will be filled with the glory of the Lord. What's more, it will be filled with millions and millions of God-glorifying reflectors from every race and tribe and tongue—the whole of God's people reflecting his light back to him in their own way and color. Thus, whatever is splendid; whatever is brilliant; whatever is luminous and clean; whatever is soft and lovely and bright; whatever is radiant and glorious—think of these things as lighting up the holy city of God.

At the center is Jesus Christ, the light of the world and the lamp of the new heaven and new earth:

> The sun will no more be your light by day,
>   nor will the brightness of the moon shine on you,
> for the Lord will be your everlasting light,
>   and your God will be your glory.
>
> Your sun will never set again,
>   and your moon will wane no more;
> the Lord will be your everlasting light,
>   and your days of sorrow will end.   (Isaiah 60:19–20)

That is why the kings and nations come marching in. It's the light that attracts them. Ahead is the city that people seek—some willingly, some almost in spite of themselves. For in this city the Lamb of God shines like a lamp, drawing people to his glory.

One day, drawn like others to this city, you and I shall get in.

Prayer

O Lord, you are the light of the world, ever shining, never going down. Draw us to your saving, healing light. Amen.

HOMEWORK

Vocabulary
84. new heaven and new earth: the place of everlasting life. This present earth will be cleansed and renewed, and heaven will come down to it. The new earth will be filled with purified culture (civilization plus its goods and services).

Questions
Day 1: What are some "old portraits" of heaven? What important change does Revelation 21:1–2 (and this reading) suggest?

Day 2: Think of a couple of examples of twisted contemporary culture and suggest possible ways of turning these things to good use.

Day 3: Why do kings come into the new city? If they come in, do all of them—even Hitler—get to stay?

Day 4: Why is the holy city described as a city of *light?*

Summary
This week please read Revelation 21 a couple of times—slowly and carefully. Think about what it will be like to live in the new earth!

23

ON

BEING

REFORMED

DAY 1

SPEAKING WITH A

REFORMED ACCENT*

Scripture
All Scripture is God-breathed and is useful for teaching, rebuking, correcting and training in righteousness.

—2 Timothy 3:16

Teachings
We receive all these books
and these only
as holy and canonical,
for the regulating, founding, and establishing
of our faith.

And we believe
without a doubt
all things contained in them—
    not so much because the church
    receives and approves them as such
    but above all because the Holy Spirit
    testifies in our hearts
    that they are from God.

—Belgic Confession, Article 5

An American who lives in England gives himself away every time he opens his mouth. The English speak English. An American speaks English with an American accent. I say "half past nine." The English say "hahf pahst noin." I say "bitter." Some English say "bih-er." One of my neighbors is a teenager named Francis. If I call her "Francis," she smiles, for her name is actually "Frahnsis."

Everybody speaks his or her language with an accent. If English isn't your native tongue, you might speak it with a Dutch or Korean or French accent. But even if English is your native tongue, you still speak it with an accent that tells people what region you come from. In the U.S., for instance, people from Boston and the deep South and the Midwest and Texas and Brooklyn all speak English. But they speak English with regional differences. Some of these have to do with pronunciation, some with rhythm, others with the length of vowels. People speak English with a regional accent.

Test yourself. A baseball fan who yells "Moida da bum on toid!" is from (a) Edgerton, Minnesota; (b) Brooklyn, New York; (c) Ripon, California.

An accent is a distinctive way of speaking. But accents and accent marks are also used in music, poetry, and painting. An artist, for example, can use a touch of color or light to bring out one part of a design. A poet shapes a line of poetry by the rhythm of stresses on syllables. A composer shapes a line of music by indicating which tones are to be struck,

*This lesson owes much to I. John Hesselink's *On Being Reformed*

or blown, or voiced, or bowed more sharply than others. The composer, painter, poet—all these use accents.

Everyone who trusts in Jesus Christ alone for salvation is a Christian. "Believe in the Lord Jesus," says the Bible, "and you will be saved" (Acts 16:31). But Christians of various kinds stress different things in the Christian religion. Catholics stress sacraments. Lutherans stress justification through faith alone. Many Methodists lay heavy stress on the need for a warm heart toward Jesus. Certain Baptists emphasize the need for being born again. Pentecostalists stress the gifts of the Holy Spirit.

All sincere believers in the gospel of Jesus Christ are Christians. But, as we can see, people speak their Christianity with different accents. To be Reformed/Presbyterian is to confess the gospel with a Reformed accent. What does this mean? Where do we lay special stress?

First I should say that Reformed/Presbyterian people join other Christians in thinking that sacraments are important. We also believe in the importance of justification through faith alone, the need for a warm heart, the necessity of being born again, and the wonder of the gifts of the Holy Spirit.

But although we believe in the importance of all these things, they are not the places in our religion where we place special stress. We accent other things. Our accents lie more on the sovereignty of God, on the authority of Scripture, on the need for disciplined holiness in personal Christian life, and, finally, on Christianity as a religion of the kingdom. In fact, these themes should be familiar to you by now. One way or another, they have appeared many times in this course. This lesson will therefore sum up much of what we have already learned.

The basis of our stress on all of these themes is the authority of Scripture. For in the Scriptures we read of God's sovereignty and kingdom. There we learn the need for disciplined personal holiness. The Scriptures correct and improve people. They *reform* us. That, in fact, is one reason we are called "Reformed." We are people who have been reshaped according to the Word of God. We are Reformed. We go by the Book.

To lay a lot of emphasis on the authority of Scripture is typical of Reformed/Presbyterian people. It's one of the ways our Reformed accent comes through.

Prayer
O God, may you always be reforming us through your Word. In Jesus' name, Amen.

DAY 2

SOVEREIGNTY

OF GOD

Scripture
The Lord reigns,
   let the nations tremble;
he sits enthroned between the cherubim,
   let the earth shake.
Great is the Lord in Zion;
   he is exalted over all the nations.
Let them praise your great and awesome name—
   he is holy.

—Psalm 99:1–3

Teachings
Our world belongs to God—
not to us or earthly powers,
not to demons, fate, or chance.
The earth is the Lord's!

—*Our World Belongs to God*, 7

S ome things are really too obvious to say: Torture hurts. Pleasure feels good. The Sahara is dry. For good eating, it's hard to beat food. Bachelors are unmarried. And so on.

The sovereignty of God might seem to fit in this category of obvious things. Sovereignty, after all, means superiority and control. A sovereign person is one who is a high and majestic ruler. To say that God is a high and majestic ruler seems all too obvious.

Still, God's sovereignty has meanings we may not think of at once or may not remember. It's wise for us to learn or recall some of them.

First, saying that God is sovereign means that the earth is the Lord's and all that is in it. This is true of the original creation. It is also true, as we have just learned, of the new heaven and new earth. It follows that we have to treat the earth with respect. Farmers, miners, foresters—even hikers—must pay attention to God's sovereignty. The earth is the Lord's. He made it. We are only long-term guests.

God's sovereignty over creation also means that animals deserve proper respect and care. It means other human beings, image bearers of God, deserve proper respect and care. They belong to God. It means we ourselves—our bodies, our minds, our consciences—deserve proper respect and care. For all these things, and all of us, come from the hand of God.

Second, God's sovereignty goes beyond creation to redemption. In the mystery of human salvation God—not we ourselves—is the main actor. We may think we have been wise to choose God; actually he has been merciful in choosing us. His will, not ours, moves us to seek him.

People sometimes get quite excited about their salvation, telling the story of it again and again to anyone who has the patience to listen. They describe what happened the day they got saved, how their pulses raced and their spines tingled as they gave themselves to Jesus. In fact, some people "get saved" anew each time they attend a rally or crusade. Perhaps it's not really salvation they are after; perhaps it's the feeling of *getting* saved.

Well, feelings are important. We all want good strong ones. But it is quite dangerous for us to think that what is important in Christianity is how it makes us feel. We are then asking, What can the faith do for *me*? How can I have an unforgettable experience in worship? How can my salvation be fun and exciting? That is, how can God make himself useful to me and my feelings and needs?

This is all backwards. This is religion centered on human beings instead of on God. These questions and attitudes miss the whole point of the Christian religion. The point is that we exist to serve and thank God, not the other way around. God is sovereign, not I. It is he who saves us, not we ourselves. The point is that we must let God be *God*.

True, thankfully serving Jesus Christ does make us happy. Worshiping God does arouse powerful feelings at times. In his mercy God does stoop to serve us in Jesus Christ.

All true. But these things become real and pure for us only when we do not try for them too hard. Try too hard to remember something you've forgotten, and it won't come back. Go on to something else—and then the thought you wanted comes to you.

In the same way we must not try too hard for salvation or happiness or fine feelings in our religion. These things may come to us—but only when we forget about them and strive to serve the sovereign God. They will come through the back door when we answer him who knocks at the front door of our lives.

God is sovereign in creation and redemption. To say this is to speak the Christian faith with a Reformed accent.

Prayer

O God, you have made us in your image. Keep us from trying to make you into our image. Let us respect you as God and not just as a person to make us happy. Amen.

DAY 3

PERSONAL

INTEGRITY

Scripture

"I have been crucified with Christ and I no longer live, but Christ lives in me."

—Galatians 2:20

Teachings

Jesus stays with us in the Spirit,
who renews our hearts,
moves us to the faith,
leads us in the truth,
stands by us in our need,
and makes our obedience fresh and vibrant.

—*Our World Belongs to God*, 31

Reformed/Presbyterian people lay a lot of stress on the disciplined life of personal holiness. Earlier we learned about training and discipline in sanctification. We learned that in sports and in our faith only disciplined people are really free.

Now I want to say this another way. We have been created by the sovereign freedom of God. God is hospitable enough to make room for us. Suppose, moreover, we feel within us the stirrings of love for Jesus Christ. This means the Holy Spirit has already been at work. Suppose, still further, that we are saved people, ready to serve God with minds and hands and energy. We know some of the pieces of this life of service and gratitude: gathering to worship, praying at home, setting aside part of our money for church and the poor, trying to obey parents (even when we don't feel like it), showing compassion to people at school who especially need someone to take an interest in them. All these things we know about. We've been reminded of them repeatedly throughout this course. They are all pieces of the Christian life.

But what puts these pieces together? What makes them not just pieces, but parts of a whole life? That is, what gives our Christian life *integrity*?

What is integrity?

Integrity is the strength that holds things together. Engineers who plan bridges or airliners worry a lot about integrity. For they understand the forces that can make a thing collapse. A bridge, for instance, must be both firm and flexible, like a long steel spring. It has to be able to give a little as the forces of wind and traffic move it. But it can't give a whole lot, or it becomes unstable.

The same goes for airliners. Jumbo jets, for instance, can develop cracks in their ribs from the force of thousands of landings. Safety requires that such aircraft be planned and built to flex just enough to absorb the force of landing but not so much that they fall apart. (Think of flexing your knees in preparation for a six-foot drop.)

Reformed/Presbyterian people care about the integrity of personal

Christian life. To keep our integrity we need two things: firm structure and inner flexibility.

The law of God gives us structure and firmness. It's like a set of ribs in an airliner or like the superstructure of a bridge. The law of God, obeyed according to the authority of Scripture, shapes our lives so that they have strong ribs. Our lives are firm and stable when we are disciplined by the law. People can depend on us. They know we won't lose our Christian shape when forces push against us or pull on us. People can predict ahead of time that we will not lie or steal. They can depend on us to show reverence for God and respect for parents. These are our ribs. This is our superstructure.

But we must also be able to flex a little. Sometimes laws and rules cannot be our final answer. We need in us a *person*—a living, guiding person to inspire us with energy and enthusiasm for vital Christian living.

For this we have in us the very Spirit of Christ. "I no longer live," says Paul, "but Christ lives in me." Elsewhere he speaks of the Holy Spirit living in us.

What does this mean? It means that at our center, in our "heart," beats the warm, personal life of God to inspire and guide us. We have the law as our skeleton. We have the Spirit of God as our vital life and breath.

Suppose you had to lie to save a life. Suppose you face a situation for which there is no rule at all. You can still adapt. You can flex a little. You can go ahead and act, if you have to, knowing that the Holy Spirit will guide you.

The Christian life needs both firmness and flexibility. It needs integrity. To say this is to speak the faith with a Reformed accent.

Prayer
Help us obey your law, Father, but also live in us through your Spirit so that we can be creative Christians in a world fouled up by sin. Amen.

DAY 4

WORLD

INTEGRITY

Scripture
He is before all things, and in him all things hold together.

—Colossians 1:17

Teachings
Jesus ascended in triumph
to his heavenly throne.
There he hears our prayers,
pleads our cause before the Father,
and rules the world.
Blessed are all
who take refuge in him.

—*Our World Belongs to God,* 29

Personal integrity is important. You can tell a person who has it. She has a strong, flexible Christian life. She can stand firm against an unholy act but love and help an unholy person. She does not change her opinions and her conversation whenever she moves to a new group or place. She is not a chameleon. She has integrity.

But personal integrity is not enough. Personal salvation isn't enough either. Of course, for a person to be saved by the grace of God and the poured-out blood of Jesus Christ is an unspeakably fine thing. If such a person possesses personal integrity as well, we rejoice.

But it is not enough. For in addition to personal integrity, Reformed/ Presbyterian people try for *world* integrity. After all, God doesn't save just individual souls. No, "God so loved the *world* that he gave his one and only Son." And this Son, Jesus Christ, is not just my personal Savior. No, he is Lord of the whole world. He is the King whose kingdom is the universe. He is the one, says Paul, in whom "all things hold together." The world has integrity, in other words, only because it is ruled and preserved by the sovereign Lord, Jesus Christ.

What does this mean?

We have learned some of what this means when we studied the kingdom of God. We learned that we must obey God the King and Christ the Lord in every part of life. Let me now say this a new way with the help of two examples.

John is a patriot. He loves his country. When his national anthem plays, John breaks out in goose bumps. When his country's flag is hoisted, John snaps smartly to attention. John would do anything for his nation. If his national leaders order John to fight in some foreign land, John asks no questions. He assumes his leaders have good reasons for their order. John simply packs up and joins the army. "My country may be wrong this time," John reasons, "but it's been right before. I've got to be loyal. I'll do anything I'm told."

John is a saved person. He also has personal integrity. But he lacks a view of world integrity. For John has not fit his country into a bigger picture of the whole world. Other countries, after all, are important too. We must respect them and not invade them for selfish reasons. They and the whole universe belong to Christ. We must seek first to be citizens of *his* kingdom.

Jim is an antipatriot. He hates his country. When his national anthem plays, Jim breaks out in a cold sweat. When his country's flag is hoisted, Jim slouches and yawns. Jim would do almost nothing for his country. If his national leaders order Jim to fight in some foreign land, Jim asks no questions. He assumes his leaders have bad reasons for their order. He simply packs up and runs and hides. "My country may be right this time," reasons Jim, "but it's been wrong before. I've got to be suspicious. I'll do nothing I'm told."

Jim is a saved person. He also has personal integrity. But Jim lacks a view of world integrity. For he has not fit his country into a bigger picture of the whole world. Other countries, after all, may be defenseless against the invasion of some murderous dictator. We have to respect those weak countries and sometimes fight to save them. For they and the whole universe belong to Jesus Christ. We must seek first to be citizens of *his* kingdom.

The gospel applies to my personal life—how I am saved and how my life holds together. But it also applies to the whole world—how the whole world is reconciled to Christ and holds together in him.

Deciding what is Christlike in the world may be terribly hard for Christians. Still, we have to try. Else for us the world has no integrity.

To speak of world integrity is to speak the faith with a Reformed accent.

Prayer
Help us grow in wisdom, O God, so that by the working of your Spirit and discussions in the church we may see what is right and wrong in the world. Amen.

HOMEWORK

Vocabulary
85. Reformed: To be Reformed is to confess the common Christian faith with a special accent. In particular, it means to accent such things as the authority of Scripture, the sovereignty of God, personal integrity in the life of holiness, and the need for a view of world integrity (sometimes called a "world-and-life view" or "kingdom vision").

Questions
Day 1: How is being Reformed like speaking English with an accent? What four things do Reformed Christians generally stress? Why is the authority of Scripture so important to us?

Day 2: How does stressing God's sovereignty affect the way we view and treat (a) the earth, (b) our neighbors, (c) our salvation?

Day 3: Explain how God's law and the Holy Spirit give us personal integrity.

Day 4: What is "world integrity" and why is it important to strive for? What's the point of the stories about John and Jim?

Summary
Talk with other adults in your family about why it is important to know what it means to be a Reformed Christian. Jot down their ideas and your own.

24

LIVING

   THE

      FAITH

DAY 1

HANDING OVER

A TRUST

Scripture

Dear friends, although I was very eager to write to you about the salvation we share, I felt I had to write and urge you to contend for the faith that was once for all entrusted to the saints.

—Jude 3

This is the first reading of the last lesson. We have covered a lot of ground. If you look back at the table of contents, you can see where we have been and which way we've come.

We began with God, as all proper religion does. We wanted to know who God is and how God speaks and acts.

Then we thought about ourselves, about humanity. We studied the human tragedy of the fall and what came from it. We discovered God's surprising rescue arrangement—a covenant of grace.

Third, in the heart of the course we looked at Christ, the Holy Spirit, and our salvation. We wanted to know how God has been at work to salvage and save. We therefore were reminded of who Christ is and what main work he does. We learned how the Holy Spirit makes this work "take" in us, and we talked about justification, faith, repentance, and sanctification. Within sanctification itself we studied the role of law and prayer.

Fourth, we saw how God organizes his people for nourishment and for doing his work in the world. That is, we learned something about the church, the sacraments, and the kingdom of God.

In the fifth and last unit we have been studying last things—that is, how history will end and what the new heaven and new earth will be like. We also spent a lesson studying our own Reformed accent.

These five units of knowledge can be summed up as three things—God, the world, and their relation. We have learned about the triune God, about the world (especially the world of human beings), and about how God and the world are related to each other in creation, fall, and redemption.

We have come a long way in learning these things. Along the way your parents and teacher and I have asked you to learn a number of concepts and terms. Why? Because we want you to understand the Christian faith. We want you to be an informed Christian. We want to trust you with the most valuable information we have. In effect, we are "handing over" the content of the Christian faith to you.

Suppose you hand over something valuable to a friend, to a bank, or to a good family. People do this all the time. They leave the country and hand over their house to someone else. They place a child in the home of adopting parents. They deposit funds in a bank. They tell a sensitive secret to a good friend.

What allows people to hand over a valuable person or thing in this way? How do they dare do it?

They do it because they have reason to trust those to whom they give the person or thing. What reasons might they have for such trust? An adoption agency would study the family who wishes to adopt a child. A bank customer would check out a bank's reputation. A homeowner would ask a tenant for references. A teenager would know from experience whether a friend could be trusted with a secret.

Without trust and reasons to trust and things handed over in trust, human life would be terrifying. It would also be hopeless and godless. For the most valuable thing ever handed over in trust is the knowledge of Jesus Christ and salvation. Without this knowledge the world becomes a maze for us. Without the faith entrusted to the church, we are like reflectors with no light source to shine on us. We are like wilderness hikers who have lost their compass. We are like sailors without a centerboard or rudder. We are like sheep without a shepherd.

The Christian faith is unspeakably precious. It is the most precious thing you have. The faith is, in fact, a *trust*. God entrusts the Christian faith to the church. All of us in the church keep handing over the faith to younger brothers and sisters, sons and daughters.

You are now in line to receive what's handed over. Everything depends on whether you can be trusted to keep the faith.

Prayer

O God, let the Christian faith be safe with us. Make us good receivers and keepers of what we've learned. Through Christ our Lord, Amen.

DAY 2

KEEPING

THE FAITH

Scripture

Timothy, guard what has been entrusted to your care. Turn away from godless chatter and the opposing ideas of what is falsely called knowledge.

—1 Timothy 6:20

E urope is full of castles. Some tower majestically over the Rhine River in Germany or over the fields and dales of England. Castles speckle the land in France, Spain, Switzerland, and Belgium. Some of these great buildings have begun to crumble, but most are so well constructed that they look just as strong today as they did seven hundred years ago.

A castle was built as a fortress *house*. Nobles would live in one of their castles for a time, till they had eaten all the fresh food and fouled up the toilets and moat. Then they would move on to another castle and start over.

But castles were built especially to be fortresses, places of safety against attack. They were ringed with water-filled ditches to make it hard for an attacker to set up ladders or to get over the wall in any other way. The only entrance to a castle was the drawbridge let down from the guardhouse. The door at the entrance to the guardhouse was double-thick and iron-reinforced. If an intruder did manage somehow to force this monster door open, he would find an unpleasant surprise just inside. For most castles were outfitted with loopholes along the passage just beyond the door. From these holes archers and gunners could assail the enemy. This passage was often also equipped with "murder holes" in the ceiling. From these, the castle's defenders could rain down rocks, spears, bowling balls, cannon shot, boiling tar, rotting animal carcasses, and other things of wonder. The intruder might wish he had dropped in some other time.

But the strongest part of early castles was a huge main tower, called a *keep*. Here the noble family had its rooms and housed its treasures. Precious lives, precious jewels, precious art—anything valuable was kept in the keep.

The keeps of surviving castles are impressively strong. Walls are four or even six feet thick. They are also slitted with arrow and gun holes—tiny at the bottom, large at the top. The spiral staircase in a castle is cunningly built to place the castle defender at an advantage. The staircase winds counterclockwise down to the left so that when facing an upcoming intruder, the defender could brace his left arm against the center post, leaving his right arm free to swing a sword in the open area of the staircase. The attacker, on the other hand, was in trouble if he wasn't left-handed; if he used his right hand, his sword got all tangled up with the center post.

In fact, most castle sieges ended before anybody got to a staircase. Most castles were almost impossible to penetrate. An attacker's best hope was to outwait the defenders, finally starving the castle into submission. Next best was to hope for treachery in the ranks of defenders.

In our text today Paul tells young Timothy to guard, to *keep* the faith that has been entrusted to him. It is a word to us as well. For when the things of the faith have been handed over to you, your Christian life has only just begun. Now you will have to guard your faith against assaults. You will have to guard it because it is the most precious thing you have—more precious than life itself.

How do we keep the faith? By studying it and knowing it well, so that we are not defeated by ignorance. By regular habits of Christian devotion—poured-out prayers, persistent Bible reading, attentive church attendance. One of the strongest keeps for the faith is a pattern of good deeds. Paul tells Timothy to be "rich in good deeds," because he knows how we are built. We are built so that when we act badly, the faith starts seeming small and unreal to us. On the other hand, when we stretch out in kindness or reach out in intelligent care for someone, Jesus Christ seems to be at home in us.

Paul tells Timothy to keep the faith. He means to guard it. And he is speaking to you and me too.

Prayer

O God, you have entrusted the Christian faith to us. Also give us a strong inner keep so that what we have may never be taken away. Through Christ, our Lord, Amen.

DAY 3

FAITH AND

EXPERIENCE

Scripture
"You asked, 'Who is this that obscures my counsel without knowledge?'
Surely I spoke of things I did not understand,
things too wonderful for me to know. . . .
My ears had heard of you
but now my eyes have seen you."

—Job 42:3,5

Most things we hear about mean a great deal more to us if we experience them. Suppose you had to describe the taste of pizza to a person who had never tried it. You could use the word "good" and all its synonyms (delicious, delectable, delightful, mouthwateringly yummy, etc.), but none of the descriptions would really do the job. You would need to escort this person to a high-quality pizza place and have the person actually anchor her teeth in a steaming, freshly baked slice of sausage and pepperoni with double cheese. Experience tells what the word "good" means.

The same goes for other items in human life. Violinists, for instance, have to learn bow techniques that are very hard to describe. Most of them, like pizza, have Italian names. A good teacher will attempt a description, giving directions for making the move, and the student will try and fail. Then, one day, when the student isn't trying too hard, the technique clicks. The student *feels* the combination of upper-arm relaxation and lower-arm firmness that makes for crisp bowing. Experience is the best teacher once again.

One could multiply examples: the strength of a hurricane gale, the soft loveliness of a morning in late May, the satisfaction of smashing a baseball with the sweetest part of the bat, the grief of death in one's family, the joy of being praised by a person you admire, the fragrance of a freshly run-over skunk, the sharp sense of shame from being caught cheating, the pleasure of losing yourself in a truly fine story. All these things can be described. In fact, you've just heard them described. But only people who have experienced these things really understand what's meant by a description of them.

Sad to say, some things in human life can be understood best when you lose them. These are things we experience all the time but take for granted—things like good health, political freedoms, or the comforts of home. You may not appreciate what these things mean till they are removed.

Other experiences, such as falling permanently in love, cannot be had till you reach a certain age. I just turned forty. Naturally, that means almost nothing to you. Indeed, it meant very little to me till it occurred one day when I was busy with something else. Now, suddenly, I know the meaning of "middle-aged."

If you have been raised in a Christian home and church—and maybe educated in a Christian school as well—you have heard a great deal about the Christian faith over the years. This course has added to the number of things you've heard.

Many of these things may have seemed empty to you—just words, just marks on paper that lack real meaning. I've been trying to describe the Christian faith to you—telling about justification, for example, and repentance and the wonder of God's grace. I have tried to interest you in the church, in the covenant, in the kingdom of God. But I know you may have found some of what I've said empty or puzzling or boring.

I know that. But I also know that if you keep on in the faith, much of what you've learned will come alive for you sooner or later. It can happen unexpectedly. You might one day be low and guilty and weak because of some foolish sin. You then experience the love of God which comes for us exactly when we are low and guilty and weak. You learn by experience the meaning of grace.

Or perhaps you join with others in a summer workshop or in a youth group project and find, to your amazement, that you are enjoying the work, that it is important to you, and that you feel like a part of a great, living body. "Church" takes on new meaning for you.

It has always been like this. The disciples of Jesus Christ were like us in this way. For instance, they had heard with their ears the prediction of Jesus' resurrection. Maybe they half-believed these words. And maybe the words didn't mean much to them. But then, on Easter morning, in a meeting that must have stopped their hearts, the disciples met the risen Lord. They saw him. And they knew him.

We can hear with the hearing of our ears. One day, in the grace of God, we shall see.

Prayer
Let us keep the faith, O God, till it comes alive for us in all its height and depth. Meanwhile, keep *us* in your care, through Jesus Christ, our Lord. Amen.

DAY 4

OPENING

THE DOOR

Scripture

"Here I am! I stand at the door and knock. If anyone hears my voice and opens the door, I will come in and eat with him, and he with me."

—Revelation 3:20

A famous Christian by the name of John Baillie once wrote about this famous verse from Revelation. I want to translate what Professor Baillie said into my own words and leave them with you as a last reading.

Every Christian is familiar with the picture in this verse. It's a picture that has inspired many drawings and paintings and even hymns. All of us know, deep inside, what the picture represents.

For we have no doubt about who is knocking at the door. This is the person for whom we are named. This is the person whom some worship and by whom others curse. Charles Lamb once said that if Shakespeare were to walk into a room, we would all rise to our feet. But if Jesus Christ were to come in, we'd all fall to our knees. For he is our Lord. And it is he who knocks.

Most of us have heard that knock for years. Every time a parent read Scripture, we were aware of that knock. Every time a talk or a reading or a sermon gripped us, we heard the knocking again. Every time God seemed to be trying to get *at* us in our conscience, or in nature, or in some experience too deep to tell—well, there again was the knocking at our door.

We hear it. We do hear the knock. But we've been hearing it for so long that it hardly makes much of an impression at times. We can eat right through the sound of it without getting indigestion. We can sleep clear through it without stirring much. Sometimes when the TV or stereo is turned up loud enough, we hardly hear the knock at all.

And, in fact, it does get blended in with other noises, doesn't it? A workman is driving roof nails, perhaps, or breaking up pavement three blocks away with a jackhammer. The windows rattle as a truck passes. The shutters bang, and a loose gate creaks. We can almost persuade ourselves at times that we were mistaken about the knocking.

Almost. But not really. Deep inside we know who's there. Deep inside we know that when we are eating or sleeping, when we are studying or playing, when we are aching or rejoicing, there he is—knocking at our inner door in that sort of patient, persistent way. We hear the sound. We know what it is. We know we are wanted. And we know who wants us.

For many weeks and months I have been writing to you about Christ and the Christian faith. I believe that what I've written is true and that it is important for you to learn. But most of it is information. You do need information to be a mature Christian, but you also need more. You need a

Savior. You need not only Christianity but also the Christ. You need the person who knocks. Nothing in this course finally matters, in fact, unless you get up and open that door. You have to give in and give up. You have to get up, lift up your head, walk over, and open that everlasting door.

And the King of glory shall come in.

Prayer
Come in, Lord Christ, and make your home in us. Amen.

HOMEWORK

Vocabulary

No new words this time. Your teacher may ask you to begin reviewing the words learned during this course.

Questions

Day 1: Why is the Christian faith so precious to us? In what ways is it "handed over in trust" to us?

Day 2: What helps *you* guard your faith? What are some of the things we have to guard our faith against?

Day 3: What does it take to make our faith "come alive"? Ask a parent how the meaning of a Christian truth that he or she had learned earlier actually "came alive" later.

Day 4: Explain: "Nothing in this course finally matters until you get up and open that door."

Summary

Look back over the table of contents of this course. Which reading or lesson or class activity was especially interesting or beneficial to you personally? Why?